Leo Gorcey's Fractured World

Leo Gorcey's Fractured World

by Jim Manago

BearManor Media
2018

Leo Gorcey's Fractured World

© 2018 Jim Manago

All rights reserved.

No portion of this publication may be reproduced, stored, and/or copied electronically (except for academic use as a source), nor transmitted in any form or by any means without the prior written permission of the publisher and/or author.

The stills illustrating this volume were issued by the original copyright owners; unless noted otherwise, they are reproduced courtesy of the author's collection (no copyright ownership implied).

Published in the United States of America by:

Bear Manor Media
P.O. Box 1129
Duncan, OK 73534-1129

BearManorMedia.com

Typesetting and layout by John Teehan

Front Cover: Leo Gorcey publicity shots. Courtesy Brandy Gorcey Ziesemer.

Back Cover: Script page from *Crashing Las Vegas* (1956). Courtesy Brandy Gorcey Ziesemer.

ISBN—978-1-62933-215-4

*To Daddy, who loved the films of
Leo Gorcey and Huntz Hall.*

I wish he could have seen this book in print.

Table of Contents

Acknowledgments ix

Preface xi

Introduction 1

1. An Accidental Actor 7
2. So Much Marital Misery 13
3. The Richard Lamparski Interview 27
4. The Brandy Gorcey Ziesemer Interview 33
5. Brandy's Thesis 43
6. Press Coverage of Stage and Screen Productions 63
7. Press Coverage of Radio Shows 83
8. The Fractured Language of Slip Mahoney 105
9. Glossary of Selected Malaprops and Other Twisted Wordplays 125
10. Afterword 163

Appendices

    Bibliography 169

    Select Radio Show Transcripts 171

    Additional Examples of Slip's Fancy Talk and Word Power 191

    Credits 197

Acknowledgments

In revealing the real Leo Gorcey, the man behind the mask, my work had only a few individuals that wished to participate. Some said they are saving material for their own possible book later. So be it.

Notwithstanding, one person stood out above all others by offering help that made this endeavor truly possible. My special thanks to Professor Brandy Gorcey Ziesemer for taking time from her busy schedule to answer my many questions regarding her father, besides sharing with me her thesis she authored in 1983. I have quoted heavily from it as it offers a fascinating insight into understanding the enigma of Gorcey.

I am indebted to Richard Lamparski for his interview with Leo Gorcey, which I quote from extensively. Once again, I am thankful for an ever-reliable associate, Randy Bonneville, who developed the credits listed in the appendix. His contribution has been indispensable.

Finally, my thanks to Donna Manago for her constant support and research assistance.

Preface

by Brandy Gorcey Ziesemer

My dad was most definitely not a "Ward Cleaver" type of father. I am, however, very fortunate to have known him after he retired from acting when he was a lot less stressed than he was while my older siblings were growing up. Leo Jr. is 9 years older and my late sister, Jan, was 7 years older than me. As a result, I was raised knowing a kinder, gentler version of my dad than my siblings knew. I idolized him and was devastated when he died on the eve of his 52nd birthday, a couple of months before my eleventh birthday.

I am pleased to write an introduction to Jim's biography of Dad because for Jim, it is a labor of love to write about the actors who he has most enjoyed watching. It is also an honor because I know Dad would be amazed and pleased that he still has fans 80 years after the release of the film version of *Dead End* in 1937.

I actually wasn't aware that Dad was famous until I was elected to a school board at the tender age of 18 and a reporter from the *Sacramento Bee* wrote an article titled: "Ringleader's Daughter is No Dead End Kid." Before then, I only had a few incidents that made me think there was something I was missing. My mom says it is because Dad was vehemently opposed to any of his children considering acting as a career. When I was about six, some older kids asked Dad for his autograph. When he finished signing I asked him why they wanted his autograph. He said, "They thought I was someone else and I didn't want to disappoint them." Then, when *It's a Mad, Mad, Mad, Mad World* was released, Leo Jr and Jan took me to see it at our local drive-in. They pointed Dad out to me in his cameo. I was "wowed," but at the same time just assumed for years that it was the only time he was ever in a movie. I wasn't sure what I thought he did before he retired because he was already retired when I was born. I just loved the fact that he and I had a lot of time to spend together.

Other than my mom telling me that when I was a toddler, I saw Dad on a huge console TV screen at a friend's house and ran behind it to find him. I never saw any of Dad's films until my 20th birthday when my then boyfriend (now husband) rented *Dead End* from Los Angeles (we were both in northern California close to where Dad retired) and borrowed a projector with screen from the local library. I was mesmerized. Then, he had cable, which I lived too far out of town to have. I learned that they ran Dad's movies on Sunday mornings, so I came to Tom's house most Sundays and watched Dad's movies.

The dad I knew was quite complex—even from my young perspective. He peppered most conversations with the mother of all cuss words, yet it was just another adjective for him, not a crude or insulting word. He loved to study words and often won small bets with people in bars by using an obscure meaning of a word or just a unique word. Someone would challenge him, and he'd go out to his car, drag his huge Webster's Dictionary back into the joint and show the challenger that indeed Dad had used the word properly. My mom explained that he started studying words early in his career so he could come up with funny malaprops. He also studied a book called *Word Wealth*. He and I were looking at words in his dictionary one night and I started giggling because I found the word shittah (a tree if I recall). I was just old enough to know that the first four letters spelled a "bad" word. My mom overheard us and said to Dad, "She doesn't think the 'F' word is a bad word but the 'S' word is." That went right over my head at the time. Mom told me much later that one day I dropped something on the floor when I was about four and came out with a singsong string of dad's favorite word.

Dad liked to write. He wrote a few play scripts that were based on 1920s New York gangster characters. He also wrote some poetry. He could be very philosophical, but what he wrote for possible publication was usually strictly for laughs or entertainment. He was a reasonably devout Catholic—taking the kids to church every Sunday and enrolling us in the Catholic version of Sunday school (CCD). Leo and Jim (his stepson, my mom's child from her marriage to her high school sweetheart) and Dad always stayed after mass to help the priest count the collection and prepare it for deposit. At the same time, he had a lot of respect for his Jewish heritage. His spirituality is another aspect of his complex personality, because he would pull pranks during mass.

Once he stacked some psalm books on the bench when his best friend's teenaged daughter stood to sing. As everyone sat down and became immediately silent, the girl was one of the last to sit, so when she did, the books crashed noisily to the floor. She turned beet red while my dad, always the gentleman in church, helped pick up the books and return them to their proper place. Another time, he folded a $5 bill into an intricate ring. After the services, the priest was frustrated because it took a while to undo the origami so it could be flattened out. Dad innocently commented that whoever the heathen was who did that during mass should go to confession.

The only time I really saw Dad's serious side with anyone who wasn't family was when he and his best friend, Denny Latimer (the local pharmacist), were talking and not aware of little ears. They had many deep conversations about the economy, politics (Dad was a financial conservative but not a social conservative), world events, business, family, and philosophy. Dad also entertained the priest (he was actually a monsignor) from our small Catholic Church on many Sundays between the second morning service and the afternoon service. They could laugh, joke, play darts or roulette, etc. with the best of them, but the two of them would sometimes have some deep conversations about spirituality and philosophy also.

Once my mom and dad divorced I spent every other weekend and part of all holidays with him. I had friends near his house, but I most enjoyed the times he and I did things together. He and I fished, rode bicycles, visited his friends, played with slot cars, went to bars, watched variety shows at night, listened to music, inventoried his coin collection, got banana splits, and went to the golf club. I also sat on the fender of his tractor while he worked the land—all 4 acres of it. He talked to me about school and asked about anything interesting I had done when I was at my mom's. I just loved to be with him.

As an adult, I grew to understand how Dad had been so tough on the older kids and so volatile with his wives. My mom always said he loved all of his children but that he was tough on Leo and Jan because he feared they might take after their mother, who hurt him deeply, but also scared him because she had some serious psychoses.

I am thankful that neither Leo nor Jan resented the fact that Dad spoiled me. I grew up idolizing Leo Jr. as much as I had my dad. I loved Jan too, and she was always very good to me. I was sad that she succumbed to alcoholism because she could have been anything she wanted to be. Jan's daughters are wonderful women whom I love very much.

Leo and I have always been close, even when months and sometimes years passed between visits. We have always enjoyed having deep philosophical and spiritual discussions, but also having great fun doing whatever presents itself as amusing when we are together.

I hope Dad would be proud of the woman I've become. My husband and I have been married since 1981 and our only child, a son, is an ICU nurse working on becoming a nurse practitioner. His wife is a wonderful daughter-in-law and is a veterinary technician. My husband is an associate professor of criminal justice and I am a professor of health information technology at a different state college.

– *Brandy Gorcey Ziesemer*

Introduction

WHEN I WAS SIXTEEN YEARS OLD, I purchased a copy of Leslie Halliwell's *The Filmgoer's Companion* (1976). I re-read and studied the pages of this reference book over the years. I still have this book, but it is now all yellowed and tattered. The entry for Leo Gorcey offered this generally accurate description: "Pint-sized American second-feature star, one of the original Dead End Kids; his screen personality was that of a tough, fast-talking, basically kindly as Brooklyn layabout, and he developed this in scores of routine films, mostly under the Bowery Boys banner."

Of course, a "layabout" is one who hangs out and does no work. Although it may be difficult for many people to consciously admit, this is something that is deep down inside all of us. That is, we all wish we can be a layabout and not feel bad about it. In other words, we all would be a layabout if it were socially acceptable. I think this is the appeal of Leo Gorcey's characters. He can be a layabout and be well-liked just the same.

My own memories of Gorcey's screen persona is that whether he was playing Spit, Muggs McGuiness, or Slip Mahoney, he indeed was a very likable street tough. The forty-one Bowery Boys films starring Gorcey typify this general attitude of his Slip Mahoney. He always tried to fix problems that arose in his neighborhood with his pals or with Louie, the owner of the Sweet Shop, which functioned as the Boys' hang out. I fondly remember scenes with him, especially when he fractured his words, or came to an impasse, insisting, "Alright! Alright! Alright!"

In addition, some of the most precious moments in Gorcey's movies occurred when he showed his sensitive and compassionate side. For instance, in *Blues Busters*, when Slip sees Sach on the street after he left him to be a famous singing star, we see the sensitive side to Gorcey as he struggles to express his connection to Sach despite the separation. The chance meeting ends with Gorcey offering a bittersweet smile. Indeed, it is one of their most touching scenes in the series and proves Slip and Sach were an inseparable pair.

The question has arisen of whether Gorcey had a problem expressing the sensitive part of himself in real life, relying instead on the tough guy image in relating to others. In regards to this, Brandy stated, "I'm not sure. I think he just felt like his public persona was what people wanted to see and hear. He was quite open, honest, and communicative with his good friends and with his family."

As an average hard-working Brooklynite struggling to make a living, my father always enjoyed Gorcey in all three of his film series (Dead End Kids, East Side Kids, and Bowery Boys). I know he would have been quite impressed to know that I too have come to find them so endearing as well, despite that I did not grow up in the streets. He would have been even more surprised and proud that I have authored this first biography of Leo Gorcey, besides the first biography of his partner, Huntz Hall.

When I listened to the only interview with Gorcey conducted by Richard Lamparski, I then realized even more so why my father liked this actor. Although he was so unlike Gorcey, as he was happily married to my mother for 38 years until his passing, and he never had any issue with alcohol or gambling addictions, my own father did have what one might consider a street-smart, crude, and common-folk manner.

My dad had grown up in the streets of Brooklyn, worked at a very early age for his father's trucking business, learned to drive and took up smoking before he was the age of 13, and he learned to survive all things. (Note: I do not intend to endorse smoking as it led to his untimely demise at the age of 61.) However, sounding very much like Gorcey in the Lamparski interview, my Dad's humorous way of relating an experience or describing something was similarly very down-to-earth. My dad shared the lack of pretensions that Gorcey, the man and his characters, exhibited.

My dad, like Gorcey—the real man and his characters—was never snobby or moralistic. In addition, he did not think too highly of himself, of who he was and his place in the world. However, I am convinced that beneath my dad's, Gorcey's, and the latter's characters' easy-going, devil-may-care façade was an underlying and powerful aspiration to be better than what they were; that is, the fantastical desire to be a truly great person appreciated and loved by everyone. However, for all of the above individuals to achieve such a greatness seemed an elusive and unreachable dream.

Gorcey himself authored his own biography in the Vantage Press title, *Leo B. Gorcey, An Original Dead End Kid Presents Dead End Yells, Wedding Bells, Cockle Shells, and Dizzy Spells*. This book is essential reading as it is both humorous and honest. In addition, Gorcey's only son, Leo, Jr., told of his harrowing life with his father in his book, *Me and the Dead End Kid* (Leo Gorcey Foundation, Spirit of Hope Publishing, 2003). That fascinating and quite tearful account is unrivaled for its honesty as well. There is no point in duplicating any of his information here. Readers wishing to understand Leo Gorcey must be sure to read both of these revelatory and insightful accounts as well.

My intent here in this biography respects Leo Jr.'s contribution to our understanding of his father. There is no intent to compete with it in any way. As far as Leo Jr. contributing to this book, his half-sister Brandy noted, "I spoke with Leo Jr. He said he doesn't have any additional information to add to your project other than his book and his preface to Dad's book. He doesn't have any problem with your writing a biography about Dad—just doesn't want to be contacted. He asked Colette as well and she said that she doesn't have anything except what will be in her documentary when it comes out, so she would rather not be contacted either." (Colette is documentarian Colette Joel.)

At first this might seem to be disappointing news. However, it does indicate that Gorcey's son has already offered everything of essence in his own powerfully moving book full of direct experiences with his dad, besides the added notes in the reprint of his dad's book. Again, anyone seeking a firsthand account of what it was like living with the real Leo Gorcey would best take time to read his son's book, where his observations and experiences are offered with much respect. I have intentionally avoided recounting all of the painful experiences that Leo Jr. suffered. Most importantly, Leo Jr.'s authorship helped him find a source of some well-deserved healing for a traumatic early life.

Brandy revealed, "Leo Jr. will appreciate you directing your readers to his book. He is a great guy and I have always admired him and enjoyed the times we get to hang out. He has an IQ that is off the charts, and he is also a talented musician. He is naturally witty and has a somewhat sensitive nature. He is doing well. He is pretty adamant about not offering any direct quotes or anything other than what is in his book and in his preface to Dad's reprinted autobiography."

What made this project so unlike my book on Huntz Hall is that so much information is circulating already on Gorcey. Brandy observed,

"In the case of Huntz, your biography was the only one dedicated to him. In the case of my dad, I'm not sure there is much of anything that hasn't already been published—albeit across many different books. There were things Gary was able to tell you about Huntz that had never been shared with the public. That isn't the case with Dad because of Leo's and my additions to his reprinted autobiography, the autobiography itself, Leo Jr.'s autobiography, my thesis (which has never been published, but Leo, Colette, and Rich Roat all read it as part of their research), Len Getz's book, Roat's three books (soon to be four), David Hayes and Brent Walker's book, and the soon-to-be documentary from Colette."

In short, so much of the story of Leo Gorcey has been told already in various and sundry articles and books that it would be best to steer clear of that material. I intentionally avoided trying to summarize or capture Gorcey's life by repeating the incidents reported elsewhere. I believe that most reading this book are familiar with many of those stories already.

Of course, a brief sketch of his life is essential, and it will be impossible to avoid recounting some facts and incidents that appear elsewhere. Nevertheless, it is my intent to offer some new and fresh thoughts about a man who had his share of troubles related to his alcoholism and bad marriages. This book is for the devoted fans, who already have knowledge of Gorcey's life and films.

I have pursued new ground here by providing information offered by his second daughter. Specifically, I have directly quoted most of Brandy's unpublished thesis. She came to study and understand her father years after his passing, and she expressed it succinctly in her thesis for her doctorate degree in English in 1983. Indeed, it sheds some new light on his life.

Secondly, I watched the Bowery Boys films in order to compile a list of Gorcey's amazing talent for mangling the English language. So much of it seems to pass quickly by viewers, and it can be easily ignored as far as understanding what is happening as regards the film plots. However, I hope that my cataloging of mangled words will reveal the intelligence and wit behind his characters.

Some may question why I did not dig deeper into all of the gossipy dark recesses in a troubled man's life. Simply put, I always liked the characters he played so much that dwelling on the actor's personal shortcomings did not seem fair, interesting, or respectful. In short, I did not think it appropriate to author an exposé of the unlikable man behind the mask.

My concern for accuracy is always uppermost in my biographical studies. Brandy: "I know you said you wanted to be sure of your facts so people didn't argue with your telling of them. I just wanted to let you know there are tons of contradictions because Dad tended to tell versions of stories or events that suited his mood and the audience. I have found many things over the years that contradict what Dad told someone else.

"For example, Dad says in his autobiography, he was working for his uncle in a plumbing business when he got fired for a job he did on the side—and botched. In that 1968 interview, Dad said he was making $6 a week for his uncle so he asked his dad if he could help him break into acting, and that they hired him for *Dead End* at $35 per week, and he asked for and got $50 per week. Dad told the same story differently depending on who the audience was. He told my mom that he would go down to the set of *Dead End* and watch David after he got off work at his uncle's shop. One day they needed a guy to fill in and they asked him to do it. Then, they made him another 2nd Ave boy like David, but had him understudy for Spit. That's just one of many, many examples.

"I have been contradicted by fans lots of times when I was just either recalling something I remember Dad directly telling me or, something Mom told me as she either witnessed firsthand or he told her. Same with some of his other close friends including some ex-girlfriends (two of whom I knew between his divorce from my mom and his marriage to wife number 5, Mary Gannon.)"

As to the origin of this book's title, *Leo Gorcey's Fractured World*, it came quickly when I learned more about Gorcey's fascination and obsession with words. He intensely studied them so that he could mangle them on screen. His Slip Mahoney character seemed to love to show off using big words—many times incorrectly or with a meaning opposite or a very different from the one he intended. I chose to use a play on words in the title. Here I thought it most appropriate to utilize the double meaning of the word "fractured." My emphasis here is on his word plays, malapropisms (or simply malaprops). However, his well-known over-indulgent use of alcohol left him "fractured" many times on and off the movie sets. I am happy to know that Brandy agreed, saying, "That sounds like a good idea."

My hope is that readers will find this book worthwhile. I am continually surprised with the feedback from my book on Huntz Hall. I have come to realize that readers can unfairly project their expectations. In their disappointment, they believe that my book failed them. My wish is that those individuals, many no doubt devoted fans, would kindly first labor in the vineyard for several years researching and authoring a book themselves before they spew their venomous darts.

Finally, I hope that the information developed here on Gorcey's birthday centennial will offer a valuable perspective to understanding a truly one-of-a-kind human being. Besides myself, I am sure that Gorcey's persona has been, and still is, meaningful and memorable to countless individuals over the years. I am grateful for those many supporters who have offered kind words regarding my biographies of Shirley Booth, Huntz Hall, Kay Aldridge, and Gale Gordon. For those supporters, I know that this book will be another enlightening and enjoyable experience.

– Jim Manago
October 2017

1 An Accidental Actor

> "Abraham Lincoln never went to college. He didn't even go to high school. And he became a pretty big man in this country. I'll do just like he did: study by flashlight."
> – Slip Mahoney, *Live Wires* (1946)

LEO BERNARD GORCEY, the physically diminutive screen actor in dozens of movies during the 1930s through the 1950s, left us with a very likeable, memorable, and unforgettable screen persona. For that reason alone, his story is an interesting one. Unfortunately, even more compelling is to learn that the real man did not adjust well to the fame and success that he secured.

Gorcey starts his own book with a saying, "It matters not his breed, race, or creed; no man knows, when he plants the seed, if it's destined to grow into a tree or a weed.

"You are about to read a simple, cynical story of an actor who has been up and down more times than a yo-yo. With a great deal of love and respect, this book is dedicated to my many wives whose excuses for leaving me were that they had sacrificed themselves on the altar of love—with my best friends. I have always figured that if a guy could take your wife away, he was automatically your friend."

With a large measure of wit (and of course booze), this actor endured five marriages, four of them ended in divorce after only a few years at most. More importantly, these failed attempts at lasting happiness left him increasingly embittered and cynical. After those opening remarks, he pictures and describes his belt buckle he had designed which memorializes his four failed marriages.

Gorcey: "As you will notice, instead of *Leo B. Gorcey* the initials read *Love Broke Gorcey*. The buckle is sterling silver. In each corner is a gold scroll indicating my former wives' names, the date of marriage, and the dollar sign in which all of them were most interested. You will notice there are two blanks (talk about gluttons) *wow!*"

Throughout his life, there is one thing that is certain about Gorcey—he managed to maintain his bad-boy screen image. In an article entitled "Bowery Boys Revisited in Book by 2 Film Buffs," Herman Wong explained, "But Leo Gorcey, who led a well-publicized, tumultuous off-screen life, was never able to break from being typecast as the street tough."

It will be evident that there is something else to this, than it being simply a matter of studio engendered and/or audience accepted typecasting.

Another matter to examine is that although the critics panned the B-movie quickies; that is, the two series of films done at Monogram Studios, it is Gorcey's work in non-series roles for other studios, done in between his regular roles, that oddly got the most attention from the press.

However, as far as the series films he did, Wong quoted author David Hayes who said, "We were struck by the great exuberance in their films. You know, many of the films were really quite marvelous spoofs, full of comic ingenuity and skillful interplay... In a way, their films are classics, despite all the years of (critical) indifference."

Furthermore, Wong said that Walker noted, "To us, the boys, as we want to remember them, live on in their films. They're real rebels, real go-getters, trying to cope with their social environment the best they know how, even if it's all for laughs... We think of them as genuine, larger-than-life screen heroes."

As far as the details of his birth and his parents, Gorcey best explained this in his book's Chapter Two, comprised of only three paragraphs, which follows here in their entirety:

Gorcey: "I was born on June 3, 1917, at 2:00 a.m. on a Wednesday morning. It was a good thing Mama had cleared the kitchen table that night, because that was where I was delivered. Stripped, I tipped the scales at twelve pounds and three ounces. Mama never let anyone forget those three ounces. Considering that Mama was only seventeen, four feet eleven inches and weighed ninety-five pounds, twelve pounds and three ounces was quite a package. The doctor must have had one helluva job introducing me into the world.

"Papa was an actor. He was away doing a play when the doctor sprung me from the cell in which I had spent my first nine months. I have had claustrophobia ever since, and do not like to be confined. Papa spent a good deal of time on the road, so we did not see too much of each other while I was growing up. But whenever he did get home, he spent most of his time with the family.

"He was in several Broadway plays: *Song of the Flame*, *Wild Flower*, and *Abie's Irish Rose*, to name a few. Papa always used to say that I would never get into too much trouble if I respected him, God, and the law—and he placed them in that order. But he forgot to add wives; they got me in more trouble than the three he mentioned."

As regards the neighborhood where he grew up, Gorcey told Lamparski: "I was born at 173rd St. and Port Washington Ave. in Upper Manhattan. I went up there and I didn't recognize that at all because it was so—it was so—well, different. When I was born there, well it was just a few people lived [sic] in apartment houses and few kids went to school across the street. Today you can't even practically walk down the street without bumping into people. Slightly different—like overpopulated."

It is true when someone once said that Gorcey was an amateur apprentice plumber and natural born actor who became an actor "by accident."

Lamparski: "Ah, one of the things that amused me and interested me was the fact that you were not unlike some of the kids from *Dead End* in a, in a school for actors. Tell them, Leo, how you got the part? I thought that was very interesting."

Gorcey: "I never studied acting. My father was an actor. Nevertheless, I started out to be a plumber. I worked with my uncle who had a plumbing shop on 23rd Street in New York. Very nice plumbing shop, but he only paid me six dollars a week. And for a while that kinda got me by. Then things—the prices they started to go up, then the six dollars didn't look so good. Went about getting a more remunerative—that's a beautiful word—remunerative job.

"Always I—a—my father was an actor and always could've got me into plays if I wished to do them, which I did not. But he always could have gotten me a job. So finally, I say, 'Hey Poppa, I don't like this pay I'm getting. All of a sudden I can't buy a pair of slacks, a pair of shoes in a month.' So he said, 'Well, I'll see what I can do.' And he happened to be sort of friends with somebody who had something to do with producing

Dead End. I can't quite remember with whom he was associated or knew, but a, he got me in the play."

Lamparski: "That was 1935?"

Gorcey: "It was in 1935, and it paid 35 dollars a week. Which in those days was a—"

Lamparski: "Equity minimum probably."

Gorcey: "Yeah, but it was a big sum of money. Sure, because I was working either six or eight dollars a week when I decided to change my occupation. (Gorcey laughs). The interesting part about [it] was that I asked for a raise [from] 35 dollars a week, I wanted 50. Big deal! So they wouldn't give it to me. They said, 'No we're going to fire you.' Sidney Kingsley said, 'We'll get somebody else. We can replace you any day in a week. It's just a bunch of kids in New York that can play the part.' And I said, 'Well find one. I want 50 dollars a week.' And they give me the 50 dollars. (Both laugh.) I thought that was funny."

While discussing some of the other actors he worked with, he tellingly went back to the tragedy of his father's demise, which effectively stopped his acting career abruptly with *Crashing Las Vegas*, the forty-first of forty-eight Bowery Boys movies. Gorcey: "As far as Poppa was concerned, he was [the] greatest. He was in *Abie's Irish Rose* in about 1926 or 1924. And it was one of the longest running plays on Broadway, and he played the starring role in *Abie's Irish Rose* uh—incidentally I'm—I come from a mixed family."

Lamparski: "Your mother's Catholic?"

Gorcey: "Russian Jew and Irish Catholic. Well, that's about as mixed as you can get without trying too hard. But Poppa was a good actor. He was just a good actor. It's too bad he got killed in an auto accident, and it was not a, you know, natural death. He made a mistake in hitting a car head on. He got killed."

Of course, Gorcey's father, Switzerland native Bernard Gorcey, played Louie Dumbrowski, owner of the sweet shop store hangout in the Bowery Boys series. Gorcey: "He was too funny for one reason uh. He didn't have too much to say in the early pictures. And one day, and if you could see this, he was a little man and he's facing a bunch of big men, and one day he said, 'I want to tell you fellows, if you don't give me more to say or more to do, I'm quitting!' (Gorcey laughs.) He's facing the moguls of the studio, whatever you call them, you know, and he says—all three, and he says, 'If you don't give me more to say I'm quitting.' (Gorcey laughs.) Quitting what? He wasn't doing anything at that time. I just thought that was funny. (Gorcey demandingly intones as Bernard): 'I'm leaving!' "

Gorcey never planned to make a career as an actor, despite the fact that his mother, Josephine Condon, married a successful stage actor.

Quickly he developed the familiar and often-imitated persona who spoke in fractured English with a Brooklyn street jargon. It seemed to begin when he played one of the street youths in the Broadway play *Dead End*. That persona would remain a part of him for the rest of his life. Oftentimes, the major newspapers have mentioned Gorcey in articles by a comparison made to other people's mannerisms, particularly to those individuals who talk like him.

For instance, an article said a pizza man in Brooklyn "looks and talks like the Leo Gorcey character in the Bowery Boys films." Another reference said that a film character played by Madonna in the 1987 release *Who's That Girl?* talks like a female Gorcey with an awful Brooklyn accent; specifically stating that the character sounds like a cross between Judy Holliday and Gorcey.

Dave Kehr in reviewing *The Two Jakes* noted in reference to Jack Nicholson, "Popping his eyes and puffing in frustration, he's starting to look like Leo Gorcey, and he remains too much of a comic figure to function as the film's moral center."

Jim Murray referred to a football player in "Dead-End Kid Is Out of Place." Murray: "You look at Jim McMahon and your first thought is, *They must be shooting a Bowery Boys somewhere nearby.* This is Leo Gorcey in pads. A great part for Mickey Rourke."

Though it is easy to belittle the B-movies that Gorcey starred in, and the limited acting skill necessary to make them successful at the box-office, Gorcey's persona brought to the films a peculiar calm and charm. Moreover, though his venture into the business of acting happened to be so accidental, it did not seem stiff and wooden, as is generally common with non-actors or those with limited dramatic skills. His sincerity and naturalness seemed to come forth in his characters effortlessly, and it seemed to require little study.

As regards to Gorcey's acting, despite the incessant mugging at times, he contributed much by imbuing his characters with some quite humorous fractured talk. This is something few have said much about, and it is the reason for this study.

2
So Much Marital Misery

> Slip Mahoney: "I don't like girls unless they are of a specific gender."
> Sach: "Yes, female."
>
> – *Jalopy* (1953)

IN CHRONICLING GORCEY'S STORY, it seems to revolve easily and intently on his problematic marriages more than his contributions as an actor or comedy performer.

Traditionally his early work received the most accolades; that is, the "A" productions at Warner Brothers with luminaries such as James Cagney, Humphrey Bogart, and others. However, the bulk of his work, the later "Poverty Row" productions at Monogram, receive short shrift. This is unfortunate, as those "B-film" productions allowed him to run the show. Indeed, the *East Side Kids* and *Bowery Boys* series are quite remarkable in their entertainment value, and are meaningful more so as the films involve Gorcey's participation, and Huntz Hall's to a greater degree than his *Dead End Kids* films.

Nevertheless, the press generously covered Gorcey's relationships as he had established a memorable place in Broadway's production of *Dead End* (1935-1937) and the Warners Bros. movies that followed. The bulk of attention paid him began with his first marriage, which took place on May 16, 1939, in Yuma, Arizona. That year saw the release of the last three of the seven *Dead End Kids* films.

From very early on, the press coverage focused on his marriages. It began with the clip entitled, "Dead End Kid Finds Out How to Get His Marriage License" (*Los Angeles Times*, May 10, 1939). The piece explained,

"Leo Gorcey, 21-year-old Dead End Kid of the movies, nosed about the marriage bureau yesterday to find out all about how to get married. But Leo, in an open-neck shirt and sweater, denied that he and his fiancée, Catherine Marvis, 17, dramatics student, had been married about five months ago in Santa Barbara, as rumor currently has it.

"Anyway, Leo was told that he would have to file his application and then wait three days. He said he wanted to be married in the Blessed Sacrament Church of Hollywood, June 4.

"'You ought to know all about this marriage business,' Leo was told by reporters. 'We understand you were married five months ago.'

"'Well,' was the answer in the best East Side brogue, 'mebbe I was and mebbe I wasn't. Anyway, Catherine and I want to be married in a church.'

"He said he'd come back a little later and file notice."

Louella O. Parsons simply reported, "Leo Gorcey, Dead End Kid, confides he'll wed Catherine Marvis, 17-year old dancer, when he gets around to it."

A few days before the marriage, a *Washington Post* article (May 13, 1939) noted, "Leo Gorcey, youthful actor who was recognized for his [work on] *Dead End Kids*, is shown with Catherine Marvis, Atlanta, Ga., dancer, as they talk over plans for their forthcoming marriage. Gorcey stopped in at [the] Los Angeles marriage bureau to ask clerks the procedure in obtaining a license."

In "*Dead End* Kid Secret Told by Bride's Paper Plate Hat, Romance Disclosed in Publicity Release on Economical Millinery" (*Los Angeles Times*, May 11, 1939), the truth came out:

"The 'Dead End Kid's' romantic secret became public property yesterday. Leo Gorcey, a member of the band of Lower East Side New York youngsters who made good in films, popped into the Marriage License Bureau to inquire into the procedure of obtaining permission to wed. But he didn't name the prospective bride.

"By nightfall the secret was out.

"In a publicity release from Paramount, Leo's sweetheart was identified as 17-year-old Kay Marvis, daughter of an Atlanta (Ga.) candy company executive. The article added that Leo and Kay were secretly married months ago—but wish to remarry publicly on June 23, the former's 22nd birthday.

"Origin of the studio's publicity release concerned a fetching little bonnet which Kay fashioned herself out of a paper plate, paper napkin, and a couple of eggshells.

"'Leo's millinery upkeep,' observed the press agent, 'is going to be pretty simple.'"

The press printed a photo with this caption: "Kay Marvis, bride of Leo Gorcey, with hat made from paper plate."

Some of the papers, such as the *Los Angeles Times*, had been incorrectly reporting Marvis as Mavis. For example, the March 29, 1939 paper stated: "Gorcey, of *Dead End Kids*, Denies Secret Marriage": "*The Times* city editor said to the rewrite man: 'We got a tip that Leo Gorcey, one of the Dead End Kids, was married secretly five months ago at Santa Barbara to Katherine Mavis. Call 'em up.'

"'Yeh, this is Leo Gorcey,' a voice said when the Hollywood telephone number answered. The rewrite man told Leo the story. Leo heard him through.

"'Well, I tell you, see, we didn't do it,' he began. 'We didn't do it,' just as if he were being cross-examined by a cop, as he is in so many film roles he plays with the rowdy film and stage kids.

"'But we've [sic] going to, sure. I hope. Kay is a swell girl. You can check all the records in at Santa Barbara and I'll bet a week's check you don't find anything.'

"'Even if we did... well I deny it. But when we do get married, it's going to happen right here in Hollywood, in front of the cameras, with the Dead End Kids all in on it. No Yuma or Reno trips for us.'

"'Well, if you did do it, Leo, we'll say, then Santa Barbara isn't the right place to check, is that it, Leo?' the rewrite man asked him.

"'No, but we expect to get married this summer,' Leo replied. 'We are engaged now.'"

Another headline at this time simply revealed, "Leo Gorcey, the Dead Ender, reported secretly wed to 17-year-old Katherine Marvis."

A photo, also missing the 'r' in her name, had the caption: "Hollywood Elopers—Leo Gorcey, one of the Dead End Kids, and Katharine Mavis, dancer, pictured during elopement to Yuma yesterday, where they took marriage vows."

Hedda Hopper offered the best response to Gorcey's first marriage, observing: "But if you want to have a day's fun and renew your youth, spend it with 400 high school jitterbugs in 'What a Life.' Jackie Cooper has his band there, too. Just for relaxation between shots, he plays the drums. Watching the cuties edge forward to get a close-up is priceless. Among them was Leo Gorcey's 16-year old bride. They were married in Santa Barbara five months ago. She's cute as Christmas. She married a

Dead-ender [sic], but she hasn't one! Wish our Hollywood gang could keep secrets like those Eastsiders!"

Surprisingly, the press did not cover what happened to mar Gorcey's first marriage. Edwin Schallert reported, "Kay Marvis, aka as Catherine Marie, divorced Leo Gorcey in June 1944 after nearly five years of marriage." Technically, the marriage to Kay ended six years after it began as the official divorce decree came a year after on June 21, 1945.

Interestingly, Kay's marriage to Groucho (July 21, 1945) ended in divorce just the same as with Gorcey. After about five years of marriage to Kay Marvis (30 years his junior), 58-year-old Groucho Marx divorced his wife, charging her with extreme cruelty, "and asserts that she caused her husband 'grievous mental suffering.' "

Gorcey's second marriage was to Evalene [referred by some newspaper reports as Evaline] (Penny) Bankston on October 24, 1945. It had the distinction of ending in divorce the quickest; that is, lasting on paper a little over 28 months, with a divorce granted on February 29, 1948. The press reported the filing of the paperwork on March 3, 1947. This meant it was ready for dissolution after only 16 months. In addition, this marriage offered the most riveting and embarrassing publicity imaginable to a movie star.

As regards to his second bride, the *Washington Post* reported in an article entitled "'Dead End Kid' in Toils" (May 23, 1948), that Gorcey "was arrested on suspicion of assault with a deadly weapon today. Police said his estranged wife, Evaline, reported he shot at her."

In "Shots in Brawl Jail Leo Gorcey," *Los Angeles Times* (May 26, 1948) reported, "Actor Leo B. Gorcey, screen tough guy who gained theatrical prominence as one of the Dead End Kids was in a prison cell yesterday and the bars were the real McCoy. He spent several hours in the Valley Division Jail in Van Nuys, where he was booked on suspicion of assault with a deadly weapon.

"The actor's arrest followed a 3 a.m. shooting at his home, 4616 Longridge Ave. At that time his estranged wife, Mrs. Evaline Bankston Gorcey, 29, and two private detectives were forcing an entrance into the family home.

"'After calling to my husband and asking him to let me in, he refused,' Mrs. Gorcey told the arresting police. 'So I broke in the rear door and he fired at me when I was in the hallway.'

"The Van Nuys officers said that the private detectives who were accompanying Mrs. Gorcey told substantially the same story. They said that the 30-year-old actor answered his wife's entreaties from outside by telling her to 'come back at a decent hour.'

"Police reported bullet holes were found in the walls four feet above the floor.

"The couple were married in October, 1945. Mrs. Gorcey filed suit March 2 for separate maintenance. Since the estrangement, she has been living in Hollywood.

"Production on a motion picture in which Gorcey is playing was held up temporarily. By midmorning, however, the actor obtained his release on a writ returnable June 3. His bond was set at $1000."

In "Alimony Cut Plea At Dead End, Too" (*Los Angeles Times*, December 16, 1948): "Former Dead End Kid Leo Gorcey, now 30, has struck a dead end deal yesterday when he moved in Domestic Relations Court to halve the $100 weekly temporary alimony he pays his estranged wife Evalene, 28.

"Last March 10, shortly after they separated, they agreed that that amount would be fair and he has been paying it. However, he contended, through Atty. Harold Lovell, he has only made $18,000 this year and has not worked since July.

"Mrs. Gorcey, who has sued him for separate maintenance, was represented by Atty. Max Fink. Fink contended that Gorcey should be able to keep up the payments for two more months when the suit goes to trial.

"Gorcey has cross-complained for divorce, charging cruelty."

"Commissioner J. B. Faulkner denied Gorcey's plea to reduce the support payments, and also refused to permit Mrs. Gorcey to move back into the family home at Sherman Oaks.

"She claimed that her husband shot at her when she tried to get in to obtain some of her belongings last May, but the actor said he only fired the gun to frighten away 'prowlers.'"

In "Wife Says Leo Gorcey Kept His Tough Role" (*Los Angeles Times*, February 1, 1949), the press reported, "Trouble with Leo Gorcey, now a 31-year-old screen veteran was that he could never forget the Dead End Kids role he first played as a teen-ager. His second wife, the former Evalene Bankston, 29, complained about the matter yesterday to Superior Judge Daniel N. Stevens when she won a decree of divorce.

"Gorcey drank to excess and carried a gun, a combination which Mrs. Gorcey said she could not relish.

"'One time a year ago,' she testified, 'he arrived home about 4 a.m., pulled the covers off my bed, threatened me with a gun and ordered me out of the house. He had been drinking, but was not drunk enough that he didn't know what he was doing.'

"Mrs. Gorcey's attorney, Max Fink, showed the court a settlement under which Gorcey agreed to pay his wife $27,500 in three installments of $2500 each and in later installments of $2000 a year. She and Gorcey were married Oct. 22, 1945, and parted Feb. 28, 1948. His first marriage was to Marvis, film actress, now wed to Groucho Marx, the film comic."

"Groucho Marx and his wife, Kay Gorcey (she still retains the surname of her first husband, Leo Gorcey) will be dance partners in a novelty number called 'Go West, Young Man' in Copacabana. Kay has danced for some years. Incidentally, she became a mother three and a half months ago."

In "Gorcey Asks Final Decree in Divorce," the press reported, "Last word in the lengthy matrimonial dispute between Leo Gorcey, 32, onetime Dead End Kid of the stage and screen, and the former Evalene Bankston, 30, film actress, yesterday was uttered by him.

"At his request, clerks of the Superior Court entered a final decree of divorce. Miss Bankston won the interlocutory decree Feb. 11, 1949, after a long contest. She charged that he drank to excess, remained away from home nights and once threatened with a gun and ordered her out of their home."

The following day, Gorcey would marry a third time. This time he tied the knot with Amelita Ward. Though this relationship brought marital misery as well, it did give him two of his three children; namely, Leo, Jr, in 1949, and Jan, his first of two daughters, two years later.

The children received press when Hopper observed, "The Christmas cards are better than ever this year. I love the ones that feature photographs of the kids. Never saw two more adorable youngsters than ex-Dead Ender Leo Gorcey's."

As regards Jan, Brandy offered this side note. "Jan lived a very sad life in many ways. She chose to live with my mom after Mom and Dad divorced, but then decided to go back with Dad after my mom punished her for sneaking out from a high school dance when she was about 16. She eloped about a year, after moving back in with Dad. She was already an alcoholic by the time she was 18. She had two daughters whom I adore—my nieces. I'm very close to them both.

"Jan tried hard to be a good mom and she had a good work ethic. She was also a talented guitarist and singer. She played lead guitar and preferred country music and mainstream top hits that had any kind of country influence. She was only 49 [in 2000] when she died from adult respiratory distress syndrome—we believe it was a complication of alcoholism which caused her immune system to weaken."

Again, Gorcey's marriage ended in a divorce granted 7 years later on February 8, 1956. A news photo had the revealing caption: "Marriage Hits Dead End—Actor Leo Gorcey, 38, who won divorce from third wife yesterday after testifying there were too many other men in her life."

"He said the house, with a swimming pool 'some people call an enlarged bathtub,' is now rented for $150 a month and that he no longer carries a gun."

"Leo Gorcey of Dead End Kids Divorces Third Wife" (*Los Angeles Times*, February 8, 1956), "Leo Gorcey, 38, onetime Dead End Kid of the screen, divorced his third wife yesterday when he testified there were too many other men in her life, including her doctor, her dentist, and a handsome cowboy.

"'She is rather fickle,' he said, wiping his tears streaming down his cheeks.

"Superior Judge Samuel R. Blake granted him the decree from the former Amelita Ward, 32… The actor testified his wife was almost constantly infatuated with one man or another and frequently remained away from home until 3 or 4 a.m. Her latest romantic interest, he said, is a married physician.

"'She is giving up our two children' Gorcey said, 'and the doctor is giving up his three children. She said she wanted to live with him for six months to see how they got along.'

"When she was in love with the dentist, Gorcey recalled, she asked his wife to give him up. But the actor added that a short time later Mrs. Gorcey declared her love for a cowboy and said she was ready to live with him in a trailer if need be.

"'But Amelita could never live in a trailer,' Gorcey observed.

"'Did you see her with these other men?' the judge asked.

"'Yes,' Gorcey replied. She didn't keep it much of a secret.

"Gorcey said his wife displayed little interest in their children, Leo Jr., 6, and Jan, 4, and took 'only about five seconds' to decide to let him have their custody.

"Under an agreement, approved by the court, however, Mrs. Gorcey reserved the right to visit the children and to have them with her during their school vacations. The contract also gave her a ranch near Red Bluff, an automobile, and $10,000 a year for five years as her share of community property.

"In addition, Gorcey agreed to pay her $700 a month alimony for a year and $200 a month when the children are in her care. He kept another ranch near Calabasas, and other valuable property, including interests in motion pictures." Attorney Harold Lovell represented Gorcey again.

His fourth marriage was to Brandy Davis. Most report that it took place in 1956. Davis is the only one of his five wives that is still alive. Brandy: "She was born Bette Jean Davis but she and Dad legally changed her name to Brandy Jean Gorcey when they married."

As regards Brandy's mom (Gorcey's fourth wife) helping to aid our understanding of Leo, Brandy explained: "She isn't able to add anything because she has been interviewed to exhaustion by Colette, Leo Jr., and Len Getz, etc. I do know most of what she has told them and have incorporated it into the answers to your questions. There are some trivial things like Dad loved to dance, and he was an excellent dancer."

This marriage gave Gorcey his third and last child, Brandy Jo, born in 1958. Brandy: "I was born Brandy Josephine Gorcey (middle name after my paternal grandmother, Josephine) and legally changed in 1981 (when I married) to Brandy Gorcey Ziesemer.

Interestingly, no press coverage seems to exist chronicling the problems with this relationship, as in the previous three. Perhaps the fact that he retired at the same time accounts for the lack of coverage. As with his prior marriages, this too ended in divorce.

His fifth and final marriage was to Mary Gannon on February 12, 1968, and it ended less than fifteen months later with Gorcey's death on June 2, 1969. Whether this marriage would have failed as well is unknown, as there was not enough time for the marriage to spiral out of control, as with the previous four.

Why did Gorcey have such misfortune as regards to finding true love? One clue given in the Lamparski interview is when he was asked, "How did you fellows fare on the Hollywood social scene when you got out there? Were you invited to Norma Shearer's parties?"

Gorcey responded, "Uh—No. I went to one, only one big party uh—I really didn't like it if you want to know the truth. Not that I'm a big judge of parties. But kind of when I go to party with a girl, I expect the girl to stay sort of side-by-side. And—um—well, most parties they don't do that. They kind of spread out the action and well, (Gorcey laughs) I don't want to sound old-fashioned or anything, but I didn't approve of it."

This is key to understanding Gorcey had set values from his upbringing. As far as what is right and wrong, he had no choice to be happy with anything else other than the stability of marriage. He was taught what was proper. Yet, he repeatedly married a partner that was incompatible in some or many ways. Not to place all the blame on Gorcey, but each woman he married somehow ignored his alcohol addiction, and they must have thought they can help him resolve the problems plaguing him. Perhaps if both Gorcey and his wives were better informed and learned of their mutual incompatibilities they would have not gotten married, and so much of the miseries engendered by tying the knot could have been avoided.

Gorcey's own admission of being "old-fashioned" meant that he would have little luck at a happy and long marriage when he kept settling down with the hip showgirls that came in his path. How could one expect for such an outgoing woman such as his first wife, actress Kay Marvis, to be happy at home cultivating a domestic life? Obviously, hindsight seems always to be perfect, and foresight is unfortunately so limited, particularly when it comes to relationships.

Was he truly a one-woman man who chose the wrong one each time, or did he have self-destructive instincts that drove him out of his marriages? Brandy: "I think both—he didn't pick well, but he wanted to find the right woman and stay faithful to her."

The multiple marriages and divorces led to financial complexities. In his book, Gorcey claimed he was earning $10,000 a week and that his total career gross was one million dollars. On the matter of his wealth, Brandy said, "I have some bits and pieces of his financial records. He liked to keep notes and ledgers. It may be an exaggeration that he was worth nearly $1 million when he died, as was quoted in some of the obits, but he certainly earned near that amount in his lifetime.

"He claims his first 3 ex-wives got most of his money. They really did get a lot from him—Amelita more so than the first two. Then, my mom refused any money except child support—no alimony and no cash payout of any kind. He allowed her to live rent-free for several months on one of his rental properties. My mom had custody of Jan by Jan's choice and Dad's acceptance, although never legal, and Jan was welcome to see Dad whenever she chose, and then, of course, she had joint custody of me, and she had a son, Jim, by a previous marriage.

"Anyway, when he died he didn't have a lot of cash, just property. He sold all of his rights when he retired so nobody received royalties from his movies, but he was pleased with the amount he got from the studio for the rights. He used the money to invest in property in northern California, but also to live off from 1957–1969. He had also invested money in rental properties and other investments during his career, but sold that off when he retired. He built his house in Los Molinos after buying the property a year or so before he retired.

"Once he died, his home and an acre were set aside as [a] life estate for his widow. He didn't do that—she successfully petitioned the court. All other property was sold at much less than it was valued because of the back-tax obligation, which was met once the property sold. The money from his estate was not distributed until I turned 21 because the estate was obligated to pay monthly child support to me (until 18 if I hadn't been in college), until 21 because I was a full-time student. Mary had petitioned a friend of Dad's in Southern California to take over as executrix of the will. Dad picked him and Dad's will was right down the line: one-fifth of everything equally to: Mary, his Mom, Leo, Jan, and me.

"By getting to be executrix, when the money was finally distributed, she [his last wife, Mary] got $20K for doing nothing as the executrix plus her share of the balance, which was about $5K for each of us. Mary did not make off well otherwise—just got away with living on the estate after she married (1971, I believe), which wasn't legal, but they had eloped. And by the time I was old enough to challenge legally her status, they said it was past the statute of limitations so she lived there until she died in 2014. The house sold and the estate was divided by fifths, but to the heirs of those who were deceased (Audrey, Jan and Mary)."

To clarify, Brandy explained, "His widow didn't have any of her own money to speak of except from some secretarial work she picked up after he died. She filed for and received a life estate, which means that she was legally allowed to live in Dad's house (even though she was only one-fifth owner) until she either moved out for at least a consecutive year, remarried, or died. It should have been terminated when she remarried, but since she eloped with her new husband, nobody knew they were married. So, she lived there until she died in 2014. At that time the house went on the market."

Although the math is involved, Brandy elaborated further for the sake of accuracy: "Instead of five equal shares, it was quite a bit more complicated than that due to the fact that some of the original heirs had died. So, when my grandmother died she gave half a share to Mary (Dad's widow who helped take care of her) and half to her daughter, my Aunt Audrey. Then Audrey died and gave her half share to each of her five kids, my cousins (2% each). When Jan died, she gave half a share to each of her two daughters. When Mary died, she had 30% due to Grandma having given her a half share and her already having a full share (20%). When Mary died, she gave half of her 1.5 shares or 15% to Earl and half to her sister. Her sister died before the house sold so that 15% was inherited by Mary's two nieces—her sister's daughters (7.5% each). Leo and I each received our full share, or 20%, when the house sold in 2015."

The issue of Gorcey's problem of a satisfactory marriage, common to many financially successful individuals, is also wrapped up in his love of the bottle. Does it really matter just when or why alcohol became such a big problem for him? The addiction took hold as it served as a method of self-medicating away his shyness, insecurities, and whatever else. Undoubtedly, it obviously empowered him enough to be quite sociable and comfortable around others.

As one can expect, especially with a complex enigma such as Gorcey, there are so many unanswered questions. The connection with, or dependency on alcohol is omnipresent in his entire adult life. Even when he discussed his difficulty of taking a trip to New York for his interview done by Lamparski, Gorcey referred to his drinking to pass the waiting time of ten hours:

Lamparski: "…My guest today just flew in from Los Angeles last night. He had a rather hectic trip from what he tells me. I don't think he had as much sleep as he should have, and I'm doubly grateful to have him here today because he hasn't been in New York what did he say 1945 [sic]. And when he starts talking, you'll know he's a New York boy. You want to introduce yourself?"

Gorcey: "Well, I'm Leo Gorcey and I did have a little difficulty in getting down here. It was my fault though, I missed the plane by five minutes and I live in a suburban area where planes do not fly out every five minutes like they do from Los Angeles. So I had to wait about ten hours to catch a plane, and meanwhile I had about ten drinks, which didn't help any. But I finally did board a plane and it got me down here and I was real excited to see the city after being away from it so long. I was just very excited to see what was going on, and boy there's plenty going on!"

At the conclusion of the interview, the devil-may-care attitude of Gorcey comes through. Lamparski: "And I look forward to our dinner tomorrow night with Huntz Hall."

Gorcey: "Good. If I last that long."

Lamparski: "And a drink with Gabe Dell." (Laughing)

Gorcey amusingly concludes, "This is an action town and I may not be alive tomorrow night. But I'm gonna try real hard."

The question remains, *why did Gorcey have to drink so much?* In addition, better still is the unanswered question, *why did he not get help?* Moreover, if he did, it apparently was to no avail. His co-star Hall eventually made it into Alcoholics Anonymous (AA) meetings in the 1970s and became sober after so many years of struggling through legal and marriage issues. The possibility of a biological/genetic predisposition would better explain his uncontrollable drinking throughout his adult life. If only he could have overcome his alcoholism before his liver failed, he might have achieved the same success as Hall and lived a quarter of a century longer.

We cannot fully know why he took to the bottle so much. The fact that he did drink incessantly would even necessitate that he was performing often while under the influence of alcohol. There are times in various Bowery Boys films where he seems to be under the influence; however, the most noticeable example is when he was "fractured" while shooting *Crashing Las Vegas*. This is his last film he did in the Bowery Boys series, made after his father died.

Even in that Lamparski interview he seemed a little off-kilter. An interesting turn came when Lamparski asked Gorcey whether his famous hat was bronzed. He was not cognizant that he had ignored a question. Gorcey does not answer that question, but talks about the hat.

He adds the amusing story that he was refused a drink (presumably before doing this interview) at a bar around the corner just because of the hat. Could it be that the bartender thought that with his funny hat that Gorcey might have been drunk already? We cannot know for sure. Once again, Lamparski asks him the question of whether he had his famous hat bronzed. Again, Gorcey does not answer it with a simple yes or no, and he instead continues to talk more about the hat. Here is that moment in the interview.

Lamparski: "Where do you keep your—I like your hat you're wearing today. But I was wishing… (Gorcey laughing) Your famous hat, I understand it's been done in bronze?"

Gorcey (still laughing): "You know what's funny about is that—I walked into a bar around the corner, wouldn't even serve me a drink. They looked at this western hat; *oh, you must be drunk wearing that hat*. I imagine that's what's—a—just presuming that's what he thought because he wouldn't serve me a drink."

Lamparski: "Is the famous one really done in bronze, the one you wore in all those pictures?"

Gorcey: "The original was an Adam's. If you wanted publicized Adam's it was man— [sic]. But the way I got it was a rather odd, but one day I was wearing that little—um—it was felt, a little felt deal that I wore in *Dead End* with holes in it and everything like—"

Lamparski: "I think they called them devil's caps, because I had one. Sure. (Overlapping Gorcey's next line.) Not as nice as yours, but—"

Gorcey: "So one day, I lost it, I lost it. So, I, the prop man had this beautiful Adam's hat on you know the, uh, Adam's hat and I said, 'can I borrow that for a minute?' I borrowed it for 30 years. (Laughing) He never got it back."

3 The Richard Lamparski Interview

> "Actually, uh, I may start going with boys because girls cost me a lot of money."
> – Gorcey told Lamparski in July of 1968

UNFORTUNATELY, THIS SOLE AUDIO INTERVIEW with Gorcey done by Lamparski, which has circulated over the years, is lacking in many ways, particularly ignoring any discussion of his contribution to his films with his malaprops, nor offering any details about the working techniques at the studios or details about his partner, Huntz Hall. At least questions about some of the many films would have shed some light on his or the studio's working methods. In addition, it would have been helpful to learn the method that Gorcey used to develop his comic bits such as the malaprops, purely a result of his own creativity.

Nevertheless, the interview does reveal some things, which make it worthy of further attention. It is precious as it does give us a chance to hear what an amusing and likeable man he was behind the actor's mask. More importantly, Gorcey revealed that he did still have some inkling of regret or lack of satisfaction with his career as an actor, even though he did like the financial remuneration.

Lamparski asked, "Did you have a good time making all those pictures. 84, that's what I counted, 84 feature films?"

Gorcey: "Roughly. But it's not a good time. It's very difficult work. You have to be in the studio two hours roughly before you work, and maybe an hour after you finished, so in another words, you put [in] maybe a twelve or fourteen-hour day, and if you count your traveling time you put in about a sixteen-hour day. And it's not easy. It's a little rough. Then they change the script on you sometimes, 'cause maybe I changed it maybe more than they did. But you'll come in the morning and you'll have all this, these pages memorized, and suddenly somebody says we can't do that uh, we're changing it. And then when they start changing it, I start changing. It became quite a hassle. It's not easy work. It's not half as easy. It's not fun, it's a job."

Lamparski: "Well, it beats uh—fooling with people's pipes, doesn't it?"

Gorcey: "Yes, it pays well. I got as much as $25 thousand dollars for a picture, which only took eight days to shoot. Nevertheless, it sounds real fantastic, twenty-five thousand dollars for eight days. I'm not complaining, but about half of that went in taxes and another portion went in uh—fees, uh agent fees. Another portion went just in, you know, operational expenses. I would say that'd uh—when I made $25 thousand a week that I'd wind up with about $25 hundred; I'd say I'd wind up with about 10 percent of it."

Lamparski: "Well, I would settle with that right now, with about $25 hundred."

Gorcey: (Laughing loudly) "Well you know something, right now I would too!"

When Gorcey talked to Lamparski about some of the stars he worked with or knew, such as Martha Raye, Ann Sheridan, and Humphrey Bogart, his accounts of those memories are filled with fondness, humor, and insight into his world.

Lamparski: "You told a story, um, it's in your book, which a, I'll give you a cue to it. I wish you would tell it, because I can't the way you wrote it. The story about the time you got the gun and shot the, you were looking for something to shoot. Martha Raye is involved in this story. Would you tell that story?" (Both laugh)

Gorcey: "Well, I bought, um, I was the treasurer of the outfit, and we used to get paid in cash, about four thousand dollars a week in cash. That's a bunch of cash. So I decided in case somebody wants to try to crash the cash, I should have a gun. So I went and bought a gun. (Laughing.) Now I wanted to see if this gun worked after I bought it. I wanted to see if it's gonna work. So I went into the dressing room. Incidentally, this was on tour with four of the children. I say now, because the, I mean, then they were children. And (laughing) my wife was on tour, we were having quite a bit of difficulty, uh, matrimonially. (Laughs) So I went in and I—"

Lamparski: "Excuse me—was this your first wife?"

Gorcey: "This, a, this was my first wife."

Lamparski: "One of the four?"

Gorcey: "The one that married Groucho Marx. But everybody knew I was having a little difficulty with her, which complicated matters more. And I bought this gun to protect the four thousand a week which I had in my keg until I could get it to the bank. And I decided to see if the gun worked. (Laughing) I wanted to see if it worked, so I filled up the toilet bowl. I kind of put on real slow until it was real full and I shot the gun into the toilet bowl, and it kinda cracked it in various and sundry ways. But everybody else came running and they thought I shot my wife. (Laughing) They figured I shot Kay. (Laughs) So then I said to them, 'get some glue, we'll put this toilet bowl back together again.'"

Lamparski: "You being the plumber. (Laughing) You would know how."

Gorcey: "No, no. I told the kids to get some glue and we'll put a toilet bowl back together again. We did. Well we didn't do such a good job because Martha Raye came in the following day and we left. And her act was going on, and obviously she used the thing and it fell down and cut her up in various and sundry places. (Laughing) She tried to sue me but she couldn't find us because we were gone by then. (Laughs) We were on the road."

Lamparski: (Laughing) "It would be an interesting case to hear in court."

Gorcey: (Laughing loudly) "She still talks about it to this day. She makes a big deal out of that. (Laughing) Very, very, very wonderful woman by the way."

Lamparski: "Yes, very funny woman. (Laughing) I guess she didn't think that was very funny."

Gorcey: "She's—for a star she's real nice. Some stars aren't. Carole Lombard was one of the nicest stars with whom I didn't work, but—uh you know the same studio. And Ann Sheridan was probably the most, she was the most. One day (Laughing) Ann Sheridan had a dental appointment and we decided that well, she shouldn't keep the dental appointment. So they have ramps on the sets where they we [sic] keep these big lights and everything. So we drove her car up on a ramp then we took the thing away. That thing that leads up to the ramp, we took it away. Whatever you call that?"

Lamparski: [Word is uncertain, it sounds like] "Stag pipe."

Gorcey: "Yeah. We took that away. And when she came out her car was sitting up 12 feet in the air with no way to get it off. That was a dirty trick. That was the only thing I did that ever regretted that I—"

Lamparski: "You like Bogart too, didn't you?"

Gorcey: "Oh, Bogart was the best. He was a prince. See Bogart was, some people didn't like Humphrey Bogart just like some people don't like, uh, did not like Frank Sinatra. And we all have friends and we all have enemies. And I don't think there's anybody that has all friends. But Bogart was, oh boy. His was uh, well I call him a prince. They called Barrymore a prince. Somebody called him, in fact they wrote a book about him."

Lamparski: "*Goodnight, Sweet Prince*, yeah."

Gorcey: "But Bogart was the nicest. He occasionally got in a little trouble for drinking, which everybody [who] drinks does. But, uh. he was a very, very nice person."

One thing certain is that Gorcey recognized the limitations of the studio system. He told Lamparski about how the actors are. "Close in particularly when they worked in the same studio, they, they have a caste system. I mean the stars don't go in with the extras, but the extras go with the extras and they have a caste system. And the stars go with the stars.

Gorcey: "You work at MGM and work with say Spencer Tracy, unfortunately I guess he's—"

Lamparski: "He died."

Gorcey: "He died. Habit of some people. Some people of having a habit of dying. Uh Spencer Tracy he would go with four or five, you know actors, or actresses in the same studio. But he would not go with actors or actresses from a different studio. He wouldn't go with anybody from 20th Century, 20th Century Fox for instance, you got a real caste system. Guys from MGM would go with the guys from MGM and the girls from MGM. The guys and the girls from 20th Century Fox would go with the guys and the girls from 20th Century Fox. It's a caste system."

Lamparski also got the uninhibited Gorcey to speak freely about his mixed Catholic and Jewish heritage and the possibility of giving up his love of women.

Lamparski: "Do you ever think what you might be doing if you stayed with Uncle Rob and his plumbing shop?"

Gorcey: "Yes I think I'd (Laughs) be better maybe because I would've married a nice Jewish girl. Rich, I never met a poor Jew."

Lamparski: "Oh, I'll introduce you to a few."

Gorcey: (Laughing) "I never met—"

Lamparski: "There's a few around here."

Gorcey: (Still laughing) "No, I'm serious, it may not sound right but uh, my family is half Jewish, half Irish Catholic and half Russian Jew, and the Irish Catholics haven't got a nickel, but all the fucking Jews are doing real good. They own half of New York, I think." (Laughing)

Lamparski: "Well, now you said in your book you're looking for a nice Irish Catholic girl?"

Gorcey: "Yeah that, I was sort of, that was satirical. That was with tongue in cheek uh, you know, just as a reversal of what I've done before. Actually uh, I may start going with boys because girls cost me a lot of money. (Laughs) They cost me $300 thousand in three years. That's a lot of money."

Lamparski: (Overlapping) "Are they cheaper, boys?"

Gorcey: "I'm beginning to study the situation. I may become a hermit." (Coughs and laughs)

Most honest perhaps is that Gorcey indicated that he certainly did not think highly of his acting ability. He told Lamparski: "Gabriel Dell was the best actor in the group. And I considered Billy Halop my equivalent, you know something like that. The actor that I thought was the worst one, actually in the final analysis did the best. The actor I thought was the worst one was me." (Gorcey laughs)

4

THE BRANDY GORCEY ZIESEMER INTERVIEW

"He wasn't a nutso conservative. I'd say financially conservative and socially a little more liberal."
— Brandy on her father

BRANDY, GORCEY'S SECOND DAUGHTER, today a full professor at a Florida college, offered much information that helps to understand her father better. First is this chapter, which is her responses to my specific questions about him. It seems that many of these details have not received attention before. In the chapter that follows, much of her thesis appears in print for the first time. She wrote about her dad more than 30 years ago in an effort to unravel the enigma of his life and more fully understand it—if that is even possible.

As regards Leo Jr.'s book about his father, he noted in it that he would be doing a follow-up book. Brandy: "My brother *did not* write a second book and, as far as I know, he isn't working on one, but he keeps some things close to the vest—even from me, and we're pretty close.

"Colette Joel is working on a documentary about the Bowery Boys (*Bowery Rhapsody*) starting with the Dead End Kids and following the actors biographically both from a personal and professional perspective. My understanding is that there is a lot more on my dad than on the other actors, but I may have just assumed that based on all the information she collected from fans, family, and friends of Dad's. Two of my cousins, Leo, and I have all been interviewed extensively on Dad for that. Colette is a wonderful person and is doing a good job.

"Also, to my knowledge, nobody else is working on a book just about my dad. If anyone is working on a book about just Dad, they haven't asked me yet. I started to write one thirty plus years ago, but it was right around the time the Bowery Boys book by Hayes and Walker was due to be released and I couldn't get a positive response from any of the most likely publishers. I didn't actually write anything except an outline and the info in my thesis (that part is repetitive and boring except for the preface and introduction)."

"Remember I was not quite eleven when Dad died. I've intensely studied how other people perceived Dad, but my perspective is from that of a child who loved her dad and who, by some grace of God, was never subjected to the strict disciplinarian side that Leo, Jan, and Jim dealt with.

"My mom says that between the alcoholism, the stress he was under before he retired, and a dreadful fear that Leo and Jan may turn out to be like their mom, he was much stricter with them and tough on them in general. By the time I came along, he was in love with my mom, he had retired so a lot less stress, and he was able to treasure his baby daughter. I believe he really loved Leo and Jan as much as he did me, but there were forces at work that made it harder for him to relax and enjoy them as he did me. [There was also] Jim [who] was a stepchild—my mom's son from her first marriage.

"So, to me he could be very funny—with both witty comments (I got a lot of his humor even though his wit was sophisticated for a child) and funny behavior. He could also be very serious. For example, he was intense about his coin collection, his stamp collection, his gun collection, and the study of language. He studied more obscure meanings of words and then worked them into his vocabulary. It's what made him so capable of using malaprops—many ad-libbed—as part of the Bowery Boys humor.

"He liked to ride a bicycle. He used to take me on bike rides all over the place; fishing in his own boat. He was an avid fisherman and that is why he chose to buy four acres on the Sacramento River in Los Molinos. It was his favorite fishing stop during vacations from Hollywood. He'd drive to Klamath and then stop at various fishing holes on the way back to Los Angeles. Los Molinos was his favorite. He'd let me ride on the fender of his tractor when he was 'working' the land; and he took me to the country club on the way back to Mom's when I was visiting.

"He enjoyed petting and talking to our horse. He loved to run the tractor. Any attachment would do over our four acres. It was the best-kept property in Los Molinos. He liked to write. He liked to cook breakfast and the meat for any meal. His favorite breakfast to make was French toast—a painstaking process, one perfect piece at a time until six of us each had a serving and then seconds. It made Leo Jr. crazy because he had to wait so long for his second piece.

"He was retired when I was born. So as I got to be a toddler, my mom would often be out doing stuff with the older kids while I followed Dad everywhere he went. My mom and dad divorced when I was six and in the first grade, but he had joint custody. I saw him a minimum of every other weekend and roughly half of all school holidays (one of two weeks at Christmas; half of spring break, etc.) He devoted a lot of time to me on the weekends. Sometimes we'd go see his friends who either had kids I liked to play with or who had grandkids, so they had fun stuff to do at their house (Dad was 41 years older than me)."

Gorcey's heavy alcohol use obviously had to affect his relationship to others, particularly his three children. Brandy observed, "I was very fortunate. It practically ruined Leo and Jan's childhood, but I was spared his temper and his extreme behaviors for some reason. I've always been thankful for, but never really knew why I was a calming effect on him."

Brandy said that her dad did not talk to her about his Hollywood days. Brandy explained: "No. He didn't want me to be interested in pursuing a career in the movies so I didn't even know he was an actor until I was about ten.

"Later on, I asked my mom a ton of questions and subsequently met the man who would become my husband. He rented a reel-to-reel film of *Dead End* for my 20th birthday."

Brandy reiterated the cute story about seeing her dad on television: "My mom says I did see him on a big console TV when I was about three and tried to go around the back of the TV to find him. I also went with Leo and Jan to see *It's a Mad Mad Mad Mad World* at a drive-in. Leo said, 'there's Dad.' I asked when Dad did that. Leo said it was long after he retired from acting. I responded, 'Dad was an actor?' [As I said earlier] at about the same time, a kid asked Dad for his autograph. I asked Dad why? He told me the kid had mistaken him for someone famous but Dad didn't want to disappoint him."

As far as Gorcey's opinion of his fans, Brandy said, "[I] don't really know except that Mom said he loved laying on the persona when they were out and anyone made a fuss over him."

Gorcey did not get into use of other drugs, as his partner Huntz Hall's regular marijuana use, as revealed in my biography. Brandy: "No, [he was] very much against any drugs. Didn't even like over the counter pain relievers and rarely took anything, even prescriptions."

Brandy: "Some of his favorite people were Jan Grippo in Los Angeles and Denny Latimer, a local pharmacist in Los Molinos."

One wonders whether Gorcey could clearly separate what he did in films from real life. That is because we are so familiar with the likeable and endlessly interesting characters of Muggs and Slip. The reality is that not much of those characters were his real self. This would be surprising to many fans. Brandy: "No. I don't think his characters were much like him, but he did emulate them, according to my mom, in public if the people around them encouraged him.

"Remember he retired before I was born. So, I never knew the actor, just the dad. Mom said that when he wrote his autobiography it was really a mix of reality with a lot of stuff that really was more other people he admired presented as though it were him. My perspective, looking back, was that he was witty, soft spoken, affectionate (with me, anyway), liked to dance, liked watching Red Skelton, liked music, was interested in current events, liked the outdoors, loved fishing. He could be very deep (philosophically) and he was a devout, although unconventional, Catholic. He took us to church but then played pranks on people during mass."

Although her parents were divorced, this was not as problematic as it could have been. Brandy: "They were both excellent about not bad-mouthing each other in front of me, and Mom was great about his joint custody. [She] never hesitated to let him have me visit extra when Dad asked."

As regards to any misgivings or things Gorcey regretted, Brandy noted, "He told my mom he wished he had stayed on as an apprentice with his Uncle Rob and been a plumber. I think he had regrets about his failed marriages."

As for his religious leanings, Brandy explained: "His mother was Catholic and his father was Jewish. He was raised Catholic and was quite devout but in an unconventional way (as I mentioned earlier). We often had the priest at our house to chill between masses on Sunday. He'd drink with Dad and play darts, plus we had a roulette wheel and a slot machine. He always joked about hiding his 'number' when he was young and the fact that it would take St. Peter a very long time to find it."

Brandy reiterated, "He was a devout Catholic, taking us to church every Sunday even though my mom didn't go; and sending us to CCD any year we weren't in Catholic School. (Catholic School children get CCD as part of the curriculum so they don't go to CCD.) [Even] inviting the priest over many Sundays in between the late morning mass and the late afternoon mass. (We went to the first mass, fasting, and then ate breakfast afterward.) His dad was Jewish so we also grew up with a healthy appreciation for and love of the Jewish traditions.

"He also joked that when he moved to Los Angeles he couldn't play golf with the Catholics because they found out his dad was Jewish, and vice a versa. He had a necklace made with a St. Christopher, a Star of David, and a cross on it. He was conservative politically but thought it was tragic when JFK was killed. He wasn't a nutso conservative. I'd say financially conservative and socially a little more liberal. He didn't approve of gays but felt people had a right to live their own lives. He was a chauvinist, but I think he would have wanted me to do whatever I wanted had he lived to see me as an adult."

Gorcey could never imagine that his films would have fans so many years later. Brandy: "I love that in 1994 the original Dead End Kids got a star on the Hollywood Walk of Fame. That would have impressed and surprised him. He never dreamed there would still be fans by then—let alone now. I guess though he would want the public to remember his malaprops. He was proud of the fact that he studied words intensely so he could easily ad lib malaprops, and the fact that even though he only had a high school diploma he was well read and extremely articulate."

As far as watching her dad's films, Brandy said, "My all-time favorite is *Angels with Dirty Faces*. He admired Cagney even though Cagney was so professional he didn't care for the antics of the Boys. Bogart, on the other hand, put them up to, and joined them in many of their pranks. I didn't see any of his movies until I was 20. Since then I've seen almost all of them. I prefer the feature films to the East Side Kids and East Side Kids to Bowery Boys, but I enjoy watching them. I've seen *Angels*, *Dead End*, and *They Made Me a Criminal* several times each."

Brandy revealed much about her mother, Gorcey's fourth wife. Brandy: "Mom turned 81 on November 16th [2016]. She was born in 1935 (Dad was born in 1917) in Southern California, [and] she is in good health. She had an interesting childhood. During the depression her family was in pretty good shape. Her mother had married young and had two sons, but her husband died of a brain aneurysm when they were fairly young.

"Grandma (née Ethel Dawson), as her first husband was a Smith and her second husband was a Davis, she went by Ethel Smith Davis. She remarried Burt Davis, who was an engineer with military subcontracts, and they had my mom and her younger brother (by 2 years), Bobby. During the depression her father had steady work. When Mom was 13, her father got a contract to work in the Philippines building infrastructure for a full year. He took my mom, her brother, and my grandmother with him. The kids loved the whole year. They attended school on a military base but had a lot of spare time. The ship hit a typhoon and the kids thought it was the most exciting adventure they could imagine, while the crew worried.

"Mom married her high school sweetheart right after graduation and they had a son, James Manning Blakesley, in 1953. Clark was in the service, and when they got together after being separated for almost a year, they really didn't have anything in common, so they had an amicable divorce. Ironically, my mom had a lifelong relationship with Clark's parents and they treated me like their own granddaughter. Clark wasn't around much, so Grandma and Grandpa spent as much time with them as their busy schedules would allow.

"My mom got the equivalent of what is now a licensed nurse practitioner and saw an ad in the paper for a nanny for the Gorcey family. She got the job. Amelita and Dad fought constantly, but Mom adored their housekeeper, Ruby, and the two became fast friends. Ruby was old enough to be Mom's mom. After Dad and Amelita divorced, Dad got full custody of the kids. Leo Jr. was born September 1, 1949, and Jan Lee Gorcey was born June 1951 (can't remember the day). Jan was named after Dad's film producer, Jan Grippo. Mom started being their nanny when her son Jim was about two.

"Leo and Jan grew to think of Mom as the only stable and sane adult in their lives. Dad was quite erratic with both schedule and behavior due in large part to alcohol, and the fact that he now had been divorced 3 times and he was angry at all three ex-wives. One night he asked my mom if she had a nice dress suitable for a party. She said no but she could get one. He took her to a party and they had a great time. Soon afterward, he asked her to marry him, and they were married in Mexico.

"I believe they were married in February 1958 and I was born that August, but Mom swears it was February 1957, and I have not seen the marriage certificate. Dad retired and moved to Los Molinos, California before I was born. He bought four acres on the banks of the Sacramento River near his favorite fishing camp. He built a house that just sold in 2015 after his last wife (Mary) died and her life estate was terminated. When I was six, Mom and Dad divorced, but Dad had joint custody and I spent a lot of time with him until he died on June 2, 1969, on the eve of his fifty-second birthday.

"Mom was too proud to take anything that wasn't specifically hers, and also did not want alimony, just child support. She had heard Dad belittle the exes for taking him to the cleaners and didn't want to be like that. She cleaned houses and rented a farmhouse for a couple of years, and then started dating Jerry Brophy, a local telephone repairman who fancied himself to be a cowboy. They got married and bought a ranch on ten acres in 1970. She had gotten a job as an eligibility worker with a welfare department, and that became her career, ending when she was 70 as a social worker in Jackson, California.

"She moved to Florida and bought a house about five miles from us in Eustis. Tom and I have been in Mount Dora, Florida since we moved here in 1993. Mom loves gourmet cooking and eating, gardening, dogs, her grandkids and great grandkids (and me of course), and she is a staunch democrat."

As regards to Brandy's memory of her dad being so much more pleasant than Leo Jr.'s experiences, Brandy explained, "I do recall Dad's temper—just was very fortunate it was never directed at me. It's not that it didn't bother me that the older kids got so severely disciplined. It's just that I didn't understand it so I just tried to ignore it. Mom says his intentions were good and that he loved all of us very much, including Jim, his stepson, but that he had an unfounded fear that Leo and Jan would turn out to be like their mother and that scared him. Jim was right in there with Leo and Jan when they did something wrong and none of them would fess up, so they all got punished.

"Meanwhile, he spent a lot of time with me and I was like his little "mini-me" in a female version. I did get into trouble occasionally, but for some reason I could crack him up so I would just get a lecture or a mild spanking before he would hug me and we'd go do something together. He got called to kindergarten one time because I had crawled under the bus seat to change seats along with several of my friends.

"He came to the principal's office and the principle said, "Mr. Gorcey, your children are always in trouble. I see your youngest is following in her siblings' footsteps. I said I hadn't crawled under the seat but my white sweatshirt was quite dirty so they knew I was lying. My dad was mad that I lied to him, not that I had crawled under the bus seat. He told me that lying was a very bad thing and that he hated liars. I don't think I ever lied to him again. I was crying all the way home, and when we got home he took me out in his boat because he knew I loved that. By the time we got back, we were laughing and life got back to normal.

"My sister was in a half-way house due to her alcoholism when I was about 20. She read a narrative she had written that explained that alcoholics with three or more children typically had one who was ignored, one who was "perfect," and one who was picked on for every perceived flaw. That would be true with Leo as the picked on one, Jan as the ignored one, and me as Miss Perfect."

What still remains are those elusive questions regarding his marital miseries and his excessive alcohol use. In the end, it really does not matter what drove him to overindulge himself. One can surmise that his alcohol abuse served as a constant companion or lifelong friend, and as an antidote to emotional conflicts. It served as a way to deal with unhappiness in his life. Whether it was just something that developed into a bad habit when he was growing up is unknown.

Brandy: "My mom says that his social drinking turned to alcoholism after he was in a bad motorcycle accident—broke ribs, arms, and legs if I recall—that he hated taking any kind of pill or drug, so he drank heavily to keep the lifelong pain at bay. His divorces and the stress he was under before he retired just exacerbated the problem."

Brandy's memory of her dad is limited to such a short time. Of course, she is curious as to what it would have been like if he would have lived until she first became an adult, or even until now. Brandy: "My whole life I have wished that. I've been curious what he would have thought of the adult I became. He was conservative politically and I am a middle of the road democrat. He was a chauvinist but I have been a lifelong tomboy, competitive and just feeling like I could do anything I wanted. I'm definitely not a feminist, though. Just firmly believe each person should be judged on their own merit, not their gender, race, religion, etc."

Brandy observed that if her dad lived: "I feel he would have stayed about the same except mellowing more with age. I am not sure if he would have become one of the angry white male Republicans that are so common today, but then he most likely wouldn't have lived this long in the best of circumstances, so hopefully not. He did mourn Kennedy's death. [Although he did not always approve] he accepted people's social behavior like gays. He was a financial conservative. He also thought the feminist movement was absurd. He wasn't really prejudicial in a hateful way, but definitely thought blacks had specific places or roles in society."

When asked if she ever remembered any of those unpleasant situations as Leo Jr. chronicled, Brandy responded, "Vaguely. Again, my thesis will explain how I saw Dad as a split image—the dark side of his personality and the side I adored that was funny and witty and philosophical and loving."

Nowadays, Brandy best expressed her feelings about her dad when she thinks about him and his short life: "I miss him so much. I am sad that his life was so short, but also understand addiction enough to realize that I couldn't have done anything to help his alcoholism even if I were an adult. I feel I knew him pretty well, but from a child's perspective. I would love to have known him from my adult perspective. I have been told I have a lot of his mannerisms. I offer you a picture of him with a snapshot of me dressed like him for Halloween when I was about 30. It's eerie. I think I have his nose and possibly mouth, but the rest of my face is my mom's."

As Brandy is sure that her dad was very different from the characters that we have all come to love and admire, then how different was he from the tough guy he played? Leo, Jr.'s book seems to imply that he was acting out the characters in real life oftentimes. Brandy: "He enjoyed entertaining the public by emulating his character(s) and he definitely had a 'tough guy' side to him. He admired Mafia figures and other tough guys. He loved boxing and wrestling (watching, not doing), but he also had a deep, philosophical side, a love of poetry, a love of language, a love of music, he loved to dance and was very good at it, variety shows, flirting with pretty women, laughing and playing games such as darts, roulette, cards, etc."

Gorcey even wrote some poetry. Brandy: "His autobiography has some samples of his poetry. I may have a play he wrote but was never published.

"He enjoyed cute things like a little coffin that you put a penny in a slot and a hand came up out of the coffin, grabbed the penny (or other coin) and took it into the coffin (bank). He was creative. He collected guns, stamps, and coins." [Author's note: Coincidentally, my dad also had one of those coffin toys, and loved demonstrating it to visiting family and friends, particularly children.]

5 Brandy's Thesis

> "Those close to him saw him, as I did, as sometimes violent and tough, at other times passive and tender; or they saw him angry and belligerent, yet again docile and loving; or they saw him merely as confused and puzzling, an enigma."
> – Brandy on her father

IN THE FALL OF 1983, Brandy submitted her thesis to the faculty at the University of California at Chico, in partial fulfillment for a master's degree in English. In addition, Brandy intended it to become part of a full-length biography of her father. The thesis, entitled *Split Image: The Dual Life of Leo Gorcey, Dead End Kid*, is divided as follows: publication rights, preface, abstract, chapters I thru V (each offering endnotes), and bibliography. The chapter breakdown is: Chapter I. Introduction. Split Image: Leo Gorcey's Divided Sense of Self, Chapter II. The Play: Beginning of a Dead End (1935-1937), Chapter III. In and Out of Focus: Hollywood Feature Films (1937-1938), Chapter IV. The Whir and Blur of It: The Last Feature Films (1939-1940), and Chapter V. Conclusion.

The preface begins the study, explaining why this study came about, particularly how some thirteen years after his burial Brandy slowly came to unravel the mystery of her father.

Brandy: "My perceptions of my father slowly began to change, however, as I learned in my teens of what others knew about my 'famous' father, the widely-known Leo Gorcey, the tough-guy actor, ex-husband, raconteur, high-stake's gambler, life-of-the-party drinker, and Hollywood drop-out. I was puzzled, hurt by the failing image. How could it be? How could my beloved father be all these things? I began to want to know the truth about him. I began to read old magazines and newspapers, to seek out old acquaintances and fans, to talk with family members and friends. I began to watch with greater purpose the television and theater reruns of the old Dead End Kids' movies, the Bowery Boys' and Eastside Kids' films starring my father and his longtime cohorts like Huntz Hall, Gabriel Dell, Bobby Jordan, Billy Halop, and Bernard Punsly. At last I fully realized that most others who knew Leo Gorcey viewed him as a talented yet troubled man of highly contradictory, turbulent, and puzzling nature."

"As a child I had been vaguely aware of my father's sometimes perplexing behavior, but I had never been the target of his anger, irrationality, or exasperating moods. I had never considered his sometimes 'odd' behavior a threat to me. During special moments with me, my father had been a most sensitive, loving, and caring human being. How ironic it now seems to me that the man who often told me bedtime stories and rocked me to sleep at night could have been responsible for the angry termination of four marriages, sudden rampages of violence, and inexplicable incidents of wild and childish 'Dead End Kid' behavior.

"How seemingly unbelievable his incessant, suicidal drinking and squandering of large sums to satisfy his gambling compulsion. How strangely inexplicable his sudden, early retirement from Hollywood at the youthful age of 38, when he was at the 'peak of his career.' How enigmatic his subsequent move to a small Southern California rural community and his ambivalent efforts over the next few years at withdrawing from national, even international, attention. The man I knew as a loving father had also been, in the eyes of many others, a very different—and often difficult—person."

"Two Leo Gorceys now appeared before my eyes, and I began to see an even bigger mystery: how could both men be one and the same person? How could I reconcile the disparate images of my father by explaining his nature and behavior? Solving this puzzle became increasingly important to me. By the time I was 21 I had begun to expend much time and effort on the matter. I read about my father, screened his films, and interviewed those who knew him. I visited many people, places, and libraries across the United States. These pursuits, together with my own knowledge of my father, made it possible for me to gradually 'discover' my father's real nature, [or] at least to come as close perhaps as any will. I have come to know Leo Gorcey well enough, I think, to explain how he could appear to be two different people, and more importantly, why."

Next, Brandy offers the purpose of the thesis, saying "...I explain how my father's erratic, contradictory, puzzling and, yes, often troublesome behavior developed during his early adult years just before and after he went on the stage and into films.... This study is concerned primarily with the first five years of Leo's acting career, 1935-1940. I am now convinced that these five years were the most important years of my father's life, for the reason that his public and private patterns of self-destructive behavior were fixed once and for all, during this period when he first gained public acclaim and national recognition. During these years as an immature and unsettled young man, he was cast in a public role as a tough Dead End Kid that overshadowed his own personality, yet served his needs until it eventually consumed him. However much he came to despise this role, he never fully outgrew it."

The abstract follows. Brandy: "Contradictory, paradoxical, enigmatic—these are the terms often employed to describe my late father, Leo Bernard Gorcey (1917-1969), who was known to millions as the feisty little ringleader of dozens of Hollywood Dead End Kid, Eastside Kid, and Bowery Boy movies."

She goes on to state her understanding of how those first five years were crucial in solidifying her father's personality. "Unfortunately, and most importantly, it was also the period when the troublesome, dual pattern of behavior that would dominate Leo's adult life for the next 30 years, and lead to his early death, originated and locked firmly in place once and for all.

"During this five-year period, when Leo was only 18–23 years of age, and through his remaining years, he would become heavily dependent on his public image—an extension of his stage and film role as the cocky, tough-talking Dead End Kid or Bowery Boy allegedly right off the streets of Hell's Kitchen in New York City. As this study reveals, he was not able to reconcile this bravura public role, which he played offstage as well as on, with the private Leo Gorcey, who was shy, insecure, and sensitive. Only a handful of closest friends and his extended 'family' ever witnessed the private Leo Gorcey, and even with them he would often retreat into the security of playing his public role at the first sign of anxiety.

"As this study reveals, Leo began to act (and apparently to think of himself) during his early adult years as a brash, belligerent, hard drinking, gambling man who could wow the ladies. Yet his increasing dependence on this type of turbulent and self-destructive behavior would bring unfortunate results: five marriages, four ending in shattering divorces;

excessive gambling and losses; serious unhappiness and frustrations with his acting career, ending in an early retirement at the age of 38 from Hollywood to a ranch in Northern California; and alcoholism, leading to an early death from cirrhosis."

Brandy concludes the abstract: "This study will have significance especially for those who worked or lived with my father, and meaning for those interested in film history, the lives of Hollywood actors, and the filmmaking process. It will have additional value for those interested in the story of the Dead End Kids. And it would seem to have poignant but ironic interest for the account it gives of one Leo Gorcey's bout with the American Dream, of his efforts to win fame and fortune, and of his failure to find what he most wanted—happiness and security. This study has further value in that, to date, no other serious biography of my father's life has been attempted. And perhaps no one will come closer to the truth than I, who did know, even as a child, many of the consequences of Leo's strongly divided sense of self."

The thesis divides Leo's first five years as an actor into three separate chapters. Brandy: "Chapter II describes Leo's childhood and family background and his very first experience with acting as a teenager when he achieved overnight acclaim in the Broadway play *Dead End*. During the highly successful two-year run of the play from 1935–1937, Leo played the role of Spit as a member of a gang of street-urchins who would become known as the Dead End Kids. The play would establish Leo in the public eye in the role he played for the rest of his acting career, and give him the public identity he could not escape in his private life. At this time, Leo's attempts at playing Spit offstage were apparently regarded as the antics of a talented, late-blooming teenager, and everyone seemed to find them amusing. For Leo, an inescapable link was being forged in his mind, however, between his stage role and the adulation he received. He was also thrust into playing this role at an especially vulnerable time before he had worked out an adult awareness of himself, and his stage identity became an easy substitute.

"Chapter III recounts Leo and the Kids' experiences in going from the Broadway stage to Hollywood films, and to greater fame and fortune. From the Samuel Goldwyn feature film of *Dead End* (1937), the Kids would move to Warner Brothers for the filming of two additional important feature films in 1938. During these two years Leo's career came sharply into focus as he reached the pinnacle of his dramatic achievement in making the three most significant and critically acclaimed films he would make, just as his personal life was starting to go out of focus. In essentials, it was the best and worst of times for Leo, though he did not know it.

"In 1937 and 1938, Leo's tough guy image was encouraged by his friends and tacitly approved by studio publicists who relayed information about his onstage and offstage antics to gossip columnists. Leo quickly realized the public liked what they saw and heard, and he played the role for all it was worth. By now, Leo had begun to drink heavily, gamble compulsively, get into minor brushes with the law, have minor traffic accidents, abuse the language with vigor, alarm his directors and producers with his pranks, play the field of movie starlets with abandon, and get plenty of publicity. His precipitous behavior might have alarmed a more mature or cautious soul, but not Leo. He had found his niche, however destructive it might prove to be.

"Chapter IV examines the transitional year for Leo of 1939, when he and the other Kids made the last four of their seven important feature films before going on to make dozens of much less significant 'B' films starting in 1940. As concern about World War II mounted, Leo could see the quality of his 1939 films gradually slipping as Warner Brothers seemed to lose interest in the type of 30s 'message' films the Kids had been making. By the end of the year, their contract options would be dropped, and they would be forced to split into two smaller groups to pursue lesser film opportunities.

"During the whir of this frenetic year Leo had serious doubts about being typecast and continuing his film career, but he nevertheless managed to achieve the leading role among the Kids, star billing, and an excellent salary. He also entered into a very profitable real estate partnership, which would make him financially independent in the years ahead. He continued with his zany offstage antics, involving himself among other things in a motorcycle crash, which would contribute to his being classified 4-F during the war. To add to the confusing blur of events in 1939, Leo also entered into the first of his troubled marriages, which was tempestuous almost from the start, setting up the pattern for his marital woes of the future."

With that introduction of the thesis chapters, what follows is specific items from each individual chapter, which provides remarkable and interesting insights that shed light on the enigma of Leo Gorcey.

In Chapter I, as regards to television reruns of his films from the 1970s through 1983, Brandy reveals, "If Leo were here to see this new burst of public interest in his films, his reaction would no doubt be heated, contradictory, and puzzling—just as his response was, I have learned, to most things in his adult life."

Brandy correctly states: "Many people attending matinees in the 1940s and 50s might also remember the transition which the Dead End Kids made after 1941, from high budget major motion pictures into two subsequent 'B' series; first, the Eastside Kids and later, the better known Bowery Boys. Only very attentive fans, however, would have noticed how the tough and unregenerate Spit, the character played by Leo in the major films, was subtly transformed into the still brash but softhearted Slip Mahoney in the 'B' series. Most fans would remember only that Leo portrayed essentially the same character throughout his twenty-year acting career.

"…Taking their cues from Leo's stage and film role as Spit in *Dead End*, gossip columnists, spurred on by studio publicists, portrayed him as a genuine Dead End Kid, as an incorrigible young tough guy—both onstage and offstage.… Most fans would not know, however, that Leo found it strongly satisfying to transfer the contentiousness of his public character into his private life. For him it was easier and more entertaining to portray Spit at Hollywood parties than to reveal his own more sensitive personality. Unfortunately, increasing reliance upon his fractious movie image set the stage for years of traumatic conflict in his private life."

Brandy: "Violent feelings, emotional scenes, and deep resentments played a role in his often stormy marriages.* Evidence reveals that these unsuccessful marriages deeply scarred Leo, who desperately wanted domestic tranquility but could not maintain a satisfactory relationship with the women he loved. Leo's marital troubles seemed to be the result of his violent temper, an insatiable need to gamble, and a severe addiction to alcohol. Yet in a divorce suit, Leo's second wife, Penny Bankston, came closer to the underlying truth when she said that his private life often reflected the character he had portrayed since adolescence."[1]

As regards to his decision to retire early, Brandy says, "Perhaps Leo's disturbing and puzzling behavior, and its effect on others, may best be illustrated by an account of his untimely and early retirement in 1955 from films and Hollywood when he was only 38. At the time, he was at the height of his popularity and financial success, at the peak of his twenty-year acting career. Nor was there much reason for Leo to believe his career would not go on indefinitely.

---

1. I offer a reminder: Marriage #1 to Kay Marvis (1939–44), marriage #2 to Penny Bankston (1945–48), marriage #3 to Amelita Ward (1949–55), marriage #4 to Brandy Jean Davis (1957–64), and marriage #5 to Mary Gannon (1968–69).

"...Instead, he chose to retire in midstream—well off but not rich. How puzzling and upsetting it must have been to those who knew Leo in 1955 when he made what could only have been seen by his associates, friends, and family as a foolish decision contradicting all professional good sense, and throwing his and many other lives into turmoil. The truth of the matter appears to be, however, the decision was a simple case of the private Leo overruling the public Leo.

"During the first months of 1955, Leo's relationship with his third wife, Amelita, had been deteriorating. As the marriage cooled, whatever stabilizing effect family life had on him diminished. His melancholia increased, made worse by his growing dependence on alcohol. Just as his life was reaching low ebb, matters were made even worse by the death of his father, Bernard Gorcey. Leo had brought his father into the Bowery Boys' films in recent years, and a close bond had sprung up between them. Bernard's death had the effect of further dampening Leo's professional drive and ambition. For these and other reasons, Leo made the absolute decision to retire, regardless of consequences, in the middle of the filming of the forty-first Bowery Boys' movie: he could no longer make motion pictures.

"The report of this decision to his wife prompted her to file for divorce. Her reasoning behind this choice is at this point irrelevant; more pertinent is its effect of further battering the already weary Leo. Leo's hopes for his wife's moral support in his decision to retire and, consequently, the return of stability to his home life were shattered. In addition, the small ranch he had purchased in Northern California several years earlier as a retreat was taken from him in the divorce settlement."

Then Brandy explains her own arrival. Brandy: "In 1956, following the divorce from Amelita, Leo repurchased the ranch in Northern California from her. Then determined, as he was to get away from his acting career, Leo moved from Hollywood, where he had been living for nearly twenty years. Off he went to the small rural community of Los Molinos and ranch life on the banks of the Sacramento River, which he believed would make him happy. Accompanying him were his two children by Amelita, his children's governess, and his mother. One year later, the governess, Brandy Jean Davis, became his fourth wife. Less than a year later, I was born, Leo's third and last child. But in 1964, when I was six years old, my mom left my dad and filed for divorce. My father was awarded joint custody of me, however, and we spent much time together over the next few years until his death. In 1969, ten months after he married for the fifth time, my father died, on the eve of his fifty-second birthday, of alcohol-induced cirrhosis of the liver. He was buried a few days later in the Los Molinos cemetery near the Sacramento River he had loved."

Although others that knew Leo thought otherwise, Brandy declared, "I believe my father enjoyed much about the last years of his life after he retired from Hollywood. He claimed to be quite satisfied with leaving the bright lights of the city for [the] fishing and ranching life he found in Los Molinos. However, others were not convinced of this at all and regarded Leo's early retirement as evidence of his irascible behavior. For example, Huntz Hall yet strongly believes that Leo was dedicated to acting and at a loss without publicity.... Huntz Hall's opinion is shared by several of Leo's Hollywood associates who agree that Leo needed an audience to entertain, and that he turned to alcohol for solace when he was deprived of one.

"This view of Leo may well be true in part, yet I have come to believe his need of an audience was only part of the truth. Evidence does exist in numerous stories, however, that after retirement Leo often entertained crowds in bowling alleys and restaurants with improvisations on his tough-guy film role. In public, Leo was, even in retirement, dependent on his stage mask. I have come to believe that Leo the Dead End Kid was a role that he took on in adolescence for self-preservation—a cloak that he could don or doff as the situation demanded, but one that became burdensome to him as the financial security he had sought became real. As in the strange case of Jekyll/Hyde, Leo was not able to throw off all the effects of playing his long-time stage persona, however, and succumbed to it ultimately.

"Nevertheless, I knew the private Leo Gorcey who would invariably present himself to his closest friends and family as a much more sensitive and complex person than Spit or Slip Mahoney. I am convinced he was contented in retirement with being relieved of having to wear his acting cloak most of the time.

"Financial and popular success had not altered Leo's apparent dislike for acting. Contrary to what some who knew him have said, my father told me again and again that he had not really enjoyed his acting career and retired as soon as he had made enough to sustain a moderate standard of living for the remainder of his days. Unlike many performers, Leo was not consumed by the 'craft' of acting. He put in a day's work at a 'job' but let nearly all other matters in his life—his family, his studies of the English language, and other pastimes—take precedence over his work.

In spite of downplaying the value of his film career, Leo never missed an opportunity, however, to appear in a cameo role or talk show after he retired. In addition, he seemed happy with the life he had chosen for retirement; yet he continued to drink in excess.

"…My memories of my father, though limited to the first ten years of my life, recall both the sensitive, subdued side of his personality, and the sparkling yet turbulent one as well. I can remember many occasions when my father entertained groups of people, delighting them with his quick wit and the characteristic mannerisms he retained from his acting days. Any gathering of an audience might provoke an imitation of the role of the tough juvenile delinquent he had played in his earlier film days. In the privacy of our home, my father would often write poetry and recite it for his children. Although he took much delight in his literary efforts, he apparently had little confidence in his creative verse, however, and invariably discarded a poem after reading it. I also recall my father's deep appreciation of classical music. He would often sit quietly for hours in our living room, listening to album after album of his favorite compositions. His older children, Leo Jr. and Jan, both began playing guitars when they were very young. Dad delighted in their efforts, and spent much time and money helping them to develop their talents.

"These memories are mixed with less pleasant ones, however, which reveal the disturbing side of my father's personality. For instance, I remember his violent temper, which was often loosed upon devices that were not functioning properly. He threw many valuables into the river because of dead batteries, rusty caps, or faulty wiring because he had no patience when it came to fixing things. They either worked properly or they were thrown with vehemence into the Sacramento River.

"At times, my father's temper was directed at my mother. One night when my parents had friends in for dinner, Leo turned the occasion into a shamble. Since he was on a diet, he reasoned that if he had to eat small portions, then everyone else would too. My mother insisted the others should have the right to eat what they wished. She had just served the roast when my father went berserk. He ranted about the large portions my mother had begun to serve. He leaped up with his martini, made for the bedroom and locked the door behind him. Of such behavior, what could one say? Similar fits of rage, usually precipitated by too much drinking, led others to believe my father was a person of troubled, violent depths, which overpowered whatever redeeming sensitivity he might have.

"Clues to the possible causes of Leo's adult behavior may be apparent in his childhood, but they do not perhaps adequately explain why he became the contradictory and self-destructive man I came to know. Although he was raised in a calm, quiet, and mostly well-ordered family, he grew to combine an unstable temperament with violent actions, causing nearly tragic results. Although he was raised in a strict home, which discouraged excessive drinking and gambling, he fell prey to both of these vices. Alcoholism may, in part, have contributed to his early retirement, and definitely caused his premature death. Where Leo had been an even-tempered, non-violent, ordinary boy, he came of age in the limelight, known for his zany antics and tempestuous nature. Nevertheless, his childhood was marred by the effects of his parent's divorce, the bite of the Great Depression, the absence of his actor-father for extended periods, and the necessity of having to work."

Of interest concerning his youth, Leo's father, Bernard, as a vaudeville actor provided his family with an upper middle class lifestyle. Bernard often had to leave home and travel, which supplied the family with a feast or famine lifestyle. This apparently contributed to Leo's insecurity about acting and money. Although his father was a Russian Jew and his mother an Irish Catholic, Leo and his brothers went to Catholic Church simply because it was closer than the Synagogue.

The satisfying childhood ended when Leo was 12 years of age as his parents filed for divorce soon after the 1929 stock market crash. Brandy explained the impact: "The couple eventually reestablished a friendship, but the security of Leo's childhood was irreparably damaged. For the next four years Leo did not see his father, nor did Bernard contribute to his family's income. Leo, unaccustomed to a lack of money, quit school when he was sixteen to become an apprentice in his uncle's plumbing shop. The six dollars per week that he earned helped support his mother and offered Leo the luxury of an occasional date, whom he usually took to the theater for a matinee. Though Leo enjoyed working for his uncle, he missed his father and desperately sought his love and respect.

"Since he had no idea where his father was, he became insecure and confused. Those feelings of insecurity were intensified in part by the shortage of money. During the Great Depression there were pitifully few high spots in the life of the average citizen, and most people could not spare a nickel for an apple or a cup of coffee. Leo's lack of security also stemmed from the cold fact that his father and mother, who had taught their sons the meaning of family and love, no longer loved one another.

"Leo's basic insecurity about acting may have resulted in part from a brutal family misunderstanding that developed over his job as an apprentice plumber. Just when he had begun to feel important and secure in his job with his uncle, Leo was persuaded by his brother and his father to trade in his plumbing tools for a script and try out for a part in a stage play. This decision, with its resulting family and personal conflict, did affect the rest of Leo's life. Although he was not inclined as a child toward show business, he had been raised in its shadow, yet he asserted in later life that he should never have allowed his brother and father to persuade him to give up his plumbing and go on the stage. Although he was able to engineer contracts, which enabled him to portray essentially one character in a static format for the next twenty years in an ever-changing business, he never developed much faith in the survival of his career and always revealed an ambivalent attitude toward his success as an actor. He never believed, ironically, that his one-character role would endure, and he tried to give it up as soon as he could afford to do so.

Brandy says her study "…reveals how the young Leo Gorcey, at a troubled time in his teen years, was cast into a stage and film role which gave him a means of hiding his underlying insecurity and sensitive nature, just as it gave him a public identity which brought him attention, acclaim, and fortune. This role became, paradoxically, both his key to success and his undoing. It reinforced some of his worst juvenile tendencies by giving him a reason to act out his rebellious behavior, violent temper, excessive drinking, compulsive gambling, and zany antics. Playing this role much of the time for his entire adult life apparently worked to arrest his maturation process at an adolescent period of his life. His efforts to shed this role and self-image later in life, especially after his retirement, were only partly successful and ultimately futile.

"…What Leo probably did not know, however, was that his stage role would determine the rest of his life, that it would continue both to serve yet conflict with his private nature, that he would never be able to shake it off. The resulting war between the two personalities of the split image, which would end in his early death, began during the first phase of Leo's professional life.

Chapter I of Brandy's thesis ends by noting that "…In a real but ironic sense, my father's life represents the fulfillment of the American Dream. His story is one of America's favorites—unknown poor boy makes good. Yet he was never really satisfied with his success. His dream was hollow. This biography explains why Leo's success was not fulfilling, but sadly tragic."

In Chapter II of Brandy's thesis, the focus initially is on Leo's first role in the stage play *Dead End*. "During these two significant years, the basic pattern of Leo's adult behavior was established, one that would not alter in any significant way during the next 33 years of his life. Three major factors contributed to hindering Leo's maturation process: the nature of the times and the play itself, the role Leo played, and the fact that his success came at a particularly vulnerable time in his life. These influences were mostly responsible for shaping Leo's 'split image' or dual nature, and the contradictory, puzzling, and erratic behavior that dominated his adult life."

On the role of Spit, Brandy notes, "Spit was the very antithesis of Leo's upbringing in that he had never experienced slum living nor been allowed to participate in gang activities. He had been much more sheltered as a child than his stage character, and his idols had been people like his father, not criminals. Leo's confusion, insecurity, and lack of direction at the time, however, enabled him to fall easily into the tough guy role that was to bring him fame and fortune. Spit's bravado was an easy cover-up or front for a mixed-up teenager. The fact that Leo's new peers encouraged Spit's deviant behavior in Leo also prompted him to play the role in his personal life."

Interestingly, Brandy offers another account of how Leo got the part of Spit—this one from his brother, David. It differs from the familiar one we have come to know that arose from Leo's autobiography. After his uncle fired him from his plumbing job, suddenly the acting job that his father wanted him and David to audition seemed to be under consideration.

Leo wrote in his autobiography (p. 28), "The plumbing shop was only ten blocks from where my brother was rehearsing in *Dead End*, so I thought I would stop in and visit him. The company was in the midst of a dress rehearsal when I found my brother backstage. He was sitting with another kid, and they were both due to go on stage in about five minutes. Suddenly, this other kid went into a dead faint. My brother explained to me that this kid only had one line and that I could probably do it as well as he did. I must have delivered that line in one magnificent manner because, in addition to the one line, I was to understudy the role of Spit. The kid who played Spit (Charles Duncan) quit (a few days later) to join a play called *Red Light*."

Brandy offers a contradictory account that Leo's brother David told her in a personal interview (January 4, 1982). Interestingly it says that Leo played Spit from the show's start—not a few months after Charles Duncan left the role. David: "Leo didn't want to act. I asked him to come down to the set to watch one of my rehearsals. Papa had already tried to get him to audition for a role in *Dead End*, but he wasn't interested. I knew he would be perfect for the part of Spit, but I couldn't persuade him to read for it. Finally, he came down to the set to watch and I used a little child psychology. I taunted him by telling him that he couldn't act if he tried. He became angry, grabbed the script I was holding and read from it. Sidney Kingsley, who already cast Charles Duncan for the part of Spit, persuaded Leo to accept the part. Kingsley fired Duncan and, in order to avoid litigation concerning Duncan's contract, he agreed to pay three months' salary and to give him billing as Spit for the first three months. But in truth, the play opened with Leo as Spit."

Brandy: "For the duration of the play, Leo-Spit swaggered, bullied, talked tough, looked mean, and played the role to the hilt. In effect he became a Dead End Kid… but would never forget how." The overnight acclaim and success was too much for Leo to process correctly. Brandy: "At 18, in an unsettled state of mind, Leo lacked the inner confidence, serenity, and sense of direction a youth needs to make a smooth transition into manhood."

Leo managed to demand pay raises, and get them, as *Dead End* continued to be a hit show on Broadway. Starting from $35 a week in 1935, he ended with nearly $300 a week by the play's end in 1937.

In Chapter III of her thesis, Brandy discusses the first three films that Leo made as a Dead End Kid with the theme of how "slums breed criminals": *Dead End* (1937), *Crime School* (1938), and *Angels with Dirty Faces* (1938). The notorious pranks that Leo and his pals engaged included not knowing how to drive and thereby crashing into Gary Cooper's $9,000.00 Duesenberg, using director William Wyler's private phone to make long-distance calls to their mothers, and so on. They even conducted sit-down strikes to stop the punishments meted out to them by the studio for their outrageous conduct.

Brandy: "As an adult, Leo attempted to compensate for his lack of formal education by intensely studying vocabulary. On most days he would thoroughly learn a new word. He used this knowledge to strengthen his deliberate comic use of malaprops."

After his first film in 1937, Brandy notes, "the scars of fame were beginning to show…. Meanwhile, Leo was encouraged by his peers and the tacit approval of the studio itself to gamble, drink, and act rowdy. His deviant behavior spurred gossip columnists to frequently mention Leo, and the studio officials saw no reason to discourage free publicity.

"At this point in Leo's career his never-to-change pattern of behavior was beginning to solidify; however, most of his pranks were still seen simply as part and parcel of an 'underprivileged' adolescent's behavior. Nobody seemed to think Leo's pranks or 'wild streak' unusual under the circumstances. As Leo grew older, however, he would never outgrow the role of Spit. He would never be quite in control of his public image."

While making his second Dead End Kid feature, *Crime School*, Leo was arrested for speeding on his newly purchased motorcycle, and given a five-day jail sentence. It would not be his only time he would receive a citation for something like this, though it was his only time he went to jail.

Brandy: "According to Leo's brother, 'Leo started drinking when he was eighteen. By the time he was twenty-one he could match most actors in Hollywood drink for drink. I wasn't very concerned about Leo's drinking then, but I later realized that he was an alcoholic at a relatively early age.' Leo never admitted to being an alcoholic. He preferred to think of himself as being 'in shape,' like a fighter, though he admitted to being a regular drinker. In his autobiography he claims, 'I have never lost a job or missed a day's work because of drinking. Good solid consistent drinkers are a lot safer to be around than the sometimes drinker.'

"Leo's view of his drinking is ironic since his dependency on alcohol brought him much grief and, ultimately, death. Later in life he would even become violent after consuming more than his limit of alcohol. Yet Huntz Hall agrees that Leo's drinking did not hinder his work. Huntz claims, 'Leo was an early riser no matter how late he had stayed out drinking the night before. After a party Leo used to have to drag me to work and keep me awake until I was able to manage on my own.'"

For his third Dead End Kid film, Brandy explained, "Leo learned much from (director Michael) Curtiz. Years after the making of *Angels with Dirty Faces*, Leo and Huntz would both agree that it was the best of all the Dead End Kids' films. Leo would feel that he, as an individual, acted better in some later films but that as a group, the Dead End Kids were at their finest...

"Leo wanted most to be like Cagney. In fact, years later, as a Bowery Boy, Leo adopted many of Cagney's mannerisms and developed or altered them to meet his needs."

Cagney stated in his autobiography, *Cagney by Cagney*, "Most of my imitators also say, 'All right, you guys!' which I don't ever remember saying. I think some of these modifications of Rocky (Cagney's character in *Angels with Dirty Faces*) came from the Bowery Boys grabbing some of those mannerisms and altering them slightly when they made their own series. Their constant repetition of those altered mannerisms might have influenced the professional imitators because, for instance, 'All right, you guys!' sounds like a Bowery Boys' line to me."

Chapter IV of Brandy's thesis offers a discussion of Leo's last four Warner Brothers films (*They Made Me a Criminal*, *On Dress Parade*, *Hell's Kitchen*, and *The Angels Wash Their Face*) before contract options for the Kids were dropped. Brandy: "At the start of 1940, the original Dead End gang split into two groups to pursue the making of different 'B' film series, bringing to an end the youngsters' five-year close association. By this time Leo was having further serious doubts about his acting career. And to complicate matters during this hectic period, Leo entered into the first of his turbulent marriages by marrying an underage bride. Through the incessant whir of activity in 1939 and early 1940, Leo's behavior did not change in any significant way, and his view of himself was now permanently locked into place—out of focus, a blur.

"…By the end of his first year in Hollywood, he had apparently resolved never to give his underlying private self a chance to emerge in public. He had won approval in his public role and no doubt feared rejection in his private one. In the privacy of his home he alternated between playing Dead End Kid and being the sensitive, shy Leo Gorcey. In his latter role, my father was loved by his wives, children, and a few close friends. But as Spit he was often drunk and unruly. Although his wives married Leo, they often lived with Spit. This pattern of behavior ultimately confused all his wives and his children, and the results were not pleasant. By the time of his first marriage in 1939, Leo's own confusion over his dual roles was such that he could not bring the split image into focus."

While working on *They Made Me a Criminal*, his third Warner Brothers feature, the nearly 22-year-old Leo met 16-year-old Kay Marvis. They secretly married, but then remarried on May 16, 1939 after Kay turned seventeen, with her parents' permission. Brandy: "Leo once claimed that he rarely argued with Kay as neither of them like to argue unless sure of the facts. This may be true, but Huntz Hall claims that Leo and Kay fought often enough in public to discourage the other Kids from getting married too soon. In fact, close examination of the details reveals that Leo's first marriage was turbulent from the very beginning. Leo once said that on his honeymoon he and Kay got into a car accident. They walked from their car to a nearby Indian reservation, where Kay's bleeding head was bandaged. She may not have blamed Leo for the accident, but on the way home they stopped to fish, when Kay hit Leo on the side of the head with a bass plug."

Of course, there are other incidents that Leo himself recounted in his autobiography, such as the time they had a crazy water fight when they took a bath together. But his desire to keep Kay out of show business, besides his incessant gambling and drinking, took their toll on the marriage.

Brandy reveals how her father learned to make some wise investments. He partnered in real estate transactions with a Max Marks, a pharmacist that Jan Grippo knew. Brandy: "The two of them invested large sums of money in property and rarely sold until they could double their investment. One outstanding purchase made by these partners was a lot on the corner of Van Nuys and Ventura Boulevards. They bought the property for about $55,000 and sold it a few years later for over $200,000."

Although Leo and the rest of the Kids worked what Brandy called "long and hard hours" on *They Made Me a Criminal*, press recognition for singling Leo out did not come until the fifth feature, *On Dress Parade*.

The change in the characterization of Spit and the Kids to reformed urchins, apparently something the public wanted, bothered some critics.

Tom Reed of the *New York Times* weighed in: "'Spit'—as he was known in the original production—was our baby—the littlest—the one most stunted by cigarette smoking—a venomous expectorator for whom the eye of the enemy was like a flying quail to a huntsman. They didn't have to take Spit away from us and reform him from a delightful beer-drinking, pool playing, butt-shooting candidate for a James Farrell conclusion, into a Frank Merriwell of Washington Military Academy. We don't regret the others so keenly, but in the case of Leo Gorcey, we feel like exclaiming sadly, 'Et tu, Spit.'"

Brandy: "Leo was probably confused by the above review. As Spit, he had rarely been reviewed as an individual. And now that he had been able to play an individual, some critics were complaining that they liked Spit better. Leo was relieved, however, when he read more favorable reviews: 'All of the Dead End Kids are in *Dress Parade*, but Leo Gorcey takes the picture right out from under them" (B. R. Crisler). Still another review made the overtures Leo wanted to hear: "Gorcey deserves a lot of credit for his finely shaded interpretations" (Robert W. Dana).

The next film, *Hell's Kitchen*, did not satisfy most critics and disappointed Leo. Before reading this opinion from a *New York Times'* critic, Leo had thought that his new image—that of a reformed street urchin—was what the public wanted.

Brandy: "The reviews bothered Leo because he had little control over the script. He worked hard, yet his part was unrewarding. He also began to realize that the studio authorities could make or break an actor, and he did not then, and never would, like being at the mercy of movie moguls. Furthermore, Leo did not like the image the writers and director gave the Kids in this picture—that of pathetic and whimpering victims of circumstance. But try as he might, Leo was helpless to fight the system. He would take his punches and hope for improvements in the future.

"Leo enjoyed making only one scene in the film. The Kids were coached by a youthful actor named Ronald Reagan, now President Reagan. Reagan was then himself a novice actor from the Midwest with some ice skating experience who instructed the Kids for a week in order to help them film an ice hockey game. Leo, who had never been athletically inclined, found that the hard training provided a release for his dissatisfaction with the film. In later years, golf would become one of Leo's favorite activities for the same reason."

The Angels Wash Their Faces, Leo's last film for Warner Brothers, was even of less significance than *Hell's Kitchen*. Brandy: "Leo's character, like that of the other Kids, was changed for this film. The Kids were less rowdy, a little more sophisticated and, at the end of the picture, made out to be heroes."

"...As the film neared completion, Leo became quite worried about his career and his personal life and had some serious decisions to make. Professionally, he had to decide if he would rather flow with the tempestuous tide of acting or take a recent offer from his uncle to return to the plumbing shop as full partner. Leo's decision to remain an actor would continue to haunt him from time to time. Until he died, he was never able to decide if he had made the best choice.

"Leo's personal life also had to change. By the end of 1939, Kay was beginning to live her own life. She rarely asked Leo about his day at work, nor did she ask to be included in his plans. He gave the matter hours of consideration, but in the end, he wound up leaving matters as they were. The result was that they continued to drift apart as they went their increasingly independent ways. In the years to come, Leo would make more of an effort to save his marriages—particularly his third one, which produced two children—a boy and a girl. As 1939 turned into 1940, however, Leo's apparent decision was to follow his own lead, and that was to continue playing the Dead End Kid role for all it was worth. As the feature films and his Warner Brothers contract came to an end, Leo hoped he would find a new path to stardom on a grander scale, but it would not come to that. Ahead lay more of the same, predicated mostly on his dual nature and puzzling behavior.

"...Leo's troubles at home were aggravated by his lack of satisfaction with his career.... He began talking with his agent and friend, Jan Grippo, about alternatives to his current situation. At this time, the two discussed the possibility of working on a series in which Leo would be the star.... Leo's newly altered role in *The Angels Wash Their Faces* accomplished at least one thing for him: it established the character that, with only slight variations, Leo would play for many years in his second 'B' series—the Bowery Boys. First, however, he would portray once again a tough slum child for the 26* films in the East Side Kids' series. As this series neared its last film, the characters would begin to mellow so that Leo's transition into the Bowery Boys' series would be less drastic.[2]

"During each of the two series, Leo would get his wish of getting star billing, but he would never attain his goal of being the caliber of star his idols were. He would be relatively satisfied for several reasons: he became financially secure, he was allowed to contribute to the writing and directing of the Bowery Boys' series, and he would be popular with his fans. However, these successes were always overshadowed by the facts that he had been typecast, his series was not reviewed by the major critics, and his stardom was limited to 'B' movie vehicles.

"...Meanwhile, offstage, Leo was kept busy with real estate transactions and other matters: gambling, drinking, and an increasingly unhappy wife. Leo's partnership with his wife was not as successful as his business partnership with Max Marks. For entertainment, Leo avoided Hollywood's social events as much as possible, preferring the company of close friends. At times Kay was included in Leo's social plans, but more often he left her at home while he went fishing with friends or flew to Las Vegas in often futile attempts to double his paycheck. His urge to gamble, even when he had extra money, disturbed Kay. When Leo gambled he also drank heavily, and Kay could not reason with him during these times. If Kay tried to discuss these matters with Leo when he was sober he usually would not

---

2. Actually, there were 22 East Side Kids films with Gorcey appearing in 21 of them.

talk about the issues at all. If he had any amount of alcohol in his system his insecurity concerning his ability to maintain a happy marriage often caused his short temper to flare, and all communication with Kay ceased.

"Leo did not intentionally alienate his wife. Kay did not like the public image her husband portrayed, yet Leo did not seem to have much control over his outlandish and irritating behavior at the time. His Dead End role had taken possession of him. Furthermore, Leo seemed to want both the convenience of having a wife and the advantages of being single. It was hard for him to compromise. Over four years after the feature films ended [Brandy referring to the Warner Brothers' productions], Kay and Leo appeared together in 1944 on a radio special with Groucho Marx. Kay found Groucho Marx irresistible and fell in love with him almost immediately. Within weeks, she had asked for, and was granted, a divorce from Leo, after which she married Groucho."

In her conclusion, Brandy restates her understanding. "The basic conflict which shaped itself during the years from 1935 to 1940 between the public and private roles Leo played certainly must have given him a divided sense of self, and he must have viewed his own identity, as Hollywood filmmakers say, in 'split image.' Those who knew Leo had to be confused by the two images or roles he played. Those close to him saw him, as I did, as sometimes violent and tough, at other times passive and tender; or they saw him angry and belligerent, yet again docile and loving; or they saw him merely as confused and puzzling, an enigma.

"The problem for Leo, and those who had to live with him, lay in trying to bring the two images into focus, that is, in trying to reconcile the two very different Leo Gorceys. On the one hand, Leo was the famous young actor always cast in the role of an unregenerate, streetwise slum kid; on the other, he was the insecure, retiring, sensitive, middle class family man. Hard as he tried, Leo could not subdue the troublesome, though lively public role, and he (and many others) would pay a stiff price for his ambivalence.

"...By the end of the five-year period (1935–1940), Leo had thus become a famous and successful movie star in a special, though limited role. He had found his place in a hazardous, toughly competitive profession that would reward him handsomely for the next 15 years. Yet Leo had also managed in the process to achieve a dual sense of self, two identities—a split image which he would never be able to bring into focus. He would never be able to subdue for long the wild behavior of his Dead End side to his quiet, private one."

6
Press Coverage of Stage and Screen Productions

"Satisfy me? It will positively inebriate me."
– Slip Mahoney, *Fighting Fools* (1949)

With the Dead End Kids' successful appearance in the Broadway show *Dead End* came the opportunity offered by Samuel Goldwyn to go to Hollywood to make the film version of the production. Apparently, those Dead End Kids productions received the most positive coverage of any of the series films.

Some sixty years later in "Huntz Hall, Perpetual Youth In 'Bowery Boys' Dies at 78" (*The New York Times*, February 2, 1999), Michael T. Kaufman explained the appeal of the Dead End Kids in the Broadway play, *Dead End* (October 28, 1935). As the Boys were "Peppering their speech with 'dese,' 'dem,' and 'dose,' the six portrayed the hard-luck solidarity of poor teenagers who, seeing few alternatives to lawlessness, find themselves impressed by criminals.

The Broadway production garnered so much respect and adulation by the press then, as well as in the years that followed. For instance, Christopher Gray in "From *Dead End* Contrast to Homogeneous Luxury" (*The New York Times*, April 30, 1995), stated its power: "Set at the foot of East 53rd Street where the new money of River House rubbed up against the then-squalid waterfront, *Dead End* captured the dramatic social contrasts that New Yorkers take for granted." In short, the production touched a nerve for its attempt to understand that reality.

Screen contract pay raises for the five Dead End Kids received approval by Superior Judge Wilson, as reported in the *Los Angeles Times*, June 18, 1937. The article specified the salaries: "Bernard Punsley, 14, $200 to $1000 per week; Gabriel Dell, 14, $150 to $750 per week; Bobby Jordan, 13, $200 to $1000 per week; Leo Gorcey, 16, $200 to $1000 per week; Huntz Hall, 15, $100 to $500 per week. These contracts are the usual film agreement with minors in which options extend over a seven-year period."

One of Gorcey's hobbies received mention in "Victims of Café Society" by John R. Franchey (*The New York Times*, January 21, 1940). Gorcey explained: "I collect hotel stuff—everything that isn't nailed down." Franchey: "He peered down at the demitasse spoon somewhat contemptuously." Gorcey: "Nix it doesn't have anything written on it. It doesn't rate my collection."

In one way, Gorcey stood apart from associates. Read Kendall (*Los Angeles Times*, February 6, 1939): "The Dead End Kids, with the possible exception of Leo Gorcey, are thinking of enrolling in North Hollywood night classes in mechanics..."

The tales of pranks played at the studios by Gorcey and the rest of his gang are legion. Even Bogart became the butt of jokes as described in my first biography of Huntz Hall.

In Gorcey's Dead End Kids period there were seven films, beginning with *Dead End*, released in 1937, which was a screen adaptation of the highly-celebrated Broadway play of the same name that ran for two years. In 1938, the second and third films appeared; namely, *Crime School* and *Angels with Dirty Faces*.

Philip K. Scheuer ("Youth Has Its Fling at Warners," *Los Angeles Times*, June 10, 1938) acknowledged, "Leo Gorcey registers strongly as Spike, the meanie..."

Lynn Foulkes in "Portrait of Leo Gorcey" referred to his "proletarian antics."

Hopper: "Dead End Kids were minus their ringleader. Leo Gorcey, at policeman's show. Leo said, 'They didn't give me any benefits the five days I spent in jail for speeding.'"

Concerning *Angels with Dirty Faces*, Hopper noted, "Leo Gorcey, one of them, just released from jail, had collected thirteen tickets for speeding—his unlucky number."

Although Gorcey protested the report that he speeded in an auto and received a jail sentence. Interestingly, it was exactly a year after the press reported the court approved his screen contract. In a photo piece, *Los*

Angeles Times, June 18, 1938, entitled "Looks Like Another Dead End," the caption read, "Leo Gorcey, boy actor from cast of *Dead End*, shown as he appeared in traffic court yesterday to get five days." The article stated, "Leo B. (Dead End) Gorcey, 20-year-old member of the team of young actors, has spent time in jail frequently—in motion pictures.

"But yesterday, for the first time, he was given a real jail sentence. He was ordered to spend five days in Lincoln Heights after pleading guilty in traffic court to a charge of speeding fifty-five miles per hour in a twenty-five-mile zone on Gower Street near Sunset Boulevard on May 26.

"Leo passed three cars and a blind intersection at that speed, and after he was given the citation drove off in the same manner, according to Officer Bigham, who arrested him. The young actor was chagrined at his sentencing.

"'Why, you couldn't go that fast down Gower at 6 o'clock in the evening in an airplane,' he said. 'And besides I was late for a broadcast. I didn't mind the ticket but the officer turned in a report that looked like the rear end of *Anthony Adverse*. And it's the first time I have ever been arrested here except for parking.'"

Over 30 years later, the reported driving speed changed from 55 to 92 miles per hour. *Washington Post*, June 4, 1969: "In his real life tough guy performances, he once served five days in the Los Angeles County Jail for driving 92 miles an hour down Wilshire Boulevard."

Kendall: "Leo Gorcey, 'speed king' of the six Dead End Kids, was not allowed by Warners to drive his car in *They Made Me a Criminal* location near Palm Springs. The answer is obvious."

Elsewhere in the press, Gorcey "has been bitten by the writing bug." In Hopper's "Kids Look for Greener Fields" (*Los Angeles Times*, July 31, 1938), "Leo Gorcey wanted to go back to his plumber's assistant job when he started his acting career. A year later, he decided to give up both plumbing and acting. Now he wants to be a writer."

Schallert: "You can't stop the Dead End Kids. If perchance their existence is menaced as screen actors, because the public sends barbs in their direction from time to time, then they have other lines. Here's Leo Gorcey, for instance, who has written a story called 'Jinx Jockey.' He is very anxious for the Warner studio to purchase their rights to the subject, but it remains to be seen what will come of it.

"Gorcey is one of the cleverest of the Dead End Kids and personally I'm for 'em. Let 'em roll on."

Hopper: "Leo Gorcey, one of the 'Dead End' gang, ordered Bert Wheeler to hurry up and change his pants. Said: 'How was I to know he was a star? I thought he was my stand-in!' Maybe we'd better tell those kids the facts of life. Leo Gorcey, who used to be a plumber's assistant in Brooklyn before he became a star, was proud of the fact that the palms of his hands were so tough he could strike a match on them. [sic] *Crime School* is frequently visited on the set by his father, Bernard Gorcey, diminutive dialect comedian from the Broadway stage."

Some fans insist that Gorcey's best films are those Warner Bros. films with the big budgets and stars. Is it simply because they are better productions overall? Brandy: "I personally find myself agreeing that *Angels* is my favorite of all of his films. When I've chatted with film professors over the years, they tend to think the feature films were socially significant and had [been] well written, well filmed, and well performed compared with the 'B' films. Then, they feel the East Side Kids were higher quality and the scripts were better than the Bowery Boys. As far as just looking at Dad as an actor, I think he had a lot more freedom to ad lib in the Bowery Boys and I think he kept the humor lively—especially playing off of Huntz Hall and Louie."

Indeed, it is the two "B" film series he did at the Poverty Row studio, Monogram, especially with the Bowery Boys films, that gave Gorcey a lot of wiggle room. He could do so much more, and the productions made him really shine as an actor/comic/etc. By comparison, the Dead End films have him in competition with the other Kids, especially with Billy Halop. Despite the production values and acting talent being seen as superior during the Dead End Kids films, Gorcey gets very limited screen time in them, especially in *They Made Me a Criminal*, and even in everyone's favorite, *Angels with Dirty Faces*.

One of the unanswered questions is why seven of the twenty-two East Side Kids comedies have never been available, anywhere. (Gorcey appeared in 21 as the first production had a different cast altogether). The titles are *Mr. Muggs Steps Out* (#15), *Follow the Leader* (#17), *Block Busters* (#18), *Bowery Champs* (#19), *Docks of New York* (#20), *Mr. Muggs Rides Again* (#21), and *Come Out Fighting* (#22).

Brandy: "In the early 80s, we found out who owned some of these but he never responded to our attempts to ask him if he was going to sell or release them. I can't find my notes on who that was."

Unlike Hall, Gorcey did not appear in *The Little Tough Guys* series of films done for Universal Studios. The press had little to say once Gorcey moved over to Monogram with the *East Side Kids* series. For what it was worth, the few mentions follow here.

For *Boys of the City*, the first East Side Kids that Gorcey appeared in had the national release title of *The Ghost Creeps*. One reviewer with initials T.M.P. (*The New York Times*, August 19, 1940) emphatically denigrated the film in saying: "wasting their time on the sort of hocus-pocus entertainment (?) that the Globe is serving this week."

Positive remarks were few and brief for the Monogram quickies. For instance, for *Spooks Run Wild*, one of the East Side Kids that combined comedy and horror (*Ghosts on the Loose* is another), a clip by G.K. (*Los Angeles Times*, October 6, 1941) noted, "Leo Gorcey, Huntz Hall, Bobby Jordan, and Sunshine Sammy Morrison, as usual, are amusing."

Strangely and incorrectly, Leonard Lyons' *Gossip* (*The Washington Post*, November 14, 1943) reported, "Lou Costello will direct the Monogram movie, *Block Busters*. It will star three of the original Dead End Kids: Leo Gorcey, Huntz Hall, and Billy Halop."

One of the few and most appreciative reviews of Gorcey's acting in this series came with *Bowery Blitzkrieg* ("East Side Kids Score in *Bowery Blitzkrieg*," *Los Angeles Times*, July 24, 1941). It gives Gorcey fine credit when he plays Muggs as a young prizefighter in trouble with racketeers: "The lads' acting, always up to or beyond par, is just as good always, with Gorcey beginning indeed to be able to convey subtleties and shadings of meanings…. Altogether, this is one of the best of the East Side Kids' endeavors."

However, just as emphatically the critics could be harsh. Bosley Crowther in "From Bad to Worse" (*The New York Times*, October 1, 1941), reviews the same title, noting: "Without meaning any offense to the parties immediately concerned, we do think the time has come to write off those erstwhile Dead End Kids. Why not make an end of these fictions? Why not let the kids go really bad, then convict them of murder, execute them and call the whole thing quits? That would be deeply satisfying—and the kids could grow up and become actors at last."

As for the *Bowery Boys* film series, the press did not see any fine moments in their limited coverage. Although there were forty-one films that Gorcey did in the series, the press clippings in the four major papers only covered some of the films during a ten-year period, and simple name-dropping comprises the bulk of the announcements. The references in these news clips report the productions underway with particular emphasis on naming who is to be in the films. In short, Gorcey and others receive attention often in name only.

In "'Dead End' Kids Grow Up to Be 'Bowery Boys'" (*Los Angeles Times*, August 18, 1945), Schallert reports, "Meet the 'Bowery Boys—Leo

Gorcey and Huntz Hall. Which, incidentally, gives the 'Dead End' kids a new career."

"The hard-boiled performers are to appear in a series of pictures. Monogram will sponsor these, and Alan Milan is working on the script of the first, which will be titled, *Stepping Around*.

"Actually, the films will be sponsored by Jan Grippo of Jewel Productions. He is the manager of the two young chaps, as well as Stanley Clements, who recently made a hit in *Salty O'Rourke*. Grippo is a clever magician on the side. Four pictures will constitute the series, per arrangement made with W. Ray Johnson, Monogram head."

In another review, Schallert notes (*Los Angeles Times*, December 5, 1948), "The picture is called *Trouble Makers*, one of the numerous branches—or twigs—that have sprung from 'Dead End' of years ago."

In reference to Adele Jergens scheduled to play in the Bowery Boys picture, *Blonde Dynamite*, Schallert acknowledges, "The Bowery Boys pictures have been getting very good playing time in the theaters."

Blonde Dynamite (*Los Angeles Times*, February 17, 1950): "…Adele Jergens is a glittering presence, and Leo Gorcey and Huntz Hall and their associates do roughshod and amusing duty. The picture provides entertainment of the secondary grade, but not too bad. William Beaudine directed."

Schallert reported (*Los Angeles Times*, July 29, 1950), "Adele Jergens has signed for the feminine lead in 'The Bowery Thrush,' with Leo Gorcey, the male star, in the Jan Grippo production at Monogram." The film would be released as *Blues Busters*.

As regards *Angels in Disguise*, Schallert reported (*Los Angeles Times*, July 6, 1949), "Copper Johnson will play a featured part in *Angels in Disguise* with Leo Gorcey at Monogram. Jean Yarbrough is directing. Miss Johnson was formerly at Pasadena Playhouse."

For *Feudin' Fools*, the *Los Angeles Times* (September 18, 1952) praised the film, saying: "It is about the best of the Bowery Boys series and delights the kids to no end."

Hopper ("Looking at Hollywood," *Los Angeles Times*, November 8, 1947), explains *Angels Alley* as, "Miss America pitches woo with Dead End Kid. That's exactly what will happen when Leo Gorcey, toughest of the Dead Enders, and Rosemary La Planche, Miss America, co-star in *Angel's Alley*, which Jan Grippo is producing."

Schallert (*Los Angeles Times*, August 12, 1948) acknowledges what Gorcey does best. He explains, "*Jinx Money* is one of the pictures descended by a long and devious route from Dead End.... Leo Gorcey massacres English efficiently for comedy, and Hall is a capable foil. The film is a rough-and-ready affair with especially good performances by the heavies, including Lucien Littlefield, Ben Welden, Ralph Dunn, John Eldredge, and others. Betty Caldwell being a moll. William Beaudine directed."

For *Let's Go Navy*, G.K. ("Tough Kids Join Navy," *Los Angeles Times*, July 31, 1951) writes: "It looks as though Leo Gorcey and Huntz Hall are qualified to become a sort of junior Abbott and Costello, if Monogram sees fit to team them, although the whole group of Bowery Kids is so popular that the organization might hesitate to dismember them. The audience howled its delight at the Bowery Boys' antics...."

"The Bowery Boys in *Let's Go Navy* are accountable for surprisingly good laugh entertainment, largely because their picture is of the timely type, and well played. It will probably afford more fun for the average audience than 'Belvedere.'"

Sometimes the film productions referred to in news clips have a change in the title. Other times Gorcey does not appear in the film after all. For instance, in one clip ("Films on Monogram, Allied Artists Schedule") reported, "Leo Gorcey and Huntz Hall will lead the Bowery Boys in four comedies, including *The Leathernecks*." The name change for this latter production is unknown.

As regards *Crazy Over Horses*, readers are simply told, "On the program are the reliable Leo Gorcey..." For *Here Come the Marines*, Schallert says the film, with a "cast headed by Leo Gorcey and Huntz Hall, is amusing."

Frequently, references in articles are to film productions whose title changes, such as *High Gear*, *High Tension*, and *Panic*. Hopper (*Chicago Daily Tribune*, November 19, 1945): "In the Dead End Kids' next picture, *High Gear*, Leo Gorcey, toughest of the lot, comes under the influence of a priest and ends up a philanthropist. The crusade against juvenile delinquency is now complete."

Schallert (*Los Angeles Times*, January 28, 1946) noted, "...*High Gear* of the Bowery Boys' series will have Leo Gorcey as an individual star, as well as various 'Dead End' kiddos of yesteryear."

Two years later, Schallert (*Los Angeles Times*, May 21, 1948) reported, "John Ridgeley gets an important heavy role in *High Tension*, per deal arranged by Jan Grip, who is producing this Leo Gorcey starring feature for Monogram."

In another clip, Schallert noted that Dan Seymour joined the cast as a spiritualist in the Jan Grippo production, *Panic*, starring Gorcey. This production made it to the screen as *Hard Boiled Mahoney*, the sixth Bowery Boys release.

Unfortunately, the limited press coverage to the Bowery Boys series did not matter to the viewing public. It is a shame that only the fans would know of the many fine moments in their last series. In fact, Gorcey plays his Slip Mahoney as an even more likeable and charming human being than his Muggs character in the East Side Kids series. Gorcey manages to exude a naturalness, a calm, and at times an engaging vulnerability that makes watching him even more enjoyable than in the previous two series.

Although his skill as an actor is evidenced in moments throughout the series, it would seem appropriate to give some examples of what the critics were missing when they ignored acknowledging the sincerity in Gorcey's roles. At times, Gorcey made his character seem so real, most especially in the Bowery Boys series. For instance, in *Angels' Alley* (1948), indeed it is a rare treat to see Gorcey's Slip actually laugh. We are treated to a tear-invoking and memorable moment when he expresses his feelings for the injured Boomer, a young fan of Slip who is in the hospital after being hit by a car.

Sach manages to cheer up a rather despondent Slip by doing imitations. Sach invites Slip: "Play some pool? How about some snooker? Wanna see my new trick? Wanna hit me with your hat?" None of these suggestions interest Slip, so Sach offers what he calls "some new imitations."

Sach first does an impression of what sounds like Ronald Colman who tells of someone who idiotically cut off his own leg without surgical equipment. He also does impressions of Jimmy Durante and James Cagney. Then he sings a silly jingle of "Figaro," ending with "I can't figure this guy out." Finally, that makes Slip laugh, and he responds happily, "You're O.K. Sach." Sach's persistence paid off as he overcame Slip being so downtrodden.

Another example is in *Blues Busters* (1950), in which Gorcey's Slip reached a rare moment of disgust and seemed to cut all ties, leaving both in a place of no return when he parted ways with Sach. The scene when they reconnect is truly unforgettable. For that reason, I repeat the exchange of dialogue here, as it is so satisfying to have Gorcey express his sensitive side. Although there are other moments in this Bowery Boys series worth singling out, this is one of the two or three best. Undoubtedly, Gorcey played this very touching scene well.

The scene happens when Sach meets up with Slip on the street and gives him a wad of money. The following exchange ends with a bittersweet smile made by Slip that makes you believe the connection between Sach and him. Yes, this is proof they truly cared about each other:

Sach: "Chief. Oh Chief."
Slip: "Hi ya Sach."
Sach: "How are you, Chief?"
Slip: "Good, I feel fine, real fine."
Sach: "I wish I felt that good. I feel rotten."
Slip: "How can you feel rotten? It's the first time in your life you're living. You're on top of the world."
Sach: "Yes, but it's lonesome up there. I want to come back, Chief. Please take me back."
Slip: "I couldn't do that. You're in the big time now. Wearing expensive clothes. Meeting important people. You reached the pineapple of your career."
Sach: "Yeah! But I wish things were like they used to be. Conning Louie out of banana splits. Going out looking for jobs and trying not to get them."
Slip: "Yeah those were the good old days. But it seems so long ago."
Sach: "Why did I have to go and get my tonsils out?"
Slip: "I don't know. I guess it was just a jerk of fate."
Sach: "How's Whitey? Is he still taking his vitamins?"
Slip: "I told you, Whitey's great, we're all in great shape."
Sach: "Here's eight hundred dollars, maybe you can use it."
Slip: "Eight hundred dollars. That's a lot of money."
Sach: "It is, well take it anyway maybe you can help pay some of Louie's debts with it."
Slip: "I couldn't take that, Sach, it would leave you broke."
Sach: "Broke, me broke? I'm loaded. I got a pocketful of nickels."
Slip: "You're holding out, huh? I was only kidding. This would help pay some of Louie's bills though."
Sach: "Gee, thanks for taking it Chief. You're a pal."
Slip: "Gives me his life savings, and then he thanks me. Good old Sach."
Sach: "Well, I gotta go Chief, so long, see ya later."
Slip: "So long Sach."
Sach: "Chief?"
Slip: "Yes." (Sach takes his hat and gives it to Slip.)

Sach: "Just one for old times' sake, please." (Slip takes his hat and weakly slaps Sach over his head.)

Sach: "Thanks a lot Chief. But you didn't have your heart in it."

On some more personal, non-film production references, a number of clips mention Gorcey. For instance, Jimmie Fidler complained, "Leo Gorcey: So you've been dancing at Charlie Foy's in your stocking feet. A charming informality, but isn't it rather silly for a grown-up man?"

"Another young sportsman is Leo Gorcey, of the 'Dead End' kids. He once met an Indian prizefighter rejoicing in the name of Joe Washington. Leo renamed his protégé King Rain-in-the-Face and is managing his fighting career."

In "Young Player Saves His Money" the public learned, "Leo Gorcey is putting all his film salary, save a budgeted sum for living expenses, into the purchase of insurance policies which should revert to the young man as a tidy fortune when he is between 35 and 38. If he is ready to retire from acting at that time, he will invest in some business. He has $17,000 sunk in annuities already… "

Dorothy Kilgallen reported, "Dead Ender Leo Gorcey is on crutches. Wrenched knee…."

In a clip entitled "New Hat Finally Wins Gorcey," the press reported that Gorcey "…becomes attached to his clothes and hates to give them up until they are embarrassingly shabby, recently bought a new hat—his first in 10 years. He was happy with it at the end of the first day. His kidding friend yanked it off, slammed it on again, pulled it down around his ears and otherwise abused it until, in the space of a few hours, it looked older than the old one."

In "Gorcey Assaults Hot Rod Record," the press reported, "Dead End Kid Leo Gorcey joins the 'crash wall' kids of the American Sport Car Association at the 5-H Speedway in Roscoe tonight. Using car No. 71, last week's winning hot rod, Gorcey in a special event will assault the speedway's one-lap track record."

In "Gorcey on the Slide," "Leo Gorcey's favorite pastime when in NY is to bet which seal in the Central Park Zoo will slide into the water first."

In "Two London Visitors Feted," Gorcey is listed among those welcoming London Picture Executives at a dinner at the Vendome, D.C. Dobide and W.J. Brown.

Gorcey participated in the Frank Borzage motion picture golf tournament at the California Country Club along with more than 150 others: "…with some of the greatest names of filmdom scheduled to swing their golf sticks for sweet charity."

He also participated in the golf tournament held in Washington, D.C.: "Dead End Kid Joins Celebs": "A 'Dead End Kid' will do his bit to help stamp out juvenile delinquency through the National Celebrities Golf Tournament and Bob Hope show this weekend.

"'Delighted to take part in the great show,' said Leo Gorcey, one of the famous Dead End Kids. Gorcey is visiting his father-in-law, Bud Ward, in Alexandria.

"Leo Gorcey, who gained fame as 'Spit' of the Dead End Kids… will add his talents to the National Celebrities Golf Tournament…. Another celebrity who joined the field, Dead End Kid Leo (Spit) Gorcey, was already in town whooping it up for the big tournament."

"'My golf's fair,' he answered. 'I break 90—and I don't mean clubs.'"

A clip referring to the deep-sea boats off Ocean Park pier stated, "Leo Gorcey, one of the Dead End Kids, had a full string of rock bass and a nineteen-pound sea bass yesterday."

Another report stated Gorcey's score at the California Country Club of 93, 51–42.

Kendall: "Leo Gorcey, 'heavy' of the Dead End Kids, and Kay Marvis were a combination at the Victor Hugo."

One of the most unusual press clips by Kendall revealed, "Leo Gorcey of the Dead End Kids operates a chain of doughnut shops on the side."

As most readers are quite familiar with Gorcey's characters in the Dead End Kids, East Side Kids, and Bowery Boys films, it seemed worthwhile to examine the press coverage of the many films he made besides the series films. To show the place of these "non-series films" in his large credits list, the titles of the series films have been repeated in a brief yearly run-down that follows in order of film release dates.

After his first film appearance playing Spit in *Dead End*, which came out in August (24) of 1937, Gorcey next appeared in a film released four months later (Dec. 14, 1937), the MGM film *Mannequin*, starring Joan Crawford and Spencer Tracy. Gorcey played Clifford Cassidy (brother of Crawford's character) in his first of many non-series parts. Crawford plays a woman who tries to make a better life for herself via marriage, only to discover true love with a millionaire having financial problems.

Schallert: "Leo Gorcey shone in *Mannequin* with Joan Crawford… Gorcey, incidentally, didn't do at all badly in *Crime School*."

Gorcey was seen as Spike Matz in *The Beloved Brat*, which concerns a problem child played by Bonita Granville and her problem parents, played by Donald Crisp and Natalie Moorhead. The film, released on April 30, 1938, was Gorcey's second non-series role. A month later (May 28, 1938) he played Charles "Spike" Hawkins in *Crime School*, the second Dead End Kids film. *Angels with Dirty Faces*, the third and best-loved film of that series came six months later (November 24, 1938).

In the Buck Jones western, *Headin' East* (1937, Columbia), Gorcey is seen as a boy boxer.

In *Portia on Trial* (1937, Republic), Gorcey's brief appearance is as the death row prisoner whose wealthy lawyer, Portia Merriman (Frieda Inescort), pleads for him to get his sentence commuted. He is seen for only a few seconds in the film, seemingly overtaken with emotion when he learns he is getting life in prison instead.

Gorcey is seen for a few seconds among the Dead End Kids (at the time of *Crime School*) in a short subject called *Swingtime in the Movies* (1938).

Roat credits Gorcey as being seen in *Land of Liberty* (1939) in archival footage; however, this could not be confirmed.

In *Private Detective* (1939), co-starring Jane Wyman, Dick Foran, and Gloria Dickson, Gorcey appeared uncredited as a newsboy.

Two months later (January 21, 1939), the fourth film of the Dead End Kids series, *They Made Me a Criminal*, gave Gorcey's Spit little to say. *Hell's Kitchen*, the fifth film of the series, came out six months later (July 3, 1939). Then less than two months later (August 26, 1939), the sixth outing in the series came, *The Angels Wash Their Faces*. Here Gorcey's character had the name of Leo Finnegan. *On Dress Parade*, the final film in the series, appeared another two months later (October 27, 1939).

Gorcey again played in a Warner Bros. crime film, this one starring George Raft, William Holden, and Humphrey Bogart. However, here he had only a bit part as the head stockroom boy named Jimmy in *Invisible Stripes*, his third non-series role, released on December 30, 1939.

Seven months later (July 15, 1940), Gorcey appeared in *Boys of the City*, where he began playing Muggs McGuiness in his first of twenty-one East Side Kids films at Monogram Studios. He finished 1940 with the release of two more East Side Kids films [*That Gang of Mine* (September 23), and *Pride of the Bowery* (December 15)], and another non-series role as "Doc" Reardon in the MGM mystery film *Gallant Sons* (November 15). It starred Jackie Cooper, Bonita Granville, Gail Patrick, and Gene Reynolds.

The New York Times Screen News announced a follow-up film to *Gallant Sons*. *Young Americans* was to be about a "group of boys and girls that uncover a spy ring in San Diego." It featured Dan Dailey, Jr and Gorcey in supporting roles. Schallert reported, "Leo Gorcey is doing a part in *Young Americans*...."

That same year Gorcey played an apartment house bellhop in the musical comedy film *Hullabaloo* (1940), starring Frank Morgan, Virginia Grey, and Dan Dailey. The latter played an actor attempting a comeback with a radio show.

In 1941, Gorcey did three more East Side Kids comedies [*Flying Wild* (March 10), *Bowery Blitzkrieg* (August 1), *Spooks Run Wild* (October 24)]. In addition, he did two non-series films; first he played Punchy Dorsey in the Republic Pictures comedy film, *Angels with Broken Wings* (May 27), co-starring Binnie Barnes, Gilbert Roland, and Jane Frazee.

In a piece entitled "*Angels With Broken Wings* Features Youthful Cast," the *Los Angeles Times* (May 29, 1941) reported, "Leo Gorcey successfully sourpusses his way through various scenes, adding to the amusement."

At the same time, Fidler observed (*Los Angeles Times*, June 3, 1941), "Republic's *Angels With Broken Wings*. Weakness of plot stymies the good work of Gilbert Roland, Binnie Barnes, and Leo Gorcey."

Later that year, Gorcey appeared as Eddie in the Warner Bros. film noir, *Out of the Fog* (June 14, 1941). The latter is the tale of fishermen (Thomas Mitchell and John Qualen) and their pier controlled by a gangster (John Garfield) in love with Mitchell's daughter (Ida Lupino). Gorcey had a cameo in the Crosby-Hope vehicle, *Road to Zanzibar*, which is not seen in circulating prints.

In 1942, Gorcey was seen in four East Side Kids comedies [*Mr. Wise Guy* (February 20), *Let's Get Tough!* (May 29), *Smart Alecks* (August 7), and *'Neath Brooklyn Bridge* (November 2)] and three non-series films. First, Douglas W. Churchill of *The New York Times* reported it under its proposed title, noting, "Metro added Leo Gorcey to *Ballad for Americans*." He played the part of Snap Collins in MGM-distributed *Born to Sing* (February 18). In addition, Gorcey reportedly sang, "I Hate the Congo," in this film about a composer of show tunes whose music was stolen by a show promoter.

Scheuer (*Los Angeles Times*, April 3, 1942) explained, "Still other youngsters, more than you can shake a script at, populate *Born to Sing*. The story is completely implausible, but you won't mind that particularly things move too fast. Leo Gorcey, leader of the gang, is as quick on the trigger in his way as Rooney is in his, which is no small compliment."

Schallert reported (*Los Angeles Times*, February 11, 1942), "Leo Gorcey wins a term contract at Metro, in addition to a job in *Sunday Punch*." This 1942 film is about the rivalry between boxers. His minor part as lightweight fighter "Biff" has importance to the story, for his character changes his mind about keeping silent about something he overheard.

In June of 1942, Gorcey played Cecil in *Maisie Gets Her Man*.

In 1943, Gorcey did only one non-series film, *Destroyer* (August 16), when he played Sarecky. The film released by Columbia Pictures starred Edward G. Robinson and Glenn Ford at odds in this tale of a Navy destroyer.

Nelson B. Bell in "The Spirit of the Navy Reflected in *Destroyer*" (*Washington Post*, September 18, 1943): "Comedy is vigorously injected by Leo Gorcey, originally of the Dead End Kids, and Ed Brophy, as a gob and the ship's engineer, respectively. . ."

Schallert writes in "*Destroyer*: Seafaring Melodrama" (*Los Angeles Times*, October 2, 1943), "Leo Gorcey and Ed Brophy aid the comedy."

Mae Tinee's review notes that the movie shows skill in acting: "Thank Edgar Buchanan, Leo Gorcey, and Ed Brophy for most of the laughs."

For the review of *Down in San Diego*, Tinee's "Kid Actors in This Picture Put It Across" (*Chicago Daily Tribune*, November 16, 1941), only mentions Gorcey for simply playing "Snap" Collins.

That same year he also appeared in four East Side Kids films [*Kid Dynamite* (February 5), *Clancy Street Boys* (April 23), *Ghosts on the Loose* (July 30), and *Mr. Muggs Steps Out* (October 29)]. For *Kid Dynamite*, the reviewer in the *Los Angeles Times* (January 16, 1943) concluded: "The lads turn in their usual characterizations and are amusing and entertaining."

In 1944, he did four East Side Kids comedies: *Million Dollar Kid* (February 18), *Follow the Leader* (June 3), *Block Busters* (July 22), and *Bowery Champs* (November 25).

In 1945, Gorcey appeared in one non-series film, playing the caretaker of a wax museum named Clutch Tracy, in *Midnight Manhunt* (July 27). Typically, Gorcey's character is replete with malaprops. The first announcement by *The New York Times* Screen News (November 18, 1944) stated, "Leo Gorcey has been signed by Pine and Thomas for the forthcoming Paramount comedy mystery *Cheese it, the Corpse*." The mystery film tells of a reporter (Ann Savage) and her boyfriend (William Gargan) who search for a criminal found dead at a wax museum.

Crowther reviewed *Midnight Manhunt* in "The Screen: Corpus Not So Delecti": "Reporters are sometimes reckless people but they are never so reckless, you may be sure as to go around stealing corpses of murdered gangsters in order to score 'scoops.' Yet that is the spurious assumption, which the Rialto's *Midnight Manhunt* makes—and, as a consequence, this very silly thriller looks even sillier to one who knows the game.

"It looks like nothing but William Gargan, Ann Savage, and Leo Gorcey playacting in a Pine-Thomas film that is as sleazy a[s] the waxworks museum in which most of it takes place. And, when one of the characters comments that American reporters will stop at nothing 'once they smell a story,' he gives a fair indication of the identifying feature of this yarn."

Also in 1945, he did the last three East Side Kids films: *Docks of New York* (February 24), *Mr. Muggs Rides Again* (July 15), and *Come Out Fighting* (September 29).

In 1946, Gorcey started the Bowery Boys series in which he appeared as the character Slip Mahoney in a total of 41 out of 48 films; [the first five are *Live Wires* (January 12), *In Fast Company* (June 22), *Bowery Bombshell* (July 20), *Spook Busters* (August 20), and *Mr. Hex* (December 7)].

As I noted in my biography of Hall, it bears repeating that as Slip, Gorcey is at his best in charm and confidence. He is a much better actor than most viewers realize. Apparently, he had his character worked out very early on. It seems that his greatest gift is the naturalness of his likeable tough guy persona. Repeatedly, Gorcey's Slip Mahoney character is unsentimental but endearing. He is always putting Sach in his place. He really does not know any more than Sach. He is not well mannered, and he does not know all the social rules of etiquette. The way he talks—part of him wants to be smart, even using words as if he is some sort of literary giant. He tries to sound intelligent, but instead mangles his speech.

Slip likes to be the leader, and he appoints himself in charge of every situation. Slip will tell Sach what to do, as if Sach does not know his ass from his elbow. Slip tends to be always watching Sach or getting someone else to watch him so that Sach does not do something stupid. Slip succeeds with others by making himself come across with a swagger that he believes he is smart. He bluffs his way through situations. If he has any doubts about his abilities, he covers it up. Yes, he is street smart, always picking up the angles.

In 1947, he continued with three more Bowery Boys films [*Hard Boiled Mahoney* (April 26), *News Hounds* (August 13), and *Bowery Buckaroos* (November 22)]. In 1948, he did one last non-series film before continuing through 1955 making only films for the Bowery Boys series. Gorcey appeared in humorist Henry Morgan's only film where he played the lead, *So This Is New York*, (June), a satirical comedy based on Ring Lardner's *The Big Town*, which offered Gorcey a minor, though plum role as a jockey named Sid Mercer.

Five years earlier, in *The New York Times* Screen News (February 21, 1942): "Metro has purchased 'the Half-Pint Kid,' a magazine story by Borden Chase, as a vehicle for Lionel Barrymore. The yarn deals with an old horse trainer who rehabilitates a dishonest jockey, and Leo Gorcey is being considered for the part of the jockey." Later one reporter noted, "Previously added were Hugh Herbert and Leo Gorcey in important roles." Gorcey and Barrymore did not appear in that film, which was released as *Harrigan's Kid* in 1943.

Thomas F. Brady (*The New York Times*, October 3, 1947): "Leo Gorcey, one of the original Dead End Kids, has been engaged for the role of 'a jockey with romantic leanings' in *So This Is New York*, the Henry Morgan vehicle Stanley Kramer is producing for Enterprise.

Schallert (*Los Angeles Times*, September 29, 1947): "All the men who make trouble for Dona Drake… include Rudy Vallee, Hugh Herbert, Leo Gorcey, Bill Goodwin, and Jerome Cowan… They constitute a quintet of suitors, more or less unsatisfactory—one or two actually disreputable."

Scheuer in "Henry Morgan Makes Bow in Wacky Satire" (*Los Angeles Times*, September 17, 1948), the combination of Ring Lardner and Morgan proves, "The compromise will not wholly please the devotees of either humorist, for it is neither legitimate Lardner nor unadulterated Morgan."

"The prospective bridegrooms, each of whom fails to make the grade are, in chronological order: Jerome Cowan, a fast-talking promoter; Hugh Herbert, a collector of trophies; Rudy Vallee, a Texan who not only breeds racehorses but also neighs them on to victory; Leo Gorcey, his lady-killing jockey; and Bill Goodwin, a thespian with a distinct odor of ham."

Among the funniest scenes: "A doubly 'fixed' race in which two jockeys whip on a lagging long shot."

Scheuer: "Tough little Leo Gorcey does one scene that is extraordinary in its holding power."

Tinee reviews *So This Is New York* in "This Airy Film Will Provide a Lot of Laughs" saying, "…Leo Gorcey does a fine bit as a jockey, who rides in a truly wonderful horse race…. It's all very light, but fast moving and sophisticated humor, an excellent bet if you're looking for some chuckles."

As would be the case, unless otherwise noted, he would make four Bowery Boys films each year. In 1948, he made *Angels' Alley* (March 7), *Jinx Money* (June 27), *Smugglers' Cove* (October 10), and *Trouble Makers* (December 10).

In 1949, he made the Bowery Boys films, *Fighting Fools* (March 17), *Hold That Baby!* (June 26), *Angels in Disguise* (September 9), and *Master Minds* (November 20).

In 1950, he made the Bowery Boys films, *Blonde Dynamite* (February 12), *Lucky Losers* (May 14), *Triple Trouble* (August 13), and *Blues Busters* (October 29).

In 1951, he made the Bowery Boys films, *Bowery Battalion* (January 24), *Ghost Chasers* (April 29), *Let's Go Navy!* (July 29), and *Crazy Over Horses* (November 18).

In 1952, he made the Bowery Boys films, *Hold That Line* (March 23 1952), *Here Comes the Marines* (June 29), *Feudin' Fools* (September 21), and *No Holds Barred* (November 23).

In 1953, he made the Bowery Boys films, *Jalopy* (February 15), *Loose in London* (May 24), *Clipped Wings* (August 14), and *Private Eyes* (December 6).

In 1954, he made the Bowery Boys films, *Paris Playboys* (March 7), *The Bowery Boys Meet the Monsters* (June 8), and *Jungle Gents* (September 5).

In 1955, he made the Bowery Boys films, *Bowery to Bagdad* (January 2), *High Society* (April 17), *Spy Chasers* (July 31), *Jail Busters* (September 18), and *Dig That Uranium* (December 25). Following the latter film's production, Gorcey's father, Bernard Gorcey, who played the Sweet Shop owner, Louie, had died from injuries sustained in a car crash.

With the release of *Crashing Las Vegas*, Gorcey's forty-first and last Bowery Boys film, on April 22, 1956, the brilliant comedic partnership of Gorcey and Hall ended. The tragic loss exacerbated Leo's erratic behavior while making that film on the movie sets. Of course, his heavy boozing only further fueled his recklessness. After 40 movies as a Bowery Boy, Gorcey could no longer competently perform, as evidenced in that first production without his father. *Crashing Las Vegas* undoubtedly proved that Gorcey's drunkenness spoiled his comic timing.

Hall's son, Gary, told me: "My father used to tell me that Leo was drunk all day long and found the last pictures with Leo very difficult. I was very young (8 years old) when the Bowery Boys movies ended, and my trips to the set were not made with a critical eye. But I can say that though he and Leo improvised a lot, they did plan what they did pretty carefully. As to improvisation—there is a lot in the movies [my father made]. They made these things in two weeks with only a little bit of rehearsal time."

The press reported that Gorcey was supposed to appear in at least three films, but he did not. First, *The New York Times* reported, "Odette

Myrtil, musical comedy actress, has been signed for the part of Angelina in *The Gentle People*, and Leo Gorcey also was added to the cast; the picture is expected to go before the cameras Thursday."

In addition, *The New York Times* revealed, "Pat O'Brien being concerned with 'Boy Meets Girl,' Warners have changed the cast of *Unfit to Print*, by Saul Elkins and Sally Sandlin. Humphrey Bogart will go into the role of the newspaper editor and Gale Page will be his wife. Leo Gorcey, one of the 'Dead End' boys, will be the tough lad regenerated by the couple."

As regards to *Unfit to Print*, *The New York Times* (July 22, 1938) noted, "The studio expects to get the newspaper yarn under way during August and today abandoned the tentative casting of Humphrey Bogart and Leo Gorcey and substituted Pat O'Brien and Bobby Jordan, one of the 'Dead End' boys."

A third film that Gorcey was supposed to have been in is Paramount's *Sealed Verdict*.

As regards to his last years, in 1963 Gorcey returned to films after a seven-year hiatus for a brief cameo in the Stanley Kramer-directed *It's a Mad Mad Mad Mad World*, released November 7, 1963. The publicity correctly noted, "Everybody who's ever been funny is in it!"

Though his scene lasts a few seconds, Gorcey is cast among so many of comedy's greatest stars, which included Milton Berle, Sid Caesar, Buddy Hackett, Phil Silvers, Terry-Thomas, Jonathan Winters, Edie Adams, Eddie 'Rochester' Anderson, Jim Backus, Joe E. Brown, Norman Fell, Stan Freberg, Sterling Holloway, Edward Everett Horton, Buster Keaton, Don Knotts, ZaSu Pitts, Carl Reiner, Arnold Stang, The Three Stooges, Jimmy Durante, Morey Amsterdam, Jack Benny, Allen Jenkins, Jerry Lewis, and so many others.

It's a Mad Mad Mad Mad World is a funny slapstick comedy about a group of strangers who learn about $350,000 in hidden loot from a dying gangster and set off on a madcap cross-country race to find it. With only two lines of dialogue, Gorcey is seen as the first cab driver, who works for Tanner Yellow Cab, who takes Melville Crump (Caesar) and Monica Crump (Adams) to the hardware store. The brief dialogue spoken in this bit are:

Gorcey: "That'll be $2.90."
Crump: "Here's $3.00. Keep the change, but wait for us."
Gorcey: "Oh, sure."

In 1966, Gorcey played a character named "Leo" in his next to his last film role, alongside Hall as stagehands in *Second Fiddle for a Steel Guitar*. The disappointing film is a letdown for a number of reasons, including poor direction, camerawork, and script. It is only a showcase of country music talents putting on a show with Gorcey and Hall offering comic relief throughout the film. The scenes with Gorcey and Hall were shoddily shot separately from the musical talents so they never appear with them on stage at the same time.

In his final film role, he played himself in an odd and unsuccessful comedy film entitled *The Phynx*, released May 6, 1970, nearly a year after his death. More than three dozen personalities appeared in this film about a rock and roll band on a mission to find celebrities seized as hostages by the communists.

Gorcey appeared among the huge assemblage of guests in this failed effort. The personalities included: George Tobias, Joan Blondell, Martha Raye, Rich Little, Patty Andrews, Busby Berkeley, Xavier Cugat, Fritz Feld, John Hart, Ruby Keeler, Joe Louis, Maureen O'Sullivan, Ed Sullivan, Rona Barrett, James Brown, Cass Daley, Louis Hayward, Patsy Kelly, Guy Lombardo, Butterfly McQueen, Richard Pryor, Colonel Harland Sanders, Rudy Vallee, Johnny Weissmuller, Edgar Bergen, Dick Clark, Andy Devine, Huntz Hall, George Jessel, Dorothy Lamour, Pat O'Brien, Jay Silverheels, Sally Struthers, I. Stanford Jolley, and others.

One of the things that probably hurt Gorcey more in retrospect is his missed opportunity to be forever immortalized on the cover art of what turned out to be a memorable moment in recording history. For in 1967, The Beatles released *Sgt. Pepper Lonely Hearts Club Band* album, and Mary Stevens in "Rounding up players of *Sgt. Pepper*" explained that The Beatles "…hired trendy pop artist Peter Blake to fashion a fantastic collage of about sixty of the group's 'favorite personalities' with whom The Beatles would be posed standing in a flower garden.

"Only Leo Gorcey of the Bowery Boys turned out to be a total stick in the mud. He demanded a fee, which EMI decided not to pay. So Gorcey was axed, while his buddy Huntz Hall basked in the glory of being part of the history-making project."

7
Press Coverage of Radio Shows

"The way Leo mangles the King's English on the Burns show, you'd think the only school he ever attended was reform school. Don't believe it. The most-thumbed books in his library are the dictionary and the encyclopedia."

– "Don't Take Him Back to Brooklyn!"
by Coy Williams (*Radio Life*, May 12, 1946)

OVER THE YEARS, Gorcey's best-known roles in films received the bulk of attention. As a result, few people even know of Gorcey's short-lived stint on radio, particularly as a regular for one entire season on Bob Burns' weekly program in the mid-1940s. Between late 1947 and mid-1949, Burns unsuccessfully attempted to revive his show with Gorcey aboard once again.

In "Burns Plans New Kind of Radio Series: Seeks Free Hand Comedian Says" (*Chicago Daily Tribune*, December 5, 1947), Larry Wolters reported: "Bob Burns, the Arkansas comedian, was in town yesterday to address National 4-H Club leaders and to do a little missionary work for his forthcoming transcribed radio series. Robin's new show is described as an 'open end' commercial. That means that it can be sponsored locally with the advertiser adding his own plugs. Also, it will not be aired in a network. Thus, Burns can select his own station in a given community.

"Burns is not only the star of the show, he is the producer, director, writer, and general supervisor. Thus he is not subject to sponsor, advertising agency, or network dictation. Last year he was so badly cast that he decided he would quit radio altogether unless he could run his own show. He thinks he found the way to do it.

"Burns will have the assistance of songstress Shirley Ross and Leo Gorcey, one of the original Dead End Kids.

"'But I'm going to soften him a little for my show,' he explained.

"Burns's show will have a bucolic flavor. His kinfolk will reappear. He may depict scenes on a farm, put on a minstrel show or raise funds for worthy causes. He hasn't worked it all out yet, but the Hollywood flavor will be taken out of it entirely, he says."

More details about Gorcey and his involvement with the Burns radio show is offered in the May 12, 1946 (Vol. 13, No. 10) issue of *Radio Life*, in an article entitled "Don't Take Him Back to Brooklyn!" by Coy Williams. The title refers to his Gorcey's weekly appearances listed for Los Angeles listeners on Thursdays at 6:30 p.m. on NBC—KFI—KFDS.

The seven photo captions in Williams' piece reveal another side to Gorcey that goes beyond the familiar Dead End/East Side Kid/Bowery Boy characterization. The articles' photos credited to Gene Lester have captions reading:

"ALWAYS IN A HURRY is Leo Gorcey, the boy who sings 'Oh, take me back to Brooklyn' on the Bob Burns show. (Leo was born in the Bronx!) With script propped on the breakfast table, and battered hat all ready to go, Leo gobbles some morning cereal."

"LEO'S NUMBER ONE hobby is the study of words! The way he kicks the King's English around on the Burns show, you'd never think he'd opened a book. But his library is well-stocked, and every day Leo sits down, as shown, to learn five new words."

"BOTH GORCEY AND HIS WIFE, PENNY, like to paint in oil. In background is Leo's nearly finished study of the ocean near Monterey. Leo also is interested in collecting rocks from all states in the union and once upon a time, back in his very young days, he wrote poetry."

"HE LIKES TO WORK IN THE GARDEN, but recently tore up a cactus bed of 150 plants, on which he'd spent years, because a newer hobby is cement work and Leo wanted to lay a sidewalk right across the cactus collection."

"PART OF GORCEY'S COLLECTION of guns includes an aluminum dart gun (at right of array). He also has five or six revolvers. The deer head is trophy of a northern hunting trip two years ago. Out at his home, Leo's interest in nature takes only a slightly different turn."

"WITH BOB BURNS AND PIGLET Burns brought in to the broadcast from his Bazooka Berk ranch. Leo carried little Lippy on stage, scared stiff that the animal would slide out of hand. But all went well, as smiles of Burns and Songstress Shirley Ross (right) indicate."

"LEO'S SALAAMING TO SHIRLEY, started as a spontaneous gag on the show, has now become a regular routine. He performs it just as he comes in singing, 'Oh, take me back to Brooklyn.' "

The article's sub-headline reads, "Confidentially, Leo Gorcey Wouldn't Know What to Do If He WERE Dropped in Brooklyn, for He's a Bronx Boy."[3]

Williams' article is worth repeating in its entirety here as it succinctly offers interesting information that has not been chronicled elsewhere.

Williams begins:

"OH TAKE ME back to Brooklyn, the land where I was born..."

"With these lyrics Leo Gorcey makes his regular Thursday night entrance on the Bob Burns program and begins a rapid-fire series of wise-cracking observations on Burns, farming, women, and animal husbandry.

"No one so far has broken down under Leo's weekly appeal and offered him passage back to his native land. It is just as well, because Leo—confidentially—wouldn't know which way to turn if he were suddenly dropped in the middle of Brooklyn. He was born and grew up in the Bronx.[3]

"This is one of those amusing facets to the Gorcey personality which provide almost as many laughs to associates off the program as on it.

"Just before Christmas Leo was telling about the gifts he'd bought his wife at the Broadway-Hollywood department store.

"The clerk said, 'And where shall I address them, Mr. Gorcey?' and I said, 'Just address them to the Broadway-Hollywood because my wife will have them all back here the day after Christmas, anyhow.'"

"On the show Leo is represented as an amateur inventor and dabbler in animal genetics. Once he reported that he'd invented a suction-cup for wives' hats so that when hubby came home late and his wife hit the ceiling, she'd stay there.

"In the interests of accuracy, that gag was not Leo's, but was cooked up by the program's writer, Vic McLeod. Leo took particular delight in it, however, for it brought him more comment, written and oral, than any he's delivered. He's acquired a lively correspondence from other amateur inventors as a result of it.

"It wasn't much funnier, though, than one of Leo's own ideas for enlarging a room of his house out in Sherman Oaks. He came to the program one day completely exhausted.

---

3. This magazine reference contradicts the Lamparski-Gorcey interview, which credits upper Manhattan as his birthplace.

"'What's the matter?' asked Burns.

"'I just finished hauling 37 wheelbarrow loads of dirt from under the house,' panted Leo.

"'What for?'

"'Well, one room is too cramped and I don't know how to lift the ceiling, so I'm lowering the floor!'

"Leo's experiments on the program with crossing various types of animals are always good for laughs. Once he announced he'd crossed a kangaroo with a beaver so he could raise fur coats with pockets. Then he was working on crossing a carrier pigeon with an owl so it could deliver night letters, and a snake with a rabbit so he could get an adder that would multiply.

"He's been collecting rocks from all the states in the Union (did you know that a rock from Maine looks just like a rock from California?) He recently pulled up a collection of 150 dwarf cacti on which he'd spent years, because he'd developed an interest in cement work and wanted to lay a sidewalk right across the cactus bed.

"Funny things always seem to happen to Gorcey. One night a colored man crawled in an open window of his house, liked the layout, stayed over until morning, and announced to Leo that the place was rundown and he ought to hang around and clean it up. He did, too; for three months.

"Leo comes to rehearsal the day of the broadcast in rough clothes and a day's growth of beard. When the show is all ready for the mic, he dashes over to his favorite barber, then knocks off a couple of fast games of pool and returns for the broadcast refreshed in mind and body.

"Once the barber turned up sick and caught Leo flat-footed. He scoured NBC until he located an electric razor, then discovered five minutes before air time that the thing wouldn't work. He wanted to drape the razor and cord around his neck, so the audience would know his intentions were good, but calmer heads prevailed. Anyhow, when he put on his ragged hat with the brim pinned back, the customers probably thought he was supposed to look that way. He's still the 'Dead End Kid' to them.

"Leo would just as soon drop that 'Dead End' tie-up, but his public won't let him. He announced after his 35th picture that he felt it was time to advance in the world, and that henceforth he would play nothing but uptown toughs. But it didn't take.

"For a time, too, he didn't want to be identified with his battered head gear, but he's finally become attached to it. He acquired it nine years ago at Universal Studios by the simple method of forgetting to return it to the property department, and it's been with him in 44 pictures out of the 51 he's made, as well as on more than a half dozen radio series and innumerable camp visits.

"That hat covers a very active brain. Leo not only stars in his pictures, but he also helps write and produce them. The poor man's Orson Welles—but he doesn't throw his knowledge around. Kidding his radio producer, Sam Pierce, about Sam's duties, Leo said, 'It doesn't take brains to be a producer. All you need to know are the rules of gin rummy.'

"The way Leo mangles the King's English on the Burns show, you'd think the only school he ever attended was reform school. Don't believe it. The most-thumbed books in his library are the dictionary and the encyclopedia. His number one hobby is the study of words, and for several years he has learned five new ones a day. He even has a notebook full of poetry he wrote in his younger days. One piece of blank verse, dashed off when he was in junior high school, sold to *Good Housekeeping* magazine. Titled "The Drought," it showed Leo's early interest in nature, starting out:

> Dry is the brook
> Shriveled are the trees
> For the sun is hot and fiery…

and going on to describe graphically the effects of a long dry spell, and what happened when the rains finally came.

"Leo never inflicts these accomplishments on his associates, however. He's more likely to talk about fishing and hunting, on which he dotes, but he's willing to listen to what you do, too. One-way conversations bore him. He once got into a hot argument with a musician who insisted on talking about nothing but music.

"'Don't you ever think of anything except music?' barked Leo. 'I bet you say your prayers in the key of F-sharp!'"

In a photo piece entitled "Bob Burns Shows Has Its Harmonious Moments," the caption reads, "Raising their voices in song and really working at it is Leo Gorcey, erstwhile Dead End Kid; Bob Burns, drawling comedian; and Shirley Ross, vocalist, who combine their talents or listeners at 7:30 P.M. on Thursday at NBC-WEAF."

Although Gorcey's shows with Burns ran from March 1, 1945 to June

27, 1946, only a few episodes of these shows circulate (see appendix). Prior to broadcasting on Burns' show, Gorcey worked on radio alongside a true comedy luminary, Groucho Marx, on *Pabst Blue Ribbon Town* from November 27, 1943 to June 17, 1944. Similarly, only several episodes of that season circulate.

Leo Gorcey studio publicity shot, late 1930s (Dead End Kids period).
Photo Courtesy Brandy Gorcey Ziesemer.

From left to right, Leo Gorcey, older brother Fred, younger brother David. Photo Courtesy Brandy Gorcey Ziesemer.

Leo Gorcey in studio publicity shot, late 1940s or early 1950s (Bowery Boys films). Photo Courtesy Brandy Gorcey Ziesemer.

Publicity pose of Leo Gorcey on the radio. Photo Courtesy Brandy Gorcey Ziesemer.

Shot of Leo Gorcey eating used in *Radio Life* article.
Photo Courtesy Brandy Gorcey Ziesemer.

Leo Gorcey Jr, and Leo Gorcey taken on Monogram set of *Hold That Line* (1952). Photo Courtesy Brandy Gorcey Ziesemer.

Publicity shot of Leo Gorcey wearing his boxing gloves.
Photo Courtesy Brandy Gorcey Ziesemer.

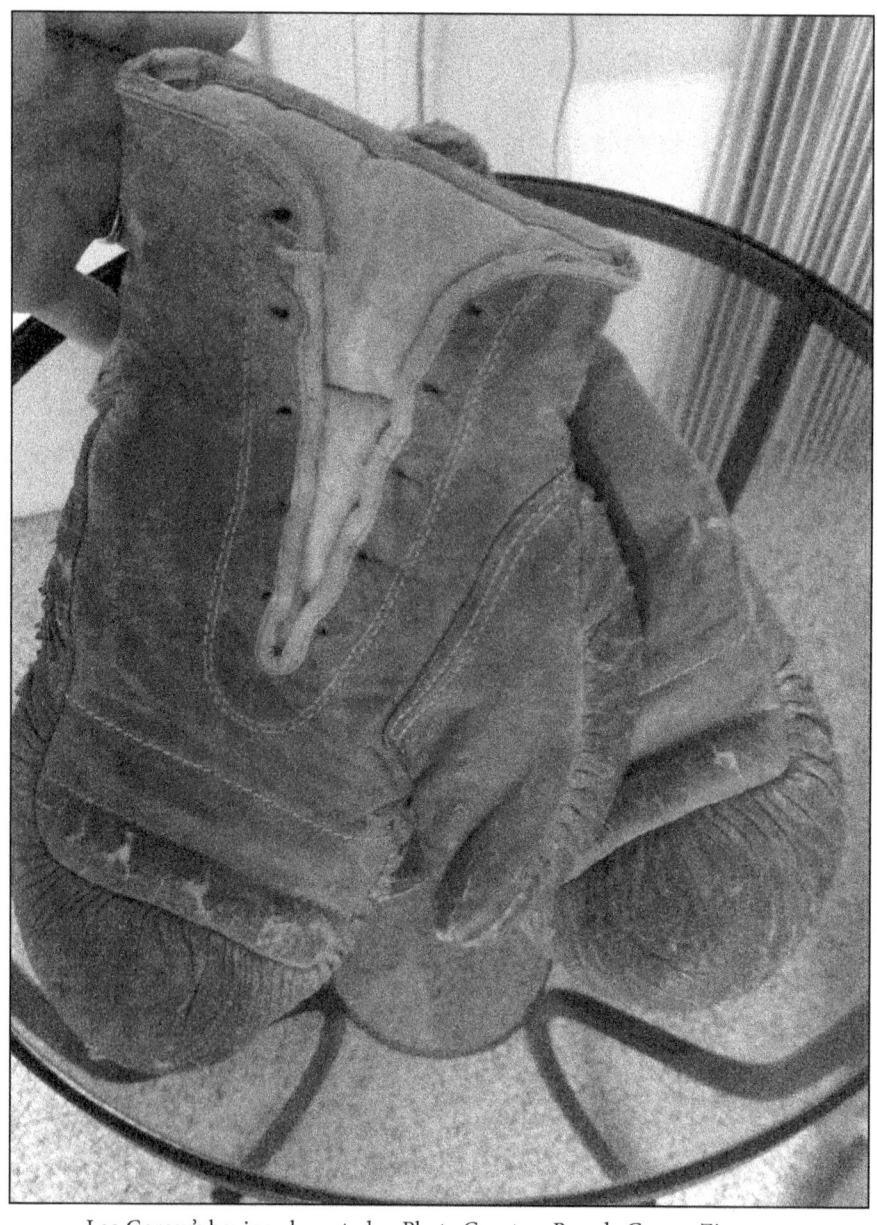

Leo Gorcey's boxing gloves today. Photo Courtesy Brandy Gorcey Ziesemer.

Leo Gorcey boxing. Photo Courtesy Brandy Gorcey Ziesemer.

Leo Gorcey with his gun collection. Photo Courtesy Brandy Gorcey Ziesemer.

Still screened for printing in *Radio Life* article showing his first deer (1945). Photo Courtesy Brandy Gorcey Ziesemer.

Press Coverage of Radio Shows • 99

Brandy's Baptism. From left to right, godfather Roland Giroux, godmother Nora Giroux, father Leo Gorcey and mother Brandy Jean (Davis) Gorcey. Lady of the Snow Church, Reno, Nevada, late August, 1958. Photo Courtesy Brandy Gorcey Ziesemer.

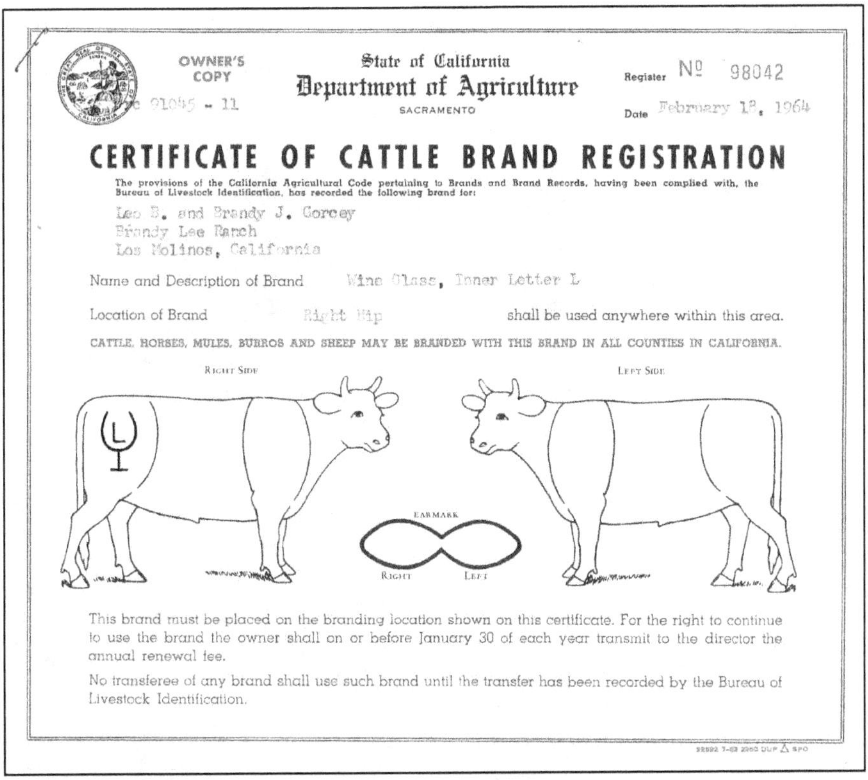

Leo Gorcey's cattle brand registration certificate. Photo Courtesy Brandy Gorcey Ziesemer.

From left to right, Leo Gorcey, Bernard Gorcey, Gabe Dell.
Photo Courtesy Brandy Gorcey Ziesemer.

Signed still of Leo Gorcey. Photo Courtesy Brandy Gorcey Ziesemer.

Leo Gorcey's personal dictionary used in developing Bowery Boys series malaprops published in 1946 as it appears in 2017. Photo Courtesy Brandy Gorcey Ziesemer.

Close-up of said dictionary showing year of publication.
Photo Courtesy Brandy Gorcey Ziesemer.

Leo Gorcey and inset of Brandy Gorcey dressing as her father.
Photo Courtesy Brandy Gorcey Ziesemer.

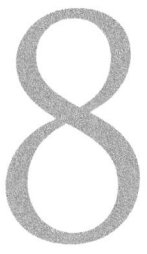

The Fractured Language of Slip Mahoney

> "Boy, some words, huh!" … Bobby Jordan's character responding to Gorcey's street hawking spiel for Pierce's Peerless Stain Remover.
> "What d'ya think, everybody can speak English as good as we do?"
>
> – Slip Mahoney *Live Wires* (1946)

IS THERE ANYTHING that she never told anyone about her dad? Brandy responded, "I'll try to think of one or more things, but I've wracked my brain to answer questions for Colette Joel's documentary on the Bowery Boys, as well as my endnotes for the reprint of Dad's autobiography, some cute stories for Rich Roat's book, and a cookbook someone was writing, containing celebrity recipes with stories."

What others have overlooked, and it is most interesting to examine, is Gorcey's fascination with language. Brandy: "I actually have his humongous dictionary and a book he liked, called *Word Wealth*. I used to help him look up words when we were together because he wanted me to share his love of the language. It rubbed off because I have a master's in English (and an advanced graduate certificate in health informatics since my career has been in health information management and technology)."

How does the malaprops, all his own invention, fit into the scripts? One certainly will wonder "what's in the scripts, and what's improvised?" Brandy: "He studied the English language. He did all of his own malaprops. His copy of a script I have does have quite a few notes. He claims they'd give them a script. He'd give it back with corrections, and then [they'd] approve some and not others of his changes, whereupon he'd deliver the lines the way he wanted to anyway."

What follows is selected malaprops used by Gorcey in the forty-one films he appeared in the Bowery Boys series. He uses a big word instead of the simple word, pronounces the correct word incorrectly, chooses the wrong word that sounds similar or part of it is similar, uses words with the opposite meaning (antonyms), offers nonsensical words, mixes up common expressions, and so on. Slip often enjoyed using fancy words—in particular, he liked to say "peruse" instead of examine, look at, or study something.

It is interesting to note that so many times his fracturing passes by so quickly that you can miss many of the subtleties of this language comedy. Although intuitively we know what he is trying to say, in fact, sometimes it takes a little thought to figure out what word he was meaning. In addition, since he will often speak so matter-of-factly and confidently, then we almost assume he is speaking correctly. On the other hand, when some other character knows he spoke incorrectly and offers a correction, he will say that he was offering the past tense, or plural form of the word, or even the feminine/masculine form of the word.

Slip is good at coming up with incorrect, though albeit humorous, explanations for events or people. From the very first Bowery Boys film, *Live Wires*, Slip shows his layabout status, as he has trouble keeping a job. To his sister's dismay, he constantly gets into fights and he cannot hold a job. A sample of some of his malaprops and poor choice of words from that film set the tone for the entire series.

He often uses the wrong word to say something. It is always obvious what he means, but clearly he is unaware that he is using the wrong word. The other characters often understand him anyway. For instance, when Slip wins at a pinball machine he tells his gang, "Decorate the mahogany." He says this expression to demand, "Pay up." They subsequently hand him the money owed.

His choice of words is often amusing. Here, when he wants the others to agree with him on selling the hawker's product, he says concerning the money matter, "This is no time for financial controversy." (*Live Wires*)

"Considering the proximity of the evening": Slip begins his question to his girlfriend as he proceeds to suggest several choices. It shows his affinity for fancy words that became commonplace in all of the Bowery Boys films.

Sometimes his descriptions are odd as here when he is demonstrating the ink removal product. He proceeds to soak the man's jacket with ink, and he says, "The man will be alright as soon as he comes out of the anesthesia."

Slip's language is often redundant. The man whose suit is ruined asks when he can get a new suit, Slip responds: "Well you see that's a matter of finances, of which mine are at a standstill. In other words, I might even add that I am a little bit broke at the moment."

His speech is full of exaggerations, as when he asks, "Can you wait here just a fraction of a second, sis?" Alternatively, when he starts warming up to fight, Slip brags, "I better not swing so hard, I might give him nemonia from here!" He means "pneumonia." It's doubly funny as it is a mispronunciation as well as inappropriate, as it is not a disease that somebody gets in a fight.

He continues, "Fellows, much to my regret, but due mostly to financial reverses, I guess we're all broke."

Then the wrong word again, "(You're nothing but a) pacifist." He means pessimist. The words are unrelated except they both begin with a "p." As usually is the case, when someone corrects him (here his sister), as with "you mean pessimist," Slip responds, "I was using the past tense."

Overall, one of my favorite expressions that Slip uses is when he retorts, "Alright! Alright! Alright!" He did that in at least nine films, including, *High Society, Feudin' Fools, Jalopy, Triple Trouble, Blonde Dynamite, Hold That Baby, In Fast Company, No Holds Barred,* and *Dig That Uranium*. In the latter film, he amusingly tells Sach, "Alright! Alright! Alright! You're a genius!" A variation of "Alright! Alright! Alright!" is "Soright! Soright! Soright!" heard in *Blonde Dynamite*.

One of Slip's constantly used malaprops is the word "depreciate" being substituted for "appreciate." Some variation of that word is present at least twenty-one times. Another frequently used malaprops is his use of the word "seclusion" to refer to "conclusion." He did that at least nine times. However, there is at least one time when he refers to an "optical seclusion," and he means "optical delusion." Another favorite seems to be his use of "seduction" as a "deduction." Interestingly, one time he misses his mark with the malaprop and actually says it correctly as "clever deduction" is in *Trouble Makers*.

Before cataloging many of Slip's fractured word plays, there are misquotes or unusual sayings. The following are some of the more interesting statements made by Slip Mahoney:

Slip says his name is "Terrence J. Montgomery Mahoney, that's my maiden name." What he meant to say is sometimes explained, others are left to the reader to decipher.

"Of course, my friends call me Slip." (*News Hounds*)

"This is the great and *insignificant* [*magnificent*] Terrence Mahoney." (*Smugglers' Cove*)

"You're not holding me here as accomplishment [*accomplice*] to the crime because I never accomplished anything in my life." (*Bowery Bombshell*)

"That's a masterpiece of understatement." (*Hold That Baby*)

"Masterpiece of understatement." (*Smugglers' Cove*)

"Some nerve giving *compounded* literature to a mental incompetent." (*Master Minds*)

"[I got the] whole case in the hollow of my head." (*Hard Boiled Mahoney*)

On baby adoption: "Tomorrow I'll take him to the humane society." (*Hold That Baby*)

"Someday I'm gonna have a layout like this Sach, sitting behind one of these big old dusky desks with my feet in the drawers, directing the secretaries, filing the files, basting the books and merging the mergers… I'm gonna take bears and bulls right by the horns. I'll probably wind up on the curb." (*Smugglers' Cove*)

"If Sach has blue blood he must of got a *transformation* from a pint of grape juice." He meant *transfusion*. (*Loose in London*)

"Sach, for some *inextracable* reason, in the Army mess means food." Did he mean *inextricable*? (*Bowery Battalion*)

"To a contagious effort, I've been able to muster up some of the most lackadaisical bon vivants in town." (*Blonde Dynamite*)

"We can go there and jitter for a jitney." (*Blonde Dynamite*)

"Just when I was beginning to think I was devastating them with my personality." (*Blonde Dynamite*)

Butler: "Whom is calling?" Slip: "Whom? Your infinitive is dangling." (*Bowery to Bagdad*)

"Don't let the feminine gender engulf you." (*Bowery to Bagdad*)

"You *meandering maniac*." (*Bowery to Bagdad*)

"You *imbecilic idiot*." (*Bowery to Bagdad*)

"Can't you see the girl's *enthralled* with me?" (*Bowery to Bagdad*)

Referring to *alumni*, he says *aluminum*. When he is corrected, he says "Guys, I was conjugating the verb." (*Hold That Line*)

"For two cents I'd dismember your head." (*Smugglers' Cove*)

"Be quiet! Whatta ya think you're in a boiler works?" (*Mr. Hex*)

He confuses famous Svengali hypnotist and Trilby, saying that Sach be Svengali and he's Trilby. (*Mr. Hex*)

"You see in my profession we are taught very young to keep our cauliflowers on the grapevine and it was in just a manner recently and very latently." (*News Hounds*)

"You see chief, I thought that maybe since the circumstantial seems to point to the fact my honorary journalistic *contemtabulism* [*contemporary*?] is among the missing this morning. Perhaps we can instigate this vicarious tale." (*News Hounds*)

"He can also toss a herring to a transman, and tell whether it's gonna land heads or tails." (*Hard Boiled Mahoney*)

When Slip asks a banker if he knows about money, the banker says he's a numismatist. Slip responds, "Come again. I don't want to get personal." (*Jinx Money*)

"Solicitors rush in where agents fear to tread." This is a re-spin of "fools rush in where angels fear to tread." (*Loose in London*)

Slip to female soldiers: "Pardon me, my cherry soufflé." (*Bowery Battalion*)

"I'm getting carnivorously hungry." (*Dig That Uranium*)

"[He] gets obstreperous when he sees a woman of the opposite set." (*Hard Boiled Mahoney*)

Describing a bull: "See the cow with a bump on its back." (*Bowery Buckaroos*)

"In a battle between brawn and brains, the brains usually comes out superior, and brains happens to be something I'm dissipated with." (*Bowery Buckaroos*)

Referring to the crooks: "putting our fingers on the bunch of the little fry." (*Angels Alley*)

"They got mere loose dognet than Ali Baba and the forty thieves." (*Angels Alley*)

"Spend a weekend, and to shoot peasants." Sach corrects him by saying you meant pheasants. Slip responds, "I was using the peasant [present] tense." (*Loose in London*)

"There's only one other thing to do, and that is to take you to the captain and make a bear breast [clean break?] of the whole thing." (*Loose in London*)

"Louie, your words reek of integrity." (*Loose in London*)

"Quick, get Louie out of that trunk before we have to send for the oxengenarian." [He needs oxygen and thinks that means send for an octogenarian?] (*Loose in London*)

"It's a pretty evaporated question Louie, but I'll try to explain to you." (*Loose in London*)

"Sach, my curiosity can no longer be repulsed." (*Loose in London*)

"Well the feeling is musilogenous." [mutual] (*Loose in London*)

"Well I guess I'll have to remonstrate [deal with] with the maniac." (*Loose in London*)

"You've been blabbing with that conniving femme fa-tally." [femme fatale] (*Loose in London*)

"I'll stay here and reconnoiter, whatever that means." (*Loose in London*)

"A nauseating suggestion." (*Loose in London*)

"That thing won't circumnavigate unless you put a dime into it." (*Clipped Wings*)

"We have to have a private filibuster with Dave and finds out the facts." (*Clipped Wings*)

Sach accuses Slip of not hearing right: "What do you think I have, a regular mitosis of the ear?" (*Clipped Wings*)

"You certainly got us in an ambidextrous mess this time." (*Clipped Wings*)

"This is a fine evolution of movement." [development of events] (*Clipped Wings*)

"I was just amusing the boys and myself with a little filet of idle banter." (*Clipped Wings*)

"Sometimes I think fate is a very declining obstacle." (*Clipped Wings*)

"Well this is the millennium. We got important matters to attend to and your teeing and fudging all afternoon." (*Clipped Wings*)

"[That's] a little disseminating to say the least" [disappointing] (*Clipped Wings*)

"We'll start the maneuver off with the old pizza movement." (*Clipped Wings*)

"And if our suspicions are well integrated, we'll outflank 'em with a pizza movement." (*Clipped Wings*)

"A personal encounter for a romantic endeavor." (*Clipped Wings*)

"You sure got us in some kettle of spinach this time." [hot water?] (*Clipped Wings*)

"You know I think this situation precludes a more cursive examination." [requires] (*Clipped Wings*)

The Fractured Language of Slip Mahoney • 111

"I think I deserve more than an undeluded share of credit." (*Clipped Wings*)

"Keep both your feet and firmly planted in terra cotta." [terra firma] (*Clipped Wings*)

"Then I won't have to infringe on your own hospitality no more." (*Private Eyes*)

"…before this conversation kindly incinerates your morale" (*Private Eyes*)

"Think I'm getting a nuisance of an idea." [notion?] (*Private Eyes*)

"Please further induce us with your problem." [advise?] (*Private Eyes*)

"Leave us continue with your enigma." [let us, problem] (*Private Eyes*)

"Then he sees her very demolishing." [devastating] (*Crazy over Horses*)

Slip to Sach: "Your amorous meanderings." (*Hold That Baby*)

"…your own indistinguishable monotones" [your own words] (*Hold That Baby*)

"This is my monetary manager and declining collaborator." (*Angels in Disguise*)

"The most anonymous mind in the annals of all modern history." (*Master Minds*)

Slip tells Sach: "I wonder, iconoclast, if you can give more enlightening tidings?" (*Master Minds*)

"Not only refund your money, but we will also be highly mortified." (*Master Minds*)

"[It] got declared a temporary mortuary and look for him at dentist." (*Master Minds*)

"[It] got declared a moratorium." (*Master Minds*)

"…but don't get a superiority [inferiority] complex." (*Master Minds*)

"This is getting very hereditary." (*Master Minds*)

Calls Sach: "Oh formidable and tedious prince." (*Master Minds*)

"The pupils in your eyes are blinking dollar and cents signs." (*Crazy over Horses*)

"Well pick it up, you canine equestrian." (*Crazy over Horses*)

"Come on. Get a move on. Time is collapsing." [running out] (*Crazy over Horses*)

"I'm a little nearsighted, I should go see a nickeologist." [optometrist?] (*Crazy over Horses*)

"Partners, I think our destinies are beginning to desitine." (*Crazy over Horses*)

"I'm very much infected with your diversified conversation." (*Jungle Gents*)

When told it was a leopard, Slip says, "I was referring to the male of the species." (*Jungle Gents*)

"I was beginning to latch onto a very impregnant idea." (*Jungle Gents*)

"I'm gonna give him an earful of fragrant colloquialisms." (*Bowery to Bagdad*)

"That's what I call a gregarious greeting committee." (*Bowery to Bagdad*)

"Get that genie to come here and to exonerate me from my incarceration." (*Bowery to Bagdad*)

With Sach outside a window on a ledge: "Stand still. Don't levitate." (*Bowery to Bagdad*)

"My inname intimate." [inane]; "That's colloquial for idiot." (*Jail Busters*)

"…if you don't mind emulsifying me a little secret…" [revealing, clarifying] (*Jail Busters*)

"What is all this subterranean noise all about?" (*Jail Busters*)

"Suppose I became so masticated to be interested in this deal?" (*Jail Busters*)

"I don't like to *dis-inform* you, but boys are supposed to dance with girls." He meant *inform*. (*Jalopy*)

"…Furthermore, I don't like to dance." (*Jalopy*)

Slip refers to a terrace as, "This is a regular plantation in the sky." (*No Holds Barred*)

"Peach sundaes ain't good for the vocal tissues." (*Blues Busters*)

"Sidewalk kinda comes up and hits us in the bust." He meant butt. (*Angels' Alley*)

"They ain't horses, they're cross-pollinated jackasses with two-toned paint jobs." When corrected he says, "Certainly, that's what I said—they're zebras." (*Jungle Gents*)

"What are you raving about, you *depraved* idiot?" (*Bowery Battalion*)

Louie says, "No! No! No!" Slip criticizes him, saying, "Louie, you're using a triple negative." (*Crazy over Horses*)

Slip pretends to have a gun on crooks, saying, "I'll *perforate* both of you." (*Hold That Baby*)

Slip quotes a famous general, saying, "If you can't join 'em, fight." (Slip has it backwards. It is really the reverse: "If you can't fight 'em, join them." (*Blonde Dynamite*)

He explains the hydrogen ray: "Well, it's a ray invented by a man named Hydrogen, what else!" (*Bowery Battalion*)

"Now I feel it is my duty to write to some of my friends in the hexagon building in Washington, D.C." Slip is referring to the Pentagon. (*Bowery Battalion*)

To a female: "Try to remember that old saying 'he who laughs the most, sometimes winds up by laughing the least.'" This is Slip's spin on it: "He who laughs last laughs the most." (*Blues Busters*)

"As the old saying goes, 'can see that the pudding has to have some proof.'" This is his twist on "the proof is in the pudding." (*Blues Busters*)

"I want you to put on your best save your fare. It's a French proposition. It means keep your trap shut." He means *savoir-faire*. (*Blonde Dynamite*)

"But after all, probation would just be *astigmatism* on our character." He means it would be a *stigma*. (*Triple Trouble*)

Slip misunderstands artificial respiration—thinks that's the problem: "could have at least given him the real thing." (*Trouble Makers*)

As a student in an English class, he offers a real tongue twister: "Professor, much of [what] you'd said is perfectly true. That is, unless the alligatin's syntax is proceeded by an objectional maxillary, which would change the contentricity of your prerogative, unless used the transitive verb. Now this is strictly a hypothetical case. [The school bell rings and Slip continues to carry on his fancy talk.] "As I just said to the psychology teacher this would either apothrokay or orangindied your date. Now I've been studying orthobeanotography, lexicography, etimology, sepantics, pathantics, pathaleonism for 27 years. On the other hand, I'll see you in the club car. (*Hold That Line*)

When a doctor uses scientific medical terms, Sach says, "he's using more bigger words than you, Chief." Slip replies, "Yeah, but he's using all plurals." (*No Holds Barred*)

"It's a mathematical *secretion* [solution] if you need money for a car, a house, or a farm you go to a bank." (*Feudin' Fools*)

"He couldn't fight his way out of a piece of bubblegum." The correct saying is "out of a paper bag." (*Fighting Fools*)

Referring to an iron bell medicine ball, Slip says, "That thing had a handle on it I would have handled that more handily." (*Hold That Line*)

"A stitch in time saves the thimble." He meant, "saves nine." (*Fighting Fools*)

Sach explains that the baby is hungry. Slip: "Well we better take him home and regurgitate him." He could have simply said, "Burp him." (*Hold That Baby*)

When introduced to a great authority on nuclear fission, Slip says, "Well I've done a lot of fishing but I never snagged a nuclear." (*Loose in London*)

After Sach breaks Louie's floor waxing machine, Slip responds, "Well, *mighty degenerated madman…* " (*Jalopy*)

Slip on Sach: "You're forgetting you're dealing with a man with the *insecticide* brain." (*Let's Go Navy!*)

He calls Sach's medical chart a diploma. (*Blues Busters*)

Tells Sach to slow down and repeat himself with, "Let's pause for station identification." (*Ghost Chasers*)

In referring to snoring, he talks fancy: "I'll *obliterate* some of the *interference*." (*Triple Trouble*)

"This place depresses my olfactory nerves." What he means is it smells bad. (*Feudin' Fools*)

An Indian insists, "Me Brave." Slip replies, "Nobody said you yellow." (*Bowery Buckaroos*)

"Algebra—a concentrated form of mathematics." (*Hold That Line*)

"Mathematics is arithmetic the hard way." (*Hold That Line*)

"Luvey la port. That means 'open the door' in Swedish." (*Angels Alley*)

"Maybe you better facilitate the acceleration a little bit lest my girl Daisy *parboiled* in her own impatience." (*Angels Alley*)

When Slip is late for a date: "Sorry I'm late. I didn't mean to *incompacitate* your patience by being deliberately *impunctual*, but my limousine had a traffic collision. I had to go back and get my town and country." (*Angels Alley*)

"Now let's curtail these *infantile* operations and get down to the stationhouse." (*Let's Go Navy!*)

"Wait until that just a minute guy—well he be *excoriated*." [infuriated?] (*Let's Go Navy!*)

"Fellows, I'm just being *infused* with a brilliant idea." (*Let's Go Navy!*)

"Get our reputations completely *unbesmirched*." (*Let's Go Navy!*)

"Just a question of recognizing my *la-tent* ability." (*Let's Go Navy!*)

[Regarding Chief Neuramo]: "I have to look up this Neurology guy." (*Let's Go Navy!*)

"Well fellows this has been very puzzling and *integrating* situation." [interesting] (*Let's Go Navy!*)

"You know something, Sach? You're precisely concisely and succinctly correct even down to the etceteras." (*Let's Go Navy!*)

"Just what are you inferring by that innuendo?" (*Let's Go Navy!*)

He refers to a dead man as a *"horizontal party"* (*Hard Boiled Mahoney*), and also as *"horizontal gentlemen."* (*Jinx Money*)

"Sach, my friend, you can think of the dumbest, stupidest, most idiotic things that have been secreted in the human mind." (*Smugglers' Cove*)

"We'll go to the famous finance company. They don't even charge interest. They just double your principle." (*Blonde Dynamite*)

"I don't like to sound *ambiguous* but I never take sides." (*Blonde Dynamite*)

"If we went to the cops with a story as *illegible* as this, they wouldn't put us in prison, they'd put us in straightjackets." (*Triple Trouble*)

"I'll sue them for some *salt and battery.*" [assault and battery] (*Blonde Dynamite*)

"You have jet-propelled engines, I'll have *jet-propelled cabooses.*" (*Smugglers' Cove*)

"Step into my web said the fly to the spider." The correct saying is "step into my web said the spider to the fly." (*Fighting Fools*)

"Remember we got to crawl before we walk, we got to run before we crawl." (*Blues Busters*)

Referring to a candlestick on the dresser, Slip says to Sach, "Pass me the *illumination*, will you?" (*Ghost Chasers*)

Sach asks Slip, "How do you whistle?" Slip responds, "Just pucker your lips and I'll bash them in." (*Ghost Chasers*)

"Sorry ma'am, but all my escorts are escorted." (*Blonde Dynamite*)

"It's not a *bagel* tiger, it's a *beagle* tiger you moron." Actually, he means a *Bengal* tiger. (*Smugglers' Cove*)

"Those that don't help themselves, just don't get no help." (*In Fast Company*)

"My heart was chirping like a quart of crickets." (*Spook Busters*)

"Men or mice." The familiar order of the phrase is "mice or men." (*Spook Busters*)

"A little short of *scratch.*" This is Slip's shortcut for saying he needs money. (*In Fast Company*)

Referring to doorman at a private casino: "The entrevous might be a little difficult." (*Lucky Losers*)

"Don't cross your bridges until you burn 'em." He meant, "Don't burn your bridges until you cross them." (*Angels in Disguise*)

"And I see the *compulsion* [complexion] of things has diminished. The *woim* [worm] has turned." (*Bowery Battalion*)

"I'm looking for four *incompetent infants* who are trying to demoralize and sabotage the United States Army by enlisting." (*Bowery Battalion*)

Looks at the officers' sleeves and says they're worsted. "It's not as worsted of this stuff." (*Bowery Battalion*)

"That tinny stuff we had on? Why you couldn't even put a press in it." (*Bowery Battalion*)

"Well this is what I call an *auspicious* beginning." (*Bowery Battalion*)

"Louie, I didn't know you are pharmaceutically inclined." (*Bowery Battalion*)

"You have to forgive my friend. He has a very *decibiliting* [rehabilitating] sense of humor." (*Bowery Battalion*)

"Don't wish to sound *deleterious*, but what's your angle?" (*Hold That Line*)

"And you just passed through the *portfolios* of our *caped* learning." (*Hold That Line*)

"Thank you. You're both very *mercenary*." (*Hold That Line*)

To the college's dean: "Happy *apperplexy*." (*Hold That Line*)

"You're liable to get javelin phobia." (*Hold That Line*)

"All I got to say is that *gargantuan* display you gave on the field today concludes one of the most startling series of *ambiguosity* I ever witnessed." (*Hold That Line*)

"O.K. You *scintillated* scientist." (*Hold That Line*)

Skip told female after she is fired, "Don't get so *promiscuous*." (*Bowery Bombshell*)

"I'll give you a *verbatim* impersonation." (*In Fast Company*)

Some words are used to mean different things. Take *perpendicular* as an example: "If I'm not being too *perpendicular*, where have you been?" Does he mean *inquisitive*? (*Spook Busters*) "In this *perpendicular* situation…" Does he mean *particular*? (*Dig That Uranium*) "If I'm being too *perpendicular*…" Does he mean *inquisitive*? (*Spook Busters*)

"So what's the charge? *Fragrancy*? [*vagrancy*] No it couldn't because I ain't *fragrant*." [*vagrant*] (*Bowery Bombshell*)

"A pasture is a place where they make pasteurized milk." (*The Bowery Boys Meet the Monsters*)

"We're going to the bank to blow the loan to finance this deal." (*Blonde Dynamite*)

"He must be going *bottomly* insane." (*Blonde Dynamite*)

To Louie: 'Who's gonna mind the store? That's such a silly question. Go out and get yourself a couple of competent clergies." (*Blonde Dynamite*)

"We have one of the most indisputable escorts." (*Blonde Dynamite*)

"On your broad shoulders befalls the honor of fulfilling on first prescription." (*Blonde Dynamite*)

"The nucleus of my idea has hatched." (*Blonde Dynamite*)

Gangster asks: "Do you own this property? Slip: "Oh, I have an *inticle* interest in it." (*Blonde Dynamite*)

"As they say in French—*mooey caliente*" (*Blonde Dynamite*)

"I guess it goes to prove that bread cast upon the waters sometimes comes back as burnt toast." (*Smugglers' Cove*)

Regarding taking a case to find a missing person, Slip does not know that a retainer is a deposit. The exchange: Slip: "Oh no, we don't retain her. We'll just find her." Client: "No, no. I mean a deposit." (*Hard Boiled Mahoney*)

Another one of his involved tongue-twisters: "You see the vautical basin which is sometimes known as the medulla oblingata transposes suggestive impulses to the patient's optical nerves, which in less professional circles is known as the eyes. Now the eyes in conjunction with the *subterranean* mind (*subconscious*) put the subject in a rather glucosed state thereby stimulating the cerebelic reflexes and indirectly working upon the corrugations of his brain." (*Mr. Hex*)

He tells a pretty woman, "You are unorthodox dynamite." (*In Fast Company*)

"I have you right by the *corpus delecti*." (*Bowery Bombshell*)

"Lead us to be departed [let us depart] down to the Chronicle building." (*News Hounds*)

For a conference with his partners, he says, "*Confence with my conferees*." (*Hard Boiled Mahoney*)

Regarding the problem of not being paid, Slip says, "That's against the interstate commerce rules." (*Hard Boiled Mahoney*)

"My means of transportation are a little liquidated. You'll have to pick me up." (*In Fast Company*)

He calls himself "a veritable monetary manipulator flat broke." (*Mr. Hex*)

"Money is just like fertilizer—doesn't do any good unless you spread it around." (*Fighting Fools*)

"Before the state realizes that time and tide wait for no homo sapiens, let the quips (chips) fall where they may, the presses shall roar tonight." (*News Hounds*)

"Then we came across another embryonic member of our select little group." (*Angels in Disguise*)

When Slip is asked, "Do you kibbutz?" he answers fancily: "In the *vernacular* of the altar, I do." (*Angels in Disguise*)

"In his *monotonous monotones*." He meant, "*In his own words*." (*Angels in Disguise*)

"My feeling is *pari-mutuel* I'm *insured*." He meant, "My feeling is *mutual* I'm *sure*." (*Angels in Disguise*)

"Get this coffee pot percolating." This is his way of saying to get the car started. (*Angels' Alley*)

On giving blood plasma, he says: "I wouldn't stand for that, Boomer's Irish, you know. Couldn't give him none of that canned stuff." (*Angels' Alley*)

"*Put on the petrol*." [*Step on the gas.*] (*Angels' Alley*)

"Nobody can sue me; I ain't got nothing to sue." (*Smugglers' Cove*)

He doesn't understand that "Esq." means Esquire.

"Back in luxury's lap." The proper expression is "Back in the lap of luxury." (*Smugglers' Cove*)

Slip coins a phrase: "The best defense would be an offense, and I was offensive." (*Smugglers' Cove*)

He calls the dog "a *trunkless* elephant." (*Smugglers' Cove*)

Looking the place over, Slip says, "Might say it is a little *promiscuous*." (*Jinx Money*)

"As neat as a barn." (*Jinx Money*)

At the racetrack, Slip says, "Let's get 'me from the *starboard* side." Of course, this is a mariner's term. He just should have said, "*right side*." (*Crashing Las Vegas*)

"A genius, he's a regular *apostrophe*. [?] Yeah, that was the famous Greek *salamander*." [philosopher?] (*Triple Trouble*)

"Whitey, I'm cognizant of the fact that you didn't sleep. But I'm begging to think it making a hyper-romantic [*hypochondriac*] out of you." (*Triple Trouble*)

"Watch your blood pressure, you'll blow a gasket." (*Triple Trouble*)

"Why don't I *vegetate* this matter over in my mind?" (*Triple Trouble*)

"Counselor Marino, we are absolutely *inebriated* with your efforts on our behalf." (*Triple Trouble*)

Explains to judge: "To elucidate and clarify the point in your legal mind I desire to wave away this probation." (*Triple Trouble*)

"You're *in the* [*using the*] wrong frequency as usual." (*Hold That Baby*)

The Fractured Language of Slip Mahoney • 119

"This *evidenced* [evidence] is strictly circumstantial." (*Triple Trouble*)

Regarding Butch's insomnia, Slip can't say the word insomnia: "in a, in a…" (*Triple Trouble*)

"Professor, that's one of the nicest paintings I've seen since Whistler hung up his *gloves*." He meant *smock*. (*Paris Playboys*)

"Don't forget Gabe, that truth is sometimes stranger than *friction*." [*fiction*] (*Triple Trouble*)

Referring to a microphone wire: "I wonder if there's a *barracuda* at the end of this line." (*Blues Busters*)

"Louie, would you please be calm before you have another attack of *angina expectorate*." [*angina pectoris*] (*Blues Busters*)

"Let's get out of the cornfield and get to work." (*Blues Busters*)

"If they're for nothing, well then we'll *fracture* a precedent." (*Blues Busters*)

"What she may lack in talent she makes up *physiogicamally*." [*physically*?] (*Blues Busters*)

"Sure got a contract. It ain't worth the infinitesimal amount of ink it was written with." (*Blues Busters*)

"Pardon me while I *depress* the idiot." (*Crazy over Horses*)

"Do as I say, act as I do." (*Crazy over Horses*)

Sach: "That sounds like a poem." Slip: "*Philologically*, it is." (*Crazy over Horses*)

"In case they're *recalcitrant* about the outcome." (*Crazy over Horses*)

"No sense getting *apoplexy*." (*Crazy over Horses*)

After getting hit with whipped cream piecake: "And that's what I call *besmirched* gratitude." (*Crazy over Horses*)

"We made the switch ourselves, if you pardon the *innuendo*." (*Crazy over Horses*)

"But *extemporaneously*, but we'll be settling accounts with those crooked horse switches." (*Crazy over Horses*)

"Louie, how can you talk that about a voice, that someday be *mortified*." [*vilified* or *immortalized*?] (*Lucky Losers*)

"If your thought waves are synthetic with his, I think it can be done. That is, if I think you were born on the right bicuspid." (*Ghost Chasers*)

"I'll flatten you right in the head if you don't stop *so-lilio-quizing*." [*soliloquizing*] (*Ghost Chasers*)

Referring to Sach: "Let's get out of here before this idiot arouses my sense of *mayhem*." (*Ghost Chasers*)

"I never knew of a moment so *innocuous* to do so." (*Spy Chasers*)

"I'm confident we're capable of handling the *ensuing* situation." (*Spy Chasers*)

"My *dictional* quality of my *total* voice" [*dictatorial, tonal*] (*Spy Chasers*)

"This is no *optical* course." (*Spy Chasers*)

"We decided to do a little *sterey-opting* investigating." (*Spy Chasers*)

"I've been kinda *cremating* this whole thing over in my mind" (*Spy Chasers*)

"I told you to follow her not to usurp her." (*Spy Chasers*)

"I hate to leave you in such an *embellished* mood." (*Spy Chasers*)

"We gather here tonight to *inebriate* each and every one of you." (*Crazy over Horses*)

"A tooth for a tooth—motto of Mahoney Collection Agency." [an eye for an eye] (*Crazy over Horses*)

"Uh, now that's what I call using words *colloquially*." (*Crazy over Horses*)

"We're not going to let any sob stories *deteriorate* from our point of attack." (*Crazy over Horses*)

"You owe our client, Mr. Dumbrowski, 250 dollars plus interest, which we're willing to disintegrate, plus court impoundments, of course." (*Crazy over Horses*)

"This place is *deforming* your *ek-wa-librium*." He meant, "*destroying* your *equilibrium*." (*Spook Busters*)

"Doctor, in other words, you're trying to *relegate* [*relay*] the thought to me that this skull impervious to injury and it might *intringically* [*intrinsically*] obliterate anything it comes in contact with." (*No Holds Barred*))

"We'll *elucidate* further with any *premature* developments." (*No Holds Barred*)

"You'll have to forgive my friend, he's still *circument* [*suffering*] from shock." (*No Holds Barred*)

"We? Ain't you using the *objectionable* verb?" (*No Holds Barred*)

"When my head clears, I'm gonna give you a shot between the eyes that will *disintegrate* your toenails." (*No Holds Barred*)

"Rhonda, we'd like better than to be a small and *mortal* service to you." (*No Holds Barred*)

"Don't be so *vee-a-ment* [*vehement?*] with the jack jerk." (*No Holds Barred*)

"Madame, I would not think of *re-deforming* [*disappointing?*] you." (*No Holds Barred*)

"If I may be so *indigenous*, I would *pardon* like to all three of you." [*indulgent, excuse*] (*No Holds Barred*)

When girl suggests to go out on the terrace: "Perhaps we can *re-fertilize* yesterday's mood." [*revisit?*] (*No Holds Barred*)

"Mind if I step over your *trousseau*?" (*No Holds Barred*)

"I don't think this man knows the negative courtesy." (*No Holds Barred*)

"Sach, there happens to be an old *maxilnary* [*axiom* or *maxim*] that says two's company and three's a crowd." (*No Holds Barred*)

"Sach, you *degenerated lunatic*, put me down." (*No Holds Barred*)

"That's a very *elucidating* [*intelligent?*] thought." (*No Holds Barred*)

"I don't know if it ever entered your minute brain." (*No Holds Barred*)

"You want all the kids on the East Side to *crink* that *unrestrained* gutter water." (*No Holds Barred*)

"Now there's a *pathetic* picture of *pandemonium*." (*Feudin' Fools*)

"You can't understand nothing with that *semi-colon* brain of yours." (*Feudin' Fools*)

"I'm trying to formulate a maneuver with a skirmish *detached*." (*Feudin' Fools*)

"All I know is we got to put a stop to this *extemporaneous* shooting." (*Feudin' Fools*)

"One thing that's certain: I got to *inculcate* [*influence?*] these guys' minds that old *salvation*." [*salvo*] (*Feudin' Fools*)

"I've beginning to *re-germinate* an idea." (*Feudin' Fools*)

"I'm just *re-germinating* an idea." (*Feudin' Fools*)

"Jones, well that's an *idiosyncrocy* of a name." (*Feudin' Fools*)

"You heard of Doctor Dumbrowsky, the famous physician in *sturgids*?" [*surgery*] (*Feudin' Fools*)

"He ranks with the Rankins, he went to medical school with Dr. Pasture." [*Pasteur*] (*Feudin' Fools*)

"Perhaps the *voiceferous* idiots would like a souvenir?" (*No Holds Barred*)

"You really got us in the *jackpot* [*jam*] now." (*High Society*)

"Our *accommodations* are rather *indigenous*." (*High Society*)

"I don't *inference* that you're *referring*." (*High Society*)

"That's a very *deleterious* accusation." (*High Society*)

"What you have on your *desultory* mind?" (*High Society*)

"minor *ejudication*" (*High Society*)

"You have to forgive my friend Louie, he's a little *indelible*." (*Here Come the Marines*)

"I don't want you guys snooping, this may be a top *drawer* secret." (*Here Come the Marines*)

After Sach gets his stripes: "Look you walking *malady*. You're in the Marine Corpse [Corps] now." (*Here Come the Marines*)

"Sach, that's his maiden name." (*Here Come the Marines*)

"You stand here and watch while I *deteriorate* this girl with the Mahoney personality." (*Here Come the Marines*)

He refers to "Séance Sara," as "Turban Mary." (*Ghost Chasers*)

"Now honey, just in-tune your *aural cavities* for an *ecclesiastical*." (*Jalopy*)

"Look, may I remind you that there's a bit of *ambivalent* justification for our *innocuous* activities." (*Jalopy*)

"*Au reservoir* [au revoir], my little antipasto." (*Jalopy*)

"I say you're gonna get *runned* [run] over." (*Jalopy*)

"Fifteen hundred dollars is something I'm very *absorbent* to forget." (*Jalopy*)

Referring to money from winning a race: "We'll have a bundle left off for *contingencies*." (*Jalopy*)

"If you need me, just call me Mata Hari Mahoney." (*Jalopy*)

"Scientific *skullduggery* has me completely *bewitched*." (*Jalopy*)

"Well, what do I owe the pleasure of this *mergealistic* appearance." (*Jalopy*)

"I'm sorry but I'll have to *recapitulate* [refuse?] your invitation." (*Jalopy*)

"The night before I have to get my adequate and *compensatory* shut-eye." (*Jalopy*)

In threatening to shoot someone, he says, "Before I *air condition* you." (*Bowery Buckaroos*)

"You must be *gaggifying me*." [putting me on] (*Dig That Uranium*)

To Sach impersonating a doctor: "You *decomposed psychomaniac*." (*Here Come the Marines*)

"Sach I'm afraid you haven't the incentive to ever become an *efernal cog* of this great newspaper." (*News Hounds*)

"Those were very *obligatory* words I think now that we're handing out bouquets." (*Fighting Fools*)

"This guy's vocabulary is almost as *condensed* [reduced] as mine." (*Master Minds*)

"You'll have to forgive the doctor, he's a little *dyspeptic*." (*Feudin' Fools*)

"Did anyone ever tell that retreat is *retrograde*?" (*Feudin' Fools*)

"Remind me later, I owe you a *retroactive* apology." (*Dig That Uranium*)

"We must not *degenerate* into panic." (*Dig That Uranium*)

Slip refers to pal Chuck as Charles Anderson: "That's his maiden name." (*Jail Busters*)

"I may be *dissuaded* to dilly-dally with these dillies for a bit." He meant *persuaded*. (*Bowery to Bagdad*)

"…in the *recoils* of the law" (*The Bowery Boys Meet the Monsters*)

"Louie that's a very *flagrant* idea." (*The Bowery Boys Meet the Monsters*)

"Before this deal is completely edible we have to draw up certain *officious* [official] documents." (*The Bowery Boys Meet the Monsters*)

"I don't like to sound congestive [combative] but we're going home, h–o–m!" (*The Bowery Boys Meet the Monsters*)

"You're full of bravado." (*The Bowery Boys Meet the Monsters*)

"*Persecute* a few calories." [eat] (*The Bowery Boys Meet the Monsters*)

"You begin to have *steeri-optical illusions*." [optical delusions] (*The Bowery Boys Meet the Monsters*)

"I'd like to present the legitimate *advocate* to the Andrew's fortune." (*Hold That Baby*)

"To get back to the *invective* of the subject, what are you doing with that reinforced hair net on your head?" (*Paris Playboys*)

"I'd like to make sure that you got those instructions *inculcated* [implanted] in your head" (*Paris Playboys*)

"The *gruesome* facts in this case is that you guys are *painting the wrong fence*." (*Paris Playboys*)

"I don't like to sound *incandescent*, but just what is this all about?" (*Paris Playboys*)

"Louie, don't be so *sartorial*." (*Paris Playboys*)

"I don't like to seem *perpendicular* about these things." [particular?] (*Paris Playboys*)

"I'll get him a meshuga doctor." (*Paris Playboys*)

"For a man you can't even carve bread, you're being pretty *parcipitant* with that sword." (*Paris Playboys*)

"It'll *dilapidate your conscious* the rest of your life." (*Smugglers' Cove*)

"Now there's a *circumspective* painting if I ever saw one." (*Smugglers' Cove*)

"Get a load of that *calcimine* job" (*Smugglers' Cove*)

"I don't think we should be too *avaricious* about this thing." (*Smugglers' Cove*)

"'The key to the mystery thou shall perceiveth whither thy fall.' That's direct from Hamlet." (*Fighting Fools*)

"There ain't no minion of law putting anything over your little one on Mahoney." (*Hold That Baby*)

Regarding Sach's disappearance: "This *holocaust* has to be kept out of the papers at any price." (*Master Minds*)

He sometimes mixes different languages, such as French & Spanish words: "*Au revoir, amigos.*" (*Bowery Buckaroos*)

Also, "*bonos dias, mon Cherie.*" (*Bowery Buckaroos*)

9 Glossary of Selected Malaprops and Other Twisted Wordplays

"On the level? I was never leveler in my life."
– Slip Mahoney, *Trouble Makers*

THE PAGES THAT FOLLOW offer many (but certainly not all) of the fancy words, misused words, or funny expressions used by Gorcey's Slip Mahoney in forty-one films in the Bowery Boys series. The first column ("SLIP SAYS") offers the word as said by Slip. Sometimes the context of the sentence is offered in brackets ([ ]). Those words with asterisks (*) are made-up words. What Slip possibly meant is listed under the second column ("SLIP MEANS"). The exact word he was aiming for is not always obvious, so perceptive readers might find a better match. The third column ("FROM FILM TITLE") indicates the location from where Slip spoke the word.

SLIP SAYS:	SLIP MEANS:	FROM (FILM TITLE):
abolished (him)	demolished	*Bowery Buckaroos*
abscess (of your imagination)	figment	*Spook Busters*
A/C – *altercating current*	alternating current	*Dig That Uranium*
(give him the) *acetate* (test)	litmus	*Master Minds*
(me and my) *accomplice*	partner	*The Bowery Boys Meet the Monsters*
accomplishment (to the crime)	accomplice	*Bowery Bombshell*
(don't like to sound) *acquiescent*	nosy	*Mr. Hex*

activating (ingredients)	*active*	*Bowery Buckaroos*
(what's that old) *adhesive*?	*adage*	*Angels in Disguise*
(bring any) *aesthetics*	*anesthetics*	*Feudin' Fools*
(part you played in this) *affray*	*affair*	*Crazy over Horses*
affiliation (between the two facts)	*association*	*Here Come the Marines*
(I think a nice cold shower will) *aggravate* (your blood circulation)	*stimulate*	*No Holds Barred*
(no time for a long) *aggression*	*discussion*	*Jungle Gents*
(they may be) *ahmad**	*armed*	*Crazy over Horses*
alien (right of every citizen)	*inalienable*	*Fighting Fools*
(successful in) *alleviating us of* (this money)	*taking*	*Jinx Money*
(the proper) *alliteration*	*pronunciation*	*Triple Trouble*
(specially) *alterated** (just for the body)	*altered*	*Let's Go Navy!*
(circumstances don't leave no) *alteration*	*alternative*	*Feudin' Fools*
(my buddy and I are having a little) *alteration*	*altercation*	*Triple Trouble*
altercation	*alternative*	*Jail Busters*
(mental) *altitude*	*aptitude*	*Spook Busters*
(perfect) *anecdote*	*antidote*	*Angels in Disguise*
(gals and uniforms are) *anonymous*	*synonymous*	*Trouble Makers*
(a very good) *anticipation*	*suggestion*	*Jinx Money*
(out of this den of) *antiques*	*iniquities*	*Blonde Dynamite*
(this den of) *antiquity*	*iniquity*	*Bowery Battalion*
(sensible) *aptitude*	*attitude*	*In Fast Company*
(it's an) *apparella** (fact)	*apparent*	*Blues Busters*
(take a pretty smart) *apple*	*cookie*	*Jinx Money*
(you must) *applicate*	*apply*	*Ghost Chasers*
[re: tattoo] (the name 'Marie') *applicated** (right on it)	*applied*	*Let's Go Navy!*
(made us) *apprentices* (to the crime)	*accomplices*	*Blonde Dynamite*
approxtimidity (in one hour)	*approximately*	*Master Minds*
(a couple of) *aqua puras*	glasses of *water*	*Lucky Losers*

Glossary of Selected Malaprops and Other Twisted Wordplays • 127

(beautiful night,) aren't it?	isn't it	In Fast Company
arf leadisen*	auf wiedersehen	Paris Playboys
(don't) arise (me no more)	arouse	The Bowery Boys Meet the Monsters
arms of Morphis*?	armed forces	Bowery Buckaroos
arrivergurci	arriverderci	Paris Playboys
(what an) arsenic	arsenal	Angels in Disguise
(give him a little) artificial perspiration	water	Private Eyes
(he can use some) artificial perspiration	respiration	Bowery to Bagdad
artillery (cirrhosis)	arterial	Clipped Wings
assault without a battery	assault and battery	Bowery Bombshell
assimulated*	assimilated	Bowery Buckaroos
(my fellow) associations	associates	Live Wires
assumulated* (that fact)	assumed/ assimilated	Lucky Losers
(my utter) astoundment	astonishment	Jail Busters
(I get) atomic ache	stomach ache	Live Wires
(mental) attics	tricks	Bowery Buckaroos
audical* (cavities)	aural	Mr. Hex
auf resivoir	au revoir	Blonde Dynamite
(never mind the) autolieography	autobiography	No Holds Barred
awfuller	awful	Crashing Las Vegas
(you look like a thief of) Badgags	Bagdad	Bowery to Bagdad
bait (your breath)	hold	Smugglers' Cove
(acute) bank rupture	bankruptcy	Spook Busters
bat's (nest)	rats	High Society
beck and command	beck and call	Spook Busters
belay (the gruesome details)	relay	News Hounds
(great public) benefracture	benefactor	No Holds Barred
(I am a) benefracturer*	benefactor	The Bowery Boys Meet the Monsters
benefracturer*	benefactor	Lucky Losers
(great) benefractury (to the human race)	benefactor	Fighting Fools

benevolent	clairvoyant	Master Minds
(don't know if he's) betwitched*	bewitched	Master Minds
bite (our time)	bide	Clipped Wings
blew (in from Miami)	flew	News Hounds
blood confusion	blood transfusion	Angels in Disguise
bona-fried	bone fide	High Society
bona-fried	bone fide	Spy Chasers
boon (companion)	bosom	Angels in Disguise
(Sach my) boon (companion)	bosom	Blues Busters
(that's what I) bought (you for)	brought	Jail Busters
(don't get your) bows (crossed)	wires	Bowery Buckaroos
(we'll get down to) brass tax	bear facts	Let's Go Navy!
brick and bracks	bric-a-brac	Master Minds
brood (brother)	blood	Fighting Fools
brung* (you something)	brought	In Fast Company
(financial) cacoons*	tycoons	Hold That Baby
(my) cahoots	cohorts	Smugglers' Cove
(thunder is something that has never) calcified (me)	terrified	The Bowery Boys Meet the Monsters
captivated (them)	captured	Jungle Gents
caps (will fall right now)	chips	Trouble Makers
(make a) carbonated (copy)	carbon	Fighting Fools
(sign of the) cardiac (you was born under)	Zodiac	Ghost Chasers
(pass me a) cartilage	cartridge	Jungle Gents
castigated	criticized	Here Come the Marines
cavaliers	chandeliers	Smugglers' Cove
(it's all a beastly) cawinkydence	coincidence	Jalopy
(30 degrees) centipede	Celsius	Jungle Gents
chaisy (lounge)	chaise	Smugglers' Cove
(look at the 15-gallon) chateau	chapeau	Dig That Uranium
chapeau	chateau	The Bowery Boys Meet the Monsters
(Louie, what are you doing with a French) chateau	chapeau	Paris Playboys
(explains that a chateau is just a small		

Glossary of Selected Malaprops and Other Twisted Wordplays • 129

chapeau, "just a matter of the *congregation* of the verb" = *conjugation*)		
"(you) *chrysantidum* (picker)"	*chrysanthemum*	*Clipped Wings*
choirpracter*	*chiropractor*	*Master Minds*
chranometer*	*chronometer* (clock?)	*Crashing Las Vegas*
(do under these) *circumferences*	*circumstances*	*Paris Playboys*
(victims of) *circumferences*	*circumstances*	*Hold That Baby*
(under these) *circumplexes*	*circumstances*	*The Bowery Boys Meet the Monsters*
circumflexes	*circumstances*	*High Society*
(doing our) *civilized* (duty)	*civil*	*Jungle Gents*
(greatest) *clairvoyage*	*clairvoyant*	*Master Minds*
(has a particular gift for the) *clairavoyage*	*clairvoyant*	*Ghost Chasers*
clam (before the storm)	*calm*	*Trouble Makers*
(going to) *coagulate* (with us?)	*cooperate*	*The Bowery Boys Meet the Monsters*
coagulating (with the press)	*cooperating*	*No Holds Barred*
cohorting	*consorting*	*Spy Chasers*
cohoots*	*cohorts*	*Spy Chasers*
(without further) *coincidence*	*incidence*	*Jungle Gents*
(put our) *collective* (brains together)	*combined*	*Crashing Las Vegas*
(now in) *collusion*	*conclusion*	*News Hounds*
(out of) *combustible goods*	*paper money*	*Dig That Uranium*
commaflaged*	*camouflaged*	*Here Come the Marines*
commotion	*emotion*	*Spook Busters*
(it's a very) *compatible* (feeling)	*comforting*	*Triple Trouble*
(different) *complexion* (on things)	*face*	*Hold That Baby*
(tries to) *comply*	*imply*	*News Hounds*
(before I lose my) *composure*	*temper*	*Mr. Hex*
comprehended… (these crooks)	*apprehended*	*News Hounds*
(I'd like to) *compress* (upon you)	*impress*	*Spy Chasers*
(doesn't sound very) *compulsory*	*compelling*	*Jinx Money*
(it's a masterpiece of) *conception*	*perception*	*Spy Chasers*
(as far as I'm) *concerted*	*concerned*	*Private Eye*
concilation* (is certain)	*conciliation*	*News Hounds*

(musical) *concoctions*	*compositions*	*Blues Busters*
concussion	*discussion*	*Private Eyes*
(letters of) *condemnation*	*commendation*	*Let's Go Navy!*
(your suggestion is more than) *condescending*	*suggestive*	*Blonde Dynamite*
(Africa—sometimes known as the dark) *condiment*	*continent*	*Jungle Gents*
(intimate) *conflagration*	*conversation*	*Fighting Fools*
(have a one-way) *conflagration*	*conversation*	*Bowery Battalion*
(you can) *confried* (in me)	*confide*	*Jail Busters*
(your very just) *confusions*	*conclusions*	*In Fast Company*
congregations (in your brain)	*convolutions*	*Spook Busters*
(I'm) *congutating**	*thinking*	*Angels' Alley*
(we'll all) *conjugate* (back here)	*congregate*	*Spy Chasers*
(don't misconstrue the) *connotation*	*investigation*	*Lucky Losers*
(alleviates my) *conscious* (to tell you this)	*conscience*	*Loose in London*
consecrate (a way to get some money)	*consider*	*Jalopy*
(I'm trying to) *consecrate*	*concentrate*	*Trouble Makers*
(our journey is) *consecrated*	*completed*	*Dig That Uranium*
(I'm) *consecrating*	*concentrating*	*Angels in Disguise*
(can't you see I'm) *consecrating*	*concentrating*	*Spy Chasers*
(little) *consecration*	*concentration*	*Bowery Battalion*
(my personal) *constructions*	*instructions*	*Hard Boiled Mahoney*
(while I) *confirm* (with our first) *patient*	*consult, client*	*Private Eyes*
(your) *confury*	*complexion?*	*In Fast Company*
consummated (by a tiger)	*consumed*	*Jungle Gents*
we'll *consume*	*resume*	*Private Eyes*
(I'm right in that) *consumption*	*assumption*	*Feudin' Fools*
(matter being highly) *contagious*	*confidential*	*The Bowery Boys Meet the Monsters*
(working in) *contusions*	*collusion*	*Jinx Money*
(prove anything) *convulsively*	*conclusively*	*News Hounds*
(my words) *contra-bandaged*	*contradicted*	*News Hounds*
consume (my place)	*assume*	*Bowery Bombshell*

Glossary of Selected Malaprops and Other Twisted Wordplays • 131

(a cold could be very) *contaminating*	*contagious*	*Paris Playboys*
contemptible (invention)	*contemporary*	*Live Wires*
(man of criminal) *content*	*conduct*	*In Fast Company*
(I arrived at the) *contusion*	*conclusion*	*Spy Chasers*
(prove anything) *convulsively*	*conclusively*	*News Hounds*
(give me your) *coordination*	*cooperation*	*Bowery to Bagdad*
(refusal to) *coordinate* (with me)	*cooperate*	*Blonde Dynamite*
(introduced in the) *coronary* (fashion)	*ordinary*	*Dig That Uranium*
corny-sewer* (of the finer arts)	*connoisseur*	*Smugglers' Cove*
corpus delicious	*corpus delecti*	*Trouble Maker*
(elevate the) *corpus delicious*	*corpus delecti*	*The Bowery Boys Meet the Monsters*
Corral (No. 5)	*Chanel*	*Jungle Gents*
Corpuscle	*Corporal*	*Here Come the Marines*
corpuses (delecti)	*corpus*	*Jungle Gents*
corrigate* (the statement)	*corroborate*	*Smugglers' Cove*
corrigations (of his brain) shell	*convolutions, skull*	*Clipped Wings*
(that's a very) *corrosive* (question)	*explosive* or *intrusive*	*Blonde Dynamite*
(it wasn't just a) *cowinkydence**	*coincidence*	*Blues Busters*
crab (our first job)	*grab*	*Spook Busters*
(by some) *creek* (of nature)	*freak*	*Blues Busters*
(bargain if I ever) *cremated* one	*created*	*Trouble Makers*
cremates a rhubarbs (with the wolves)	*creates a brouhaha*	*The Bowery Boys Meet the Monsters*
crime (purpose)	*prime*	*Clipped Wings*
(take us on a) *crook's* (tour)	*Cook's*	*The Bowery Boys Meet the Monsters*
crucial (position)	*critical*	*Angels in Disguise*
(the facts) *crucified* (in my mind)	*crossed*	*Here Come the Marines*
crudely (interrupted)	*rudely*	*News Hounds*
(in my) *crumbled* (opinion) [Louie corrects him. Slip responds that he was using the past tense.]	*humble*	*Triple Trouble*

D/C – *dirty and crinkly*	direct current	*Dig That Uranium*
(best of my) *dability**	ability	*News Hounds*
(best of my) *debility**	ability	*Let's Go Navy!*
(make his first public) *debutant*	debut	*Blues Busters*
(meet a couple of) *debutramps*	debutantes	*High Society*
(financially) *decapitated*	incapacitated	*Jinx Money*
(financially) *decapitated*	incapacitated	*Fighting Fools*
deceived (by men)	conceived	*Live Wires*
(hands of the) *deceivers*	receivers	*Spook Busters*
(got a wonderful) *deception*	perception	*Clipped Wings*
deception	inception	*High Society*
(sometimes he gets very) *deciduous*	insidious	*Jalopy*
(a very) *declamatory reduction*	inflammatory deduction	*Clipped Wings*
(interior) *declarations*	decorations	*Jinx Money*
(girl that's so) *declined*	inclined	*Live Wires*
(very musically) *declined*	inclined	*Mr. Hex*
(so) *declined*	inclined	*Hard Boiled Mahoney*
declined (to agree with you)	inclined	*Here Come the Marines*
declined (to agree with you)	inclined	*Spy Chasers*
declined (to get a) *deflated* (head)	inclined, inflated	*News Hounds*
(your) *deef* (as a post)	deaf	*Jail Busters*
defected	infected	*Private Eyes*
(serious) *defense*	offense	*Here Come the Marines*
(this is strictly) *deferential*	confidential	*News Hounds*
(lie) *deflector*	detector	*Private Eyes*
deform (him of our good luck)	inform	*Let's Go Navy!*
deform (me of one fact)	inform	*Private Eyes*
deform (you)	inform	*Bowery Bombshell*
deform (you)	inform	*Jungle Gents*
deform	inform	*Crashing Las Vegas*
(I hate to) *deform* (you)	inform	*Jungle Gents*
deform Horace of the invitation	inform	*High Society*
deformed (you of the news)	informed	*Blues Busters*
(just) *deformed* (me)	informed	*Master Minds*

Glossary of Selected Malaprops and Other Twisted Wordplays • 133

(if somebody) *deforms* (the police)	*informs*	*Jail Busters*
(let's not) *defrenchiate**	*differentiate*	*Bowery Battalion*
defused (by this whole thing)	*confused*	*Jinx Money*
defusing (me a little)	*confusing*	*Trouble Makers*
(only one thing that's) *defusing*	*confusing*	*Bowery Battalion*
degenerated (opinion)	*educated*	*Jinx Money*
deject (your)	*reject*	*In Fast Company*
dehales* (carbon monoxide)	*exhales*	*In Fast Company*
dehydrate (my thoughts)	*process*	*Bowery Bombshell*
delectable (friend)	*dependable*	*Jalopy*
deject (it)	*eject*	*Private Eyes*
delicious anemia	*pernicious anemia*	*Angels' Alley*
(Sach is socially) *delinquent*	*deficient*	*Jalopy*
(but I think Corp. Stacy is having) *delirium trumans*	*delirium tremens*	*Here Come the Marines*
deloped *(the greatest voice)	*developed*	*Blues Busters*
(bringing this case to a successful) *delusion*	*conclusion*	*Crazy over Horses*
(jumping at) *delusions*	*conclusions*	*In Fast Company*
(facing only one unjustifiable) *demeanor*	*misdemeanor*	*Dig That Uranium*
(ultimately) *demised*	*dismissed*	*Here Come the Marines*
Demograts	*Democrats*	*Loose in London*
demolish (the refreshments)	*devour*	*Private Eyes*
(vitamins in) *demoltified* (form)	*demulsified*	*Hold That Line*
denominated by Indians	*inhabited*	*Bowery Buckaroos*
(your verbal) *denunciation*	*pronunciation*	*Ghost Chasers*
(there's nothing I would) *deplore* (more)	*adore*	*Bowery to Bagdad*
deponents	*opponents*	*News Hounds*
(proper) *deportation*	*importance*	*Hard Boiled Mahoney*
deposed (the uranium)	*exposed*	*Dig That Uranium*
(I do) *depreciate* (all that)	*appreciate*	*Hold That Baby*
(don't) *depreciate* (every little thing)	*appreciate*	*Triple Trouble*
(we) *depreciate* (everything)	*appreciate*	*Let's Go Navy!*
(we can) *depreciate* (that fact)	*appreciate*	*Crazy over Horses*

(I'll) *depreciate* (your cooperation)	*appreciate*	*Here Come the Marines*
(I can certainly deeply) *depreciate*	*appreciate*	*No Holds Barred*
(I don't think you) *depreciate*	*appreciate*	*Jalopy*
(I certainly) *depreciate* (the fact)	*appreciate*	*Jalopy*
depreciate	*appreciate*	*Loose in London*
depreciate (the fact)	*appreciate*	*Private Eyes*
(you don't) *depreciate*	*appreciate*	*High Society*
(I deeply) *depreciate*	*appreciate*	*Spy Chasers*
(at least I) *depreciate*	*appreciate*	*Dig That Uranium*
depreciate more if you didn't *segregate* your adjectives	*appreciate, separate*	*Clipped Wings*
(we) *depreciate* (this) *invective*	*appreciate, incentive*	*The Bowery Boys Meet the Monsters*
(the gift is deeply) *depreciated*	*appreciated*	*Lucky Losers*
depreciated	*appreciated*	*Crashing Las Vegas*
(this money will be) *depreciated*	*appreciated*	*Bowery Battalion*
(show my) *depreciation*	*appreciation*	*Angels in Disguise*
(lack of) *depreciation*	*appreciation*	*Angels' Alley*
(I don't wanna be) *depreciative*	*unappreciative*	*Live Wires*
(get a very good) *depression*	*impression*	*Private Eyes*
(electrical) *dequipment**	*equipment*	*Crazy over Horses*
derailing (my train of thought)	*disturbing*	*Live Wires*
(we can) *derange* (to stay)	*arrange*	*The Bowery Boys Meet the Monsters*
derange (that)	*arrange*	*Crashing Las Vegas*
(be able to) *derange*	*arrange*	*Ghost Chasers*
(a little more) *deranging*	*arranging*	*Hard Boiled Mahoney*
(done something) *derisive*	*decisive*	*Fighting Fools*
my *derogative*	*prerogative*	*In Fast Company*
derogatory (sum) (when Bobby Jordan corrects him, Gorcey says *prerogative* is the feminine tense)	*designated*	*Jinx Money*
*desicrate**	*donate*	*Jinx Money*
desist	*resist*	*Jinx Money*
(I was) *desponsible*	*responsible*	*Hold That Baby*

Glossary of Selected Malaprops and Other Twisted Wordplays • 135

(matter of great) *despondency*	urgency	Hard Boiled Mahoney
(you'll find all the) *destructions*	instructions	Jalopy
(your facial) *destruction*	construction	Ghost Chasers
(architectural) *destruction*	construction	Trouble Makers
(importance) *detached*	attached	Spy Chasers
(usual) *detaining* (fee)	retaining	Hard Boiled Mahoney
(this may be) *detergent*	urgent	Jail Busters
deadteriating (climax)	deteriorating	Spook Busters
detracted (those guys gunfire)	distracted	Jungle Gents
detrained (slightly)	detained	Fighting Fools
(assets and) *detriment* (of my vast estate)	debts	Smugglers' Cove
(difficulty and) *diffusion*	confusion	Spook Busters
(very) *diligently*	delicately	Bowery Buckaroos
(you got the) *discrepancy* (to call it dirt)	audacity	Smugglers' Cove
(we have to) *discriminate* (exactly what they're up to)	investigate	Spy Chasers
discriminations	incriminations	Bowery Bombshell
(few hints of etiquette that we have to) *disgust*	discuss	Blonde Dynamite
(I don't want to) *dis-eliminate* (you)	disenchant	Jalopy
disencourage (us)	discouraged	Dig That Uranium
(this is where we) *disintegrate*	separate	Clipped Wings
(I like to) *disgust* (with you)	discuss	The Bowery Boys Meet the Monsters
disinclined (to think)	inclined	Bowery Buckaroos
(alright boys, let's) *disintegrate*	disappear	Ghost Chasers
disintegrate (some of that dust)	eliminate	Spook Busters
disintegrated (into thin air)	vanished	Hard Boiled Mahoney
(serious) *dilamania*	dilemma	Bowery to Bagdad
dislocated (without a tuppets)	disinherited	Loose in London
(that's very) *disparaging*	discouraging	News Hounds
(give you a little) *dispatch*	news	Angels' Alley
(do it with) *dispatch*	speed	Crazy over Horses

disreputable (news)	*bad*	*In Fast Company*
(why do you have to go around) *dis-rupturing* (things?)	*disrupting*	*Spy Chasers*
diffused	*confused*	*Jinx Money*
(you are cordially) *disinvited*	*uninvited*	*Jail Busters*
disseminating (it among the charities)	*distributing*	*Jinx Money*
(have a private) *dissipation* (with the warden)	*conversation*	*Jail Busters*
(long) *dissipation* (on the subject)	*dissertation*	*Jalopy*
dissolved (with an enigma)	*involved*	*Dig That Uranium*
(fire is) *distinguished*	*extinguished*	*Jungle Gents*
(get that fire) *distinguisher*	*extinguisher*	*Jail Busters*
ditict attorney	*district attorney*	*Angels' Alley*
(points I'd like to) *distress*	*discuss*	*Here Come the Marines*
diversifying (question)	*difficult*	*Spook Busters*
diverted (sense of humor)	*perverted*	*Dig That Uranium*
divisiting*	*visiting*	*Crashing Las Vegas*
(born and) *dragged*	*upraised*	*Clipped Wings*
(puts on the) *drape shade*	*disguise*	*News Hounds*
(insane) *drissle**	*drivel*	*Bowery to Bagdad*
(famous) *earmark*	*landmark*	*Loose in London*
(we got an) *ears dropper*	*eavesdropper*	*News Hounds*
(you're) *edible* (for the Olympics)	*eligible*	*Triple Trouble*
(for your) *edification*	*information*	*Live Wires*
(for your) *edification*	*information*	*Crazy over Horses*
(he's been so inadequately) *edicated*	*educated*	*News Hounds*
(everyone is getting) *e-fixiated**	*asphyxiated*	*Hold That Line*
electricution (lessons)	*elocution*	*Ghost Chasers*
(final word of) *elimination*	*information*	*Paris Playboys*
(without the) *elephant* (of a doubt)	*element*	*Jail Busters*
(ready to) *elucidate* (yourself)	*explain*	*Bowery Buckaroos*
embalmers (re: the king's men)	*enforcers*	*Bowery to Bagdad*
embellishes (the lives of the kids)	*endangers*	*The Bowery Boys Meet the Monsters*

Glossary of Selected Malaprops and Other Twisted Wordplays • 137

(sign) *embezzled* (on the whole car)	*emblazoned*	*Jalopy*
(beginning to get the) *emblem* (of an idea)	*sign* or *indication*	*Private Eyes*
Emory Post	*Emily Post*	*Hold That Baby*
(we're barking up an) *empty* (tree)	*wrong*	*Let's Go Navy!*
emuzzle	*embezzle*	*High Society*
(circle the whole) *entrampment*	*encampment*	*Jungle Gents*
enforced (in our work)	*involved*	*Bowery Bombshell*
(monetary) *enigma*	*crisis*	*Crashing Las Vegas*
ensuring (millions)	*ensuing*	*Dig That Uranium*
(disturb your) *equanimity*	*sleep*	*Angels' Alley*
(geographical) *era*	*area*	*Bowery Bombshell*
escapade (from wild beasts)	*escape*	*Jungle Gents*
(inner sanctums of them) *Esmeric** (arts)	*Mesmeric*	*Mr. Hex*
es-spinach (agents)	*espionage*	*Spy Chasers*
es-spinach (agents)	*espionage*	*Bowery Battalion*
(get ready to) *evaporate*	*disappear*	*Paris Playboys*
(we're going to) *excavate*	*investigate*	*Spook Busters*
(most) *excavating* (match)	*exciting*	*Angels in Disguise*
(view is absolutely) *excruciating*	*invigorating*	*No Holds Barred*
exhaled	*exiled*	*Spy Chasers*
exhibition (A)	*exhibit*	*Bowery Buckaroos*
(weekend hunting) *exhibition*	*expedition*	*Feudin' Fools*
exhilarate (the literature)	*examine*	*No Holds Barred*
(we were so) *exhilarated*	*exhausted*	*Jungle Gents*
(put my foot on the) *exhilarator*	*accelerator*	*Jalopy*
(accelerate the) *exhilarator*	*accelerator*	*Dig That Uranium*
(little personal business to) *expatiate*	*discuss in detail*	*Hard Boiled Mahoney:*
expedition (papers)	*extradition*	*Bowery Buckaroos*
expel (the whole thing to you)	*explain*	*News Hounds*
*exploriating** (that crockery)	*excavating*	*Jungle Gents*
*exportorate** (he notes that it is slang for spit)	*expectorate*	*Bowery Bombshell*
expounding (what is common)	*explaining*	*News Hounds*
extemporaneous (equipment)	*excavating*	*Dig That Uranium*
(my) *exterminated* (honor)	*extreme*	*Spy Chasers*

extinct (improvement)	*distinct*	*The Bowery Boys Meet the Monsters*
extinguish	*distinguish*	*In Fast Company*
extinguish (right from wrong)	*distinguish*	*News Hounds*
extinguished	*distinguished*	*High Society*
extinguished (guests)	*distinguished*	*News Hounds*
extinguished (guest)	*distinguished*	*Spy Chasers*
(nice to have such an) *extinguished*	*distinguished*	*Private Eyes*
(your attention is) *extracted*	*distracted*	*Bowery Bombshell*
(terribly) *extracting*	*distracting*	*No Holds Barred*
Extreme Court	*Supreme Court*	*Bowery Bombshell*
Extreme Court	*Supreme Court*	*News Hounds*
eyeball witness	*eyewitness*	*Trouble Makers*

falsify (my emotions)	*hide*	*Spook Busters*
(absolutely) *fanatic*	*fantastic*	*Crashing Las Vegas*
(thank you my) *fatalistic* friends	*fantastic*	*News Hounds*
female prohibition	*female intuition*	*Angels in Disguise*
fiesta	*siesta*	*Spy Chaser*
filament (of your imagination)	*figment*	*Loose in London*
(the big) *finance-smear*	*financier*	*High Society*
(with our) *financial static*	*financial status*	*Bowery Bombshell*
finger of speech	*figure of speech*	*In Fast Company*
(get the knife in the boiling water and get it) *fertilized*	*sterilized*	*Feudin' Fools*
(get) *flabbered* (once in a while)	*flabbergasted*	*Angels Alley*
flabbergasted Sach's receiving apparatus	*impaired or shocked his telepathic ability*	*Private Eyes*
(be alone for a) *fleecing* (moment)	*fleeting*	*Spy Chasers*
(Florence) *Nightingams*	*Nightingale*	*Blues Busters*
(wanna go) *formally*?	*formal*	*Live Wires*
fortifying (combination)	*formidable*	*Bowery Bombshell*
(committed your last) *fox pox*	*faux pas*	*High Society*
fragis	*fragile*	*Crazy over Horses*
(gonna be a) *freakus*	*fracas*	*Crashing Las Vegas*
fracture (of your Bill of Rights)	*infraction*	*Hard Boiled Mahoney*

Glossary of Selected Malaprops and Other Twisted Wordplays • 139

(no more) *fractures* (of the rules)	infractions	*Hold That Line*
(what's the charge?) *Fragrancy?**	vagrancy	*Bowery Bombshell*
(I ain't) *fragrant*	vagrant	*Bowery Bombshell*
(juvenile) *fragrants*	delinquents	*Fighting Fools*
(kicking up a) *fraykus*	fracas	*Jungle Gents*
fritter (away)	flitter	*Angels in Disguise*
(Sergeant's out on a) *furlong*	furlough	*Clipped Wings*
gander	look	*Spook Busters*
(take a) *gander* (at those)	look	*News Hounds*
garter	goiter	*Private Eyes*
(he's studying) *gastronomy*	astronomy	*Bowery to Bagdad*
(took off like) *gazilles**	gazelles	*Angels in Disguise*
(wild) *geese* (chase)	goose	*Angels in Disguise*
genius	genie	*Bowery to Bagdad*
geranium	uranium	*Dig That Uranium*
*germalism**	journalism	*News Hounds*
*germalist**	journalist	*News Hounds*
(attack with your) *golf stones*	gallstones	*Blues Busters*
(rattle your) *golf stones*	gallstones	*Jungle Gents*
(search every nook and) *granny*	cranny	*Trouble Makers*
(intestinal) *gratitude*	fortitude	*Spook Busters*
griddle (that guy)	grill	*Bowery Buckaroos*
(ladies') *griddles*	girdles	*Jungle Gents*
(keep our noses to the) *ground stone*	grindstone	*Spy Chasers*
Gullible's Travels	Gulliver's	*Loose in London*
(writ of a) *habeus corporal**	habeas corpus	*Clipped Wings*
(make our) *habitude* (someplace else)	habitat	*Let's Go Navy!*
habitude	habitat	*Hard Boiled Mahoney*
habitude	habitat	*Jungle Gents*
habitude	habitat	*Jinx Money*
habitude	habitat	*Ghost Chasers*
hair and hairs	heir and heirs	*Loose in London*

(Halls of) *Ivory*	*Ivy*	*Loose in London*
(you're having) *hallukinations*	*hallucinations*	*Jinx Money*
(you're suffering from) *hallukinations*	*hallucinations*	*Blues Busters*
(having) *hallukinations*	*hallucinations*	*Loose in London*
hallukinations	*hallucinations*	*Smugglers' Cove*
hallukinations	*hallucinations*	*Trouble Makers*
hallukinations	*hallucinations*	*Bowery to Bagdad*
hallukinations	*hallucinations*	*Paris Playboys*
hash (note)	*mash*	*Paris Playboys*
hasty mañana (as the French would say)[actually Spanish phrase]	*hasta mañana*	*Angels' Alley*
hasta banana	*hasta mañana*	*Spy Chasers*
(justified bone in his) *head*	*body*	*Hard Boiled Mahoney*
(dishonest bone in his) *head*	*body*	*Mr. Hex*
helicropter*	*helicopter*	*Clipped Wings*
(Oh I never get dizzy that only happens to be people with) *highdrophobia**	*acrophobia*	*No Holds Barred*
historical (yelling)	*hysterical*	*Jungle Gents*
(don't get) *historical*	*hysterical*	*Trouble Makers*
(make yourselves) *homely* (boys)	*at home*	*Bowery Battalion*
(set your) *hooks*	*sights*	*Jalopy*
Hopeless diamond	*Hope diamond*	*Master Minds*
(find new) *horror-zons**	*horizons*	*Jinx Money*
(Western) *hospitility**	*hospitality*	*Bowery Buckaroos*
(it's Slip Mahoney), *hostess*	*host*	*Blues Busters*
(holding him as a) *hostess*	*hostage*	*Bowery Buckaroos*
(as a) *hostess*	*hostage*	*Jungle Gents*
Hostess	*host*	*Dig That Uranium*
(I am the) *hostess*	*host*	*Loose in London*
hot seat	*electric chair*	*Master Minds*
(sense of) *human*	*humor*	*No Holds Barred*
(going to be very) *humidified*	*humiliated*	*Bowery Battalion*
(you're a true) *humilitarian**	*humanitarian*	*Fighting Fools*
(wasn't only the heat, it was the) *humility*	*humidity*	*News Hounds*

Glossary of Selected Malaprops and Other Twisted Wordplays • 141

(you're going about this in a) hypercontriacle* (manner)	hypermanical	Dig That Uranium
(in the matter of) hypercontriacle* (interest)	hypermanical	Crashing Las Vegas
(this is a very) hypercontriacle* (situation)	hypermanical	Trouble Makers
(this whole predicament is your fault, you, you) hypermaniac	hypochondriac	Blues Busters
hypographical* (knowledge)	geographical	Dig That Uranium
(nature and her) idiot-syncrasies*	idiosyncracies	Dig That Uranium
(he's traveling) igfognito*	incognito	No Holds Barred
(nothing like being) illiterate	literate	Live Wires
illuminate (the guards)	eliminate	Jail Busters
(process of) illumination	elimination	Loose in London
(process of) illumination	elimination	Crazy over Horses
(process of) illumination	elimination	Live Wires
ilukanations*	hallucinations	Spook Busters
immaterial (witnesses)	material	Jinx Money
"your name will go down through time immaterial"	immemorial	Fighting Fools
impertinent interrogations	important questions	Clipped Wings
(latch onto a very) impertinent (idea)	important	Jungle Gents
(have all those) impertinent (facts)	important	Loose in London
impertinent	important	Smugglers' Cove
(Why do women have to be so) imperceptible?	perceptive	Angels' Alley
inadequate	adequate	Jinx Money
(were you) incapacitated?	injured	Crashing Las Vegas
("Do you happen to know where they) incarcerate (these) incinerating (documents)	keep, incriminating	High Society
(are you) incinerating	insinuating	In Fast Company
(keep the fire) incinerating	burning	Jungle Gents
(this whole) incineration (is absolutely ridiculous)	insinuation	Paris Playboys

(make a serious) *incision*	decision	*Crashing Las Vegas*
(never live to regret your) *incision*	decision	*Hold That Line*
(trained to a point of) *incision*	precision	*Here Come the Marines*
(final) *incision*	decision	*Private Eyes*
(grave) *incision* (to make)	decision	*Bowery to Bagdad*
incompassened* (in this tent)	encompassed/ inside	*Master Minds*
(I'd like to be) *incompetent* (enough)	competent	*Hold That Baby*
inconsequential (knowledge)	substantial	*Jail Busters*
inconsequential (conclusion)	consequential	*Bowery Buckaroos*
inconvenience	convenience	*Master Minds*
inconvertible (suggestion)	inconvenient	*Angels' Alley*
(cause a lot of) *inconveyance**	inconvenience	*Crazy over Horses*
inculcating	impressing upon	*Crashing Las Vegas*
(pardon the) *indeception** (sir)	interruption	*Here Come the Marines*
indefinite (charge)	definite	*Bowery Bombshell*
(so we'll be easily) *indemnified*	identified	*Jail Busters*
(never been) *indemnified*	identified	*The Bowery Boys Meet the Monsters*
(case of mistaken) *indemnity*	identity	*Private Eyes*
(mistaken) *indemnity*	identity	*Paris Playboys*
(you have been completely) *indicated*	vindicated	*Jungle Gents*
[when he's corrected, he says he was using the singular verb]		
(looking so) *indigenous* (about?)	indignant	*Blonde Dynamite*
(won't stay in the trunk) *indigenously*	indefinitely	*Loose in London*
indiscriminate	discriminate	*Trouble Makers*
(it is a matter of) *indiscrimination*	indiscretion	*In Fast Company*
(it's an) *indisruptive** (feast)	indisputable	*No Holds Barred*
indu-bubbly*	indubitably	*Jinx Money*
(absolutely) *inedible*	incredible	*Bowery to Bagdad*
(it's absolutely) *inedible*	incredible	*Clipped Wings*
(the thought is absolutely) *inedible*	incredible	*Crazy over Horses*
(very) *ineffectual*	effective	*Jinx Money*

Glossary of Selected Malaprops and Other Twisted Wordplays • 143

(show my) *ineptitude*	*gratitude*	*Bowery Buckaroos*
inextracable (reason)	*inextricable*	*Bowery Battalion*
(sinus) *infatuation*	*infection*	*Jungle Gents*
inferences	*references*	*News Hounds*
(address your) *inferior* (officer)	*superior*	*Spy Chasers*
Infernal Revenue (agents)	*Internal Revenue*	*In Fast Company*
(students of the) *inferior* (arts)	*interior*	*Hold That Line*
inferred (to)	*referred*	*Jungle Gents*
(we're) *inferring* (to different kinds of lodges)	*referring*	*Loose in London*
(I'm very much) *infested*	*interested*	*The Bowery Boys Meet the Monsters*
(I have) *infinitesimal* (fortitude)	*intestinal*	*Loose in London*
infinitesimal (fortitude)	*intestinal*	*Jungle Gents*
(and that makes an) *infirmary*	*affirmative*	*Crazy over Horses*
(scared into) *infirmity*	*eternity*	*Spy Chasers*
(thanks for the) *inflammation*	*information*	*Crazy over Horses*
(as) *influenzas* (as they are)	*influential*	*The Bowery Boys Meet the Monsters*
(pardon the) *infusion*	*intrusion*	*Hold That Baby*
(I'm) *inmagneto**	*incognito*	*Bowery Buckaroos*
(born with an) *inmate* (curiosity)	*innate*	*Trouble Makers*
(one of my) *inmates*	*intimates*	*Lucky Losers*
(thought was completely) *inoculated*	*innocuous*	*Private Eyes*
(don't think I like your) *innuendo*	*suggestion*	*The Bowery Boys Meet the Monsters*
(like it's an) *inuindo**	*innuendo*	*Fighting Fools*
(state of) *inoccupancy**	*occupancy*	*Spook Busters*
(making) *inoculating* (remarks)	*insulting*	*Here Come the Marines*
(don't want to sound) *inquerious**	*inquisitive*	*Jungle Gents*
(don't want to sound) *inquerious**	*inquisitive*	*Crazy over Horses*
(just a little) *inqueerious**	*inquisitive*	*Lucky Losers*
*inqueerious**	*inquisitive*	*Angels' Alley*
(I'm) *inqueerious**	*inquisitive*	*Fighting Fools*
*inqueerious**	*odd* or *suspicious*	*Hold That Baby*
*inqueerious**	*inquisitive*	*Jinx Money*
*inqueerious**	*inquisitive*	*High Society*

inqueerious*	*inquisitive*	Jungle Gents
insange (ruling)	*insane*	Loose in London
inside (a riot)	*incite*	Live Wires
(thought we'd) *instigate* (it)	*investigate*	Triple Trouble
instigate (the matter)	*investigate*	Crashing Las Vegas
(real) *instinct* (pleasure)	*distinct*	Feudin' Fools
(it's my) *instinguished** (welcome)	*distinguished*	Blues Busters
instiguished*	*distinguished*	Paris Playboys
(but my female) *institution*	*intuition*	Ghost Chasers
institutional (rights)	*constitutional*	Bowery Bombshell
(you'll be completely) *insulated*	*isolated*	Feudin' Fools
(maybe I better) *insult* (my attorney)	*consult*	Here Come the Marines
insult subordination	*insubordination*	Clipped Wings
insulted	*consulted*	Jungle Gents
(I'll absolutely) *insure* (you)	*assure*	Hold That Line
(rest) *insured*	*assured*	Jungle Gents
(Madame you can rest) *insured*	*assured*	Private Eyes
(you're going to be) *disintegrating* (with the hoi polloi)	*integrating*	Loose in London
(I don't like to sound like a) *inter-alligator*	*interrogator*	Paris Playboys
interject (her)	*interpret*	Jungle Gents
(stop) *intercepting* (me)	*interrupting*	Bowery Battalion
(stop) *interjecting*	*interrupting*	Bowery Bombshell
(stop) *interjecting*	*interrupting*	Jalopy
(pardon the) *interjection*	*interruption*	Lucky Losers
intermediary (result)	*immediate*	Jungle Gents
interpolating	*interrupting*	Triple Trouble
(pardon the) *interpolations*	*interruptions*	Spy Chasers
interrogatory	*derogatory*	Angels in Disguise
interrupting	*interpreting*	Jungle Gents
(refuses to be) *intimated*	*intimidated*	Bowery to Bagdad
(mean to) *intimidate* (that Sach)	*intimate*	Loose in London
intrimidated	*intimidated*	Spy Chasers
(do you think you could) *introduct** (us to your boss?)	*introduce*	Jail Busters

Glossary of Selected Malaprops and Other Twisted Wordplays • 145

(well that's an) *introductory* (piece of repartee if I ever heard it)	interesting	*Dig That Uranium*
invigorating (to your said sister)	upsetting	*Hard Boiled Mahoney*
invigorating (ceremonies)	important?	*Loose in London*
(wouldn't get so) *irrigated*	irritated	*Blues Busters*
(they'll really be) *irrigated*	irritated	*Feudin' Fools*
(never been so highly) *irrigated*	irritated	*Jalopy*
irrigated (into thin air)	evaporated	*Private Eyes*
(very) *irrigating* (creature)	irritating	*Trouble Makers*
(the) *irrigation* (department)	immigration	*Hold That Line*
(I) *iterate*	repeat	*Blues Busters*
(take a little) *itinerary*	inventory	*Smugglers' Cove*
(it was just a) *jerk* (of fate)	twist	*Blues Busters*
journal of recess	adjourned	*News Hounds*
Juniper	Jupiter	*Trouble Makers*
justified (reward)	just	*News Hounds*
(how about getting me a) *knockdown*	introduction	*News Hounds*
*lapple** (of his coat)	lapel	*Live Wires*
(little) *larengeetis**	laryngitis	*News Hounds*
(you're speaking with your) *larnix** (and not your) *diagram*	larynx, diaphragm	*Ghost Chasers*
(down the) *latch*	hatch	*Paris Playboys*
(somebody's been) *leavesdropping**	eavesdropping	*Crashing Las Vegas*
leg-lease	legalese	*Bowery Buckaroos*
(tripping the light) *fanatic*	fantastic	*Bowery to Bagdad*
(spraining the) *liniments* (of my arm)	ligaments	*Bowery to Bagdad*
liquidate (the problem)	eliminate	*Spook Busters*
(regain my) *liquidequibrium**	equilibrium	*Bowery to Bagdad*
lizard (of finance)	wizard	*Blonde Dynamite*
(financial) *lizards*	wizards	*Mr. Hex*

(a bunch of) *lubrications*	*fabrications*	*Hard Boiled Mahoney*
ludicrous	*lucrative*	*Private Eyes*
lunk* (in my throat)	*lump*	*Spook Busters*
(fooling around with) *Macaroni's* (pet invention)	*Marconi's*	*Triple Trouble*
magnanimosity*	*generosity*	*In Fast Company*
(my inmate) *magnanimosity**	*generosity*	*Smugglers' Cove*
magnanimous (offer)	*generous*	*Trouble Makers*
magnanimous (gesture)	*generous*	*Fighting Fools*
(you're very) *magnanimous*	*generous*	*No Holds Barred*
(insult to my) *manlihood**	*manhood*	*Blonde Dynamite*
(my) *maternal* (duty to warn you)	*paternal*	*No Holds Barred*
(fellow) *matriculators**	*matriculates*	*Spook Busters*
(card) *manipulations*	*maneuvers*	*Bowery Buckaroos*
major bromo*	*major domo*	*Smugglers' Cove*
magany*	*mahogany*	*Smugglers' Cove*
(your) *Magestic* [When Slip is corrected, he replies, "I was using the past tense."]	*majesty*	*Spy Chasers*
(supposed to have) *magnesia*	*amnesia*	*Paris Playboys*
(this is a plain case of) *magnesia*	*amnesia*	*Jail Busters*
(white handkerchief) *magnifies* (truce)	*signifies*	*Feudin' Fools*
malpartition*	*malnutrition*	*Hold That Baby*
airay (of) *mascalinatude**	*array, masculinity*	*Blonde Dynamite*
masticate (the escape plans)	*mastermind*	*Private Eyes*
(rehash this for my own) *mastication*.	*understanding*	*Hold That Baby*
mater d'chef*	*maître d*	*Dig That Uranium*
(young) *matron*	*maiden*	*Spy Chasers*
maul (around in my head)	*mull*	*Angels' Alley*
mauselinoleum*	*mausoleum*	*The Bowery Boys Meet the Monsters*
(take some drastic) *measurements*	*measures*	*In Fast Company*
(suffering from that) *melody*	*malady*	*Triple Trouble*

Glossary of Selected Malaprops and Other Twisted Wordplays • 147

melodynamic*	melodramatic	Bowery Bombshell
(before he flips his) *melon*	wig	Blues Busters
(thanks for the) *memorandum*	information	Jinx Money
menial (of arms)	manual	Spy Chasers
mentally (art of) *self-offense*	manly, self-defense	Private Eyes
(mentally) *insufficient*	deficient	Hold That Baby
migrating headaches	migraine	Clipped Wings
(old) *minimum*	maxim	Angels in Disguise
(United States) *Mink*	Mint	Jinx Money
minus (details)	minor	Hard Boiled Mahoney
(must be some) *misamputation**	misunderstanding	Private Eyes
(been a little) *misapprehension*	misunderstanding	Angels' Alley
(under a) *misapprehensive**	misunderstanding	Hard Boiled Mahoney
(hope it won't be) *misconstewed**	misconstrued	Feudin' Fools
(example of) *misinterpolation**	misinterpretation	Bowery to Bagdad
mommaterily*	momentarily	Loose in London
Monseur*	Monsieur	Paris Playboys
getting *monotonous*	dangerous?	Spook Busters
(got a) *monotomy** (on the town) [When asked, "Don't you mean *monopoly*?" Slip replies, "I was using the past tense."]	monopoly	Bowery Buckaroos
(bolster up my) *moraley**	morale	Master Minds
mortifried* (man)	mortified	Trouble Makers
mouseyleum*	mausoleum	Jungle Gents
mug (is always open)	morgue	Trouble Makers
musicalley	musicale	High Society
nasty turshims*	nasturtiums	Angels' Alley
natereilly*	naturally	Master Minds
nebulous (career)	fabulous	Angels in Disguise
(I got a) *nebulous* (idea)	fabulous or brilliant	Fighting Fools
(get a) *necklace* (of an idea)	inkling	Crashing Las Vegas
necklace (of a very wonderful idea)	inkling	Spy Chasers

(I was just getting a) *necklace* (of an idea)	*inkling*	*No Holds Barred*
(beginning to get a) *necklace* (of an idea)	*inkling*	*Hold That Line*
(I'm getting a) *necklace* (of an idea)	*inkling*	*High Society*
(I just got the) *necklace* (of an idea)	*inkling*	*Clipped Wings*
(you make me feel very) *neuralgic*	*nostalgic*	*Jalopy*
*nervous intigestion**	*nervous indigestion*	*Bowery Bombshell*
neuros (of money involved)	*oodles*	*Loose in London*
neurotic (hairdo)	*erotic?/hypnotic?*	*Angels in Disguise*
*newspaperment's** (award)	*newspapermen's*	*News Hounds*
(dumb) *nincompoodle**	*nincompoop*	*Bowery Battalion*
nom de prune	*nom de plume*	*Spook Busters*
*normanclature** (of the Navy)	*nomenclature*	*Let's Go Navy!*
(did you) *nullify* (the cops?)	*notify*	*Spy Chasers*
(pleased to) *nullify* (your acquaintance)	*make*	*Bowery to Bagdad*
numerologist	*numismatist*	*Spy Chasers*
oblivious	*obvious*	*Spook Busters*
oblivious	*obvious*	*Bowery Buckaroos*
oblivious	*obvious*	*Jinx Money*
oblivious	*obvious*	*Jail Busters*
oblivious	*obvious*	*Loose in London*
obliviously (you have forgotten)	*obviously*	*Crashing Las Vegas*
obliviously (I gotta) *disenlighten*	*obviously, disappoint*	*Paris Playboys*
obliviously	*obviously*	*Dig That Uranium*
obliviously	*obviously*	*Dig That Uranium*
(it's pretty) *oblivious*	*obvious*	*Blues Busters*
by the tone of your *imbiguosity**, (that it's quite) *oblivious* (to me)	*impetuosity?, obvious*	*Feudin' Fools*
(money's no) *objection*	*object*	*Live Wires*
*obstentatious**	*ostentatious*	*Master Minds*
*obstinatrition**	*obstetrician*	*Hold That Baby*

Glossary of Selected Malaprops and Other Twisted Wordplays • 149

octopus	*oculist/optometrist*	Jinx Money
octopus	*oculist/optometrist*	Jungle Gents
(see an) *octopus*. (I need glasses)	*oculist*	Let's Go Navy!
offensive (little guy)	*defenseless*	Bowery Buckaroos
offensive (plan)	*defensive*	Feudin' Fools
omnivorous (situation)	*serious*	Bowery to Bagdad
(my own) *optics*	*eyes*	Spook Busters
(my own) *optics*	*eyes*	Angels in Disguise
(my own) *optics*	*eyes*	Trouble Makers
(cast your) *optics* (on that cell)	*eyes*	Jail Busters
(eyes are bad…see an) *optimist*	*optometrist*	Bowery Bombshell
(see an) *optimist*	*optometrist*	Spook Busters
(maybe an) *optimist*	*optometrist*	Master Minds
optimistic	*pessimistic*	News Hounds
(all go to a) *optomestrist**	*optometrist*	Live Wires
(my own) *orbits*	*eyes*	Jinx Money
(living the life of) *O'Riley*	*Riley*	Clipped Wings
(foremost) *oscitecture's*	*architect's*	Loose in London
(a medium that) *over-mediated*	*over-meditated*	Ghost Chasers
(stone) *overturned*	*unturned*	Fighting Fools
(anyone bring an) *ox-cilating* (fan?)	*oscillating*	Loose in London
(stop being such a) *pacifist*	*pessimist*	Crazy over Horses
(probably) *pantomime poisoning**	*ptomaine poisoning*	Spy Chasers
parsimonious (gesture)	*generous*	Bowery Buckaroos
(very) *parsimonious* (of him)	*generous*	Trouble Makers
(filing a) *partition* (for bankruptcy)	*petition*	Crashing Las Vegas
(nomination to your) *paternity*	*fraternity*	Hold That Line
up on a *pedestrian*	*pedestal*	Live Wires
pent-up house	*penthouse*	Crashing Las Vegas
perambulate (an idea)	*consider/study*	Crazy over Horses
(let's) *perambulate*	*study*	Smugglers' Cove
(let's) *perambulate*	*study*	Crazy over Horses
perambulating (is good for little babies)	*carriage strolling*	Hold That Baby
(armed robbery was) *permeated*	*perpetrated*	Let's Go Navy!
(if you) *persist*	*insist*	Angels in Disguise

(we have to go about this in the regular) *perspectives* (of the law)	*process*	*Clipped Wings*
(you're not very) *perspicacious*	keen or sharp	*Spy Chasers*
(use these tickets before they) *perspire*	expire	*Master Minds*
(give him a little artificial) *perspiration*	respiration	*Ghost Chasers*
(it's very) *perspiring*	perplexing	*Loose in London*
perturbed	disturbed	*Smugglers' Cove*
peruse (these preliminaries)	watch (what I do)	*Lucky Losers*
peruse (the contents)	study/examine	*Lucky Losers*
perused my girl	looked over	*Crazy over Horses*
peruse (that skull of yours a little more) *infinitesimally*	study, intimately?	*No Holds Barred*
peruse my *perambulations*	study, thoughts	*Here Come the Marines*
peruse (the terrain)	study	*Clipped Wings*
(we can) *peruse* (your problems further)	examine	*Private Eyes*
(we'll) *peruse* (the contents)	examine	*Spook Busters*
peruse that frail and human wreck	examine	*No Holds Barred*
(closer) *perusal* (of the details)	study	*Mr. Hex*
pervade (a terrain)	patrol	*Dig That Uranium*
(That is) *perversely* (the vernacular of the situation)	precisely	*Bowery to Bagdad*
(kitchen) *petroleum*	linoleum	*Live Wires*
(pardon the) *petrusion**	intrusion	*Ghost Chasers*
(Chief) *Petting* (Officer)	Petty	*Let's Go Navy!*
nature's *phenomeni** [explains it's the plural for *phenomena*]	phenomenon	*Bowery Buckaroos*
(surge of) *philantropics**	philanthropy	*Jinx Money*
(adolescent) *phrase*	phase	*News Hounds*
(natural) *philmoni**	phenomenon	*Trouble Makers*
(it's a supernatural) *philomonia**	phenomenon	*Blues Busters*
(arrived at the) *physiological* (moment)	logical	*Jungle Gents*
(the) *pineapple* (of your career)	pinnacle	*Blues Busters*

Glossary of Selected Malaprops and Other Twisted Wordplays • 151

pinochle (of our endeavor)	pinnacle	*Angels in Disguise*
pinochle (of my success)	pinnacle	*News Hounds*
pins and noodles	pins and needles	*Angels' Alley*
(that bowl—I guarantee that's pure) *poisonaire*	porcelain	*High Society*
(lose by a large) *pleurisy*	plurality	*Jinx Money*
pollinated (by cannibals)	inhabited	*Let's Go Navy!*
pomade (in the park)	promenade	*Live Wires*
(a little) *pomenade*	promenade	*Hold That Baby*
(I'm leaving) *post hasty*	immediately	*Spy Chasers*
(he's going to pop his) *pretzels*	blood vessels	*No Holds Barred*
poultry (sum)	paltry	*No Holds Barred*
poultry (sum)	paltry	*Smugglers' Cove*
*prebosis**	proboscis	*Jungle Gents*
(we've been) *precedingly** *deferred* (to each other)	previously referred	*Dig That Uranium*
(precisely what I) *precipitated*	anticipated	*Smugglers' Cove*
precipitated at the moment	preoccupied	*News Hounds*
(don't be) *precipitant*	fall headlong	*Trouble Makers*
(don't be so) *precipitant*	fall headlong	*Fighting Fools*
(don't be) *precipitant*	fall headlong	*Spy Chasers*
precipitant	fall headlong	*Paris Playboys*
precluded	concluded	*Smugglers' Cove*
precludes (the) *foregone* (matinee)	concludes, last	*Master Minds*
predominately (what I'm thinking)	precisely	*High Society*
(it's strictly) *pulminary**	preliminary	*Private Eyes*
premature (engagement)	prior	*Angels' Alley*
(got this whole situation) *premedicated*	premeditated	*Dig That Uranium*
(what's your) *preposition*?	proposition	*Private Eyes*
(absolutely) *preprosperous**	preposterous	*Ghost Chasers*
(hidden) *preserves*	reserves	*Mr. Hex*
(one good) *press* (deserves another)	turn	*News Hounds*
(edge of a terrific) *press-a-pineapple*	precipice	*Dig That Uranium*
prevaricate (about it in person)	converse	*The Bowery Boys Meet the Monsters*
preying (on your imaginations)	playing	*Spook Busters*
(guarantee you lots of better) *procrastinations*	predictions	*Master Minds*

*profeal** (to match)	*profile*	*Blues Busters*
(charitable) *projectiles*	*projects*	*The Bowery Boys Meet the Monsters*
(figures of national) *promiscuosity**	*prominence*	*Triple Trouble*
pronounced (pugilist)	*renounced*	*Fighting Fools*
prosecute (for the gold)	*prospect*	*Bowery Buckaroos*
pardon my friend's *protrusion*	*intrusion*	*Jungle Gents*
(pardon the) *protrusion*	*intrusion*	*Blues Busters*
(pardon the) *protrusion*	*intrusion*	*No Holds Barred*
(if you'll pardon the) *protrusion*	*intrusion*	*Blues Busters*
(if you pardon the) *protrusion*	*intrusion*	*Private Eyes*
(pardon my friend's) *protrusion*	*intrusion*	*Jalopy*
slightly *psychiatrical**	*psychotic*	*News Hounds*
*psychoalkalyzed**	*psychoanalyzed*	*Ghost Chasers*
*psychoalkalyzed**	*psychoanalyzed*	*Bowery Buckaroos*
*psychopatrick** research	*psychopathic*	*Spook Busters*
P.T. *Barney*	P.T. *Barnum*	*Master Minds*
(practice makes) *puffect**	*perfect*	*Dig That Uranium*
pulmonary (examination)	*preliminary*	*Paris Playboys*
pulmonary (hearing)	*preliminary*	*Triple Trouble*
(is it my) *purgatory* (to refuse this probation)	*prerogative*	*Triple Trouble*
(stop having) *purpleplexy**	*apoplexy*	*Bowery Bombshell*
*purpletrated**	*perpetrated*	*Blonde Dynamite*
quick (of time)	*nick*	*Hard Boiled Mahoney*
(work my fingers to the) *quirk*	*quick* or *bone*	*Clipped Wings*
(work my fingers to the) *quirk*	*quick* or *bone*	*Crazy over Horses*
(touched me to the) *quirk*	*quick*	*News Hounds*
(cut me to the) *quirk*	*bone*	*Fighting Fools*
(can come here on a new) *quotation*	*quota*	*Hold That Line*
radium	*radius*	*Hold That Baby*
(grab the) *range*	*reins*	*Crazy over Horses*
(you've been working in this) *rat's skull?*	*rat's nest*	*Blonde Dynamite*

Glossary of Selected Malaprops and Other Twisted Wordplays • 153

(serious) *rebate*	*debate*	*Bowery Buckaroos*
(don't be) *recalcitrant*	*ridiculous*	*Bowery Buckaroos*
(I just want you to) *rekapidulate*	*repeat*	*Hold That Baby*
(my eyes must be) *receiving* me	*deceiving*	*Loose in London*
*receptible** (mood)	*receptive*	*Blues Busters*
recite (a riot)	*incite*	*Blues Busters*
reconcile (that number)	*remember*	*Jinx Money*
*recongirder**	*reconnoiter*	*Spy Chasers*
(my eyes must be) *receiving* (me)	*deceiving*	*Jungle Gents*
reclining (years)	*declining*	*Crashing Las Vegas*
(try to) *re-compute* (the circumstances)	*figure out*	*Crazy over Horses*
(sit and) *reconnoiter*	*reconsider*	*Private Eyes*
(everyday) *recurrence*	*occurrence*	*Blues Busters*
(Alright mental giant, come over here and I'll) *re-engage* (you from those handcuffs)	*release*	*Private Eyes*
(he's still) *refined* (to quarters)	*resigned*	*Clipped Wings*
*refirmative**	*affirmative*	*Angels in Disguise*
refrains (to)	*refers*	*The Bowery Boys Meet the Monsters*
refreshing (course)	*refresher*	*Hard Boiled Mahoney*
(I seriously) *refugee* (the fact)	*refute*	*Jungle Gents*
regurgitate (myself)	*repeat*	*Crashing Las Vegas*
(I) *regurgitate*	*repeat*	*The Bowery Boys Meet the Monsters*
(I better) *regurgitate* (the details)	*repeat*	*Crazy over Horses*
(I) *regurgitate*	*repeat*	*No Holds Barred*
regurgitating (that last question)	*repeating*	*Dig That Uraniunn*
(So I) *regurgitate*	*repeat*	*Feudin' Fools*
(I) *regurgitate*	*repeat*	*Loose in London*
(I) *regurgitate*	*repeat*	*Clipped Wings*
(I) *regurgitate* (again)	*repeat*	*Paris Playboys*
regurgitating (over that matter)	*rethinking*	*Ghost Chasers*
(don't like to) *rehabilitate* (you)	*disappoint*	*Paris Playboys*
(Louie has to be) *reimbursted**	*reimbursed*	*Crazy over Horses*
*reincarcerated**	*reincarnated*	*Ghost Chasers*
(I'm going to) *re-irrigate*	*reiterate*	*Crazy over Horses*

(I) *re-irritate*	reiterate	*No Holds Barred*
reiterate (that one)	repeat	*Crashing Las Vegas*
(I keep) *reiterating* (to you)	repeating	*Bowery Buckaroos*
(meeting just about) *rejourned**	adjourned	*Dig That Uranium*
rejuvenated	recuperated	*Jail Busters*
re-medicated (damage)	remedial	*Jungle Gents*
(must be) *repaired*	prepared	*Spy Chasers*
repent houses	penthouses	*Hard Boiled Mahoney*
(exact) *replications*	replica	*Bowery Buckaroos*
(good) *requestrians*	equestrian	*Jungle Gents*
resistance (to you)	assistance	*Jinx Money*
resistance	assistance	*Bowery Buckaroos*
(they rest on their) *resources*	laurels	*Hold That Baby*
(how many) *resolutions* (does the fan make)	revolutions	*Jalopy*
(let's not get too) *resuscitated*	excited	*Crashing Las Vegas*
retail prescription	detailed description	*Private Eyes*
retail prescription	detailed description	*Spy Chasers*
(I) *retaliate* (which means to repeat)	repeat	*The Bowery Boys Meet the Monsters*
reviving (me from my sleep)	waking	*The Bowery Boys Meet the Monsters*
(your) *romantical inflatuation**	romantic infatuation	*Bowery to Bagdad*
roost (of all evil)	root	*Mr. Hex*
roost (of all evil)	root	*Jinx Money*
(guard duty) *roaster*	roster	*Spy Chasers*
(very clever) *rouge*	ruse	*Bowery Buckaroos*
roustabout (way)	roundabout	*News Hounds*
rumor (on the brain)	tumor	*Private Eyes*
(gun stuck in my) *sacred iliac*	sacroiliac	*Bowery to Bagdad*
tell her you're *Sagintarium*	Sagittarius	*Ghost Chasers*
salvaged (the lives)	saved	*The Bowery Boys Meet the Monsters*
sanctimony (of his Sweet Shop)	sanctuary	*Master Minds*

Glossary of Selected Malaprops and Other Twisted Wordplays • 155

(let's go into the inner) *sanction*, (and get the) *see-ancee* (equipment)	*sanctum, séance*	*Ghost Chasers*
sane dribbling	*insane driveling*	*Clipped Wings*
sanitary (confinement)	*solitary*	*Triple Trouble*
sanitorium*	*sanitarium*	*Jail Busters*
(put on your best) *save your fare*	*savoir faire*	*Blonde Dynamite*
(all this) *scientific friction*	*science fiction*	*The Bowery Boys Meet the Monsters*
secluding (ourselves)	*including*	*Dig That Uranium*
(correct) *seclusion*	*conclusion*	*Hard Boiled Mahoney*
(logical) *seclusion*	*conclusion*	*News Hounds*
(logical) *seclusion*	*conclusion*	*Master Minds*
(You know Sach, I came to) *seclusion* (that you are not very intelligent)	*conclusion*	*Lucky Losers*
(I've come to the) *seclusion*	*conclusion*	*Blonde Dynamite*
(coming to the) *seclusion*	*conclusion*	*Crazy over Horses*
(let us not jump to) *seclusions*	*conclusions*	*Jinx Money*
(jumping to) *seclusions*	*conclusions*	*Live Wires*
seclusions	*conclusions*	*Trouble Makers*
(optical) *seclusions*	*delusions*	*Spook Busters*
(mathematical) *secretion*	*solution*	*Feudin' Fools*
(serve as a nerve) *sediment*	*sedative*	*Feudin' Fools*
(we need is a good) *sediment*	*sedative*	*The Bowery Boys Meet the Monsters*
(this is no time for) *sediment*	*sentiment*	*Loose in London*
(conditions of this prison, they're not) *seductive* (to the prisoners)	*conducive*	*Triple Trouble*
(a brilliant) *seduction*	*deduction*	*Blonde Dynamite*
(a brilliant) *seduction*	*deduction*	*Crazy over Horses*
(a very brilliant) *seduction*	*deduction*	*Feudin' Fools*
(one scientific) *seduction*	*deduction*	*No Holds Barred*
(came to that) *seduction* (myself)	*deduction*	*Paris Playboys*
(clever) *seduction*	*deduction*	*Bowery to Bagdad*
(clever) *seduction*	*deduction*	*Jail Busters*
seduction	*deduction*	*Spy Chasers*
(optical) *seduction*	*delusion*	*Jungle Gents*
(we'll) *segregate*	*separate*	*Jinx Money*

(just act) *self-insured*	*self-assured*	*Bowery Bombshell*
self-offense	*self-defense*	*Jungle Gents*
(I'm gonna wind up in a) *seminary*	*sanitarium*	*Bowery to Bagdad*
(a very) *sendentary* (apartment house)	*sedentary*	*Jinx Money*
(that's how people get) *septic ulcers*	*peptic ulcers*	*Hold That Line*
sewing (your weight around)	*shoving*	*Hold That Line*
(nervous) *shakedown*	*breakdown*	*Private Eyes*
shallow (of a doubt)	*shadow*	*Spy Chasers*
(forgive my) *sideclick**	*sidekick*	*Dig That Uranium*
(we finished a) *siesta*	*semester*	*Hold That Line*
siesta	*semester*	*Hold That Line*
similar [referring to a person]	*familiar*	*News Hounds*
(a) *skillion** (times)	*million*	*Private Eyes*
skitsophreniac*	*schizophrenic*	*Loose in London*
(after a five-minute) *slojurn**	*sojurn*	*Dig That Uranium*
(see) *snorerena**	*senorita*	*Bowery Buckaroos*
somambulance* (attacks)	*somnambulist*	*Bowery Buckaroos*
sopeeny* (him)	*subpoena*	*Spy Chasers*
spam (of my life)	*span*	*Spook Busters*
speedetrician* [Whitey said word first]	*pediatrician*	*Master Minds*
(motley looking) *spittoon*	*platoon*	*Spy Chasers*
(whole) *spittoon* (of soldiers)	*platoon*	*Bowery Battalion*
(I will) *sopeeny** (him)	*subpoena*	*Spy Chasers*
(just) *spook* (when you're spoken to)	*speak*	*Jungle Gents*
(you had a little) *spring off*	*offspring*	*Fighting Fools*
spurn (of the moment)	*spur*	*In Fast Company*
(horse of a different) *stable*	*color*	*In Fast Company*
(stars and their) *stalletites**	*constellations*	*Master Minds*
statuary	*statues*	*Smugglers' Cove*
(search this place from) *stem to stone*	*top to bottom*	*Loose in London*
sterile (silver)	*sterling*	*Smugglers' Cove*
stickly coinfidential*	*strictly confidential*	*Triple Trouble*
stinking (of an idea)	*inkling*	*Hard Boiled Mahoney*

Glossary of Selected Malaprops and Other Twisted Wordplays • 157

stooping (around)	*snooping*	*Angels in Disguise*
(don't break my) *strain* (of thought)	*train*	*Hold That Baby*
*stupersonic** (sound barrier)	*supersonic*	*Jalopy*
*stuperstitious**	*superstitious*	*Lucky Losers*
*stupidstitions**	*superstitions*	*Jungle Gents*
(plastic) *sturgeon*	*surgeon*	*High Society*
subjunctive (about it)	*subjective*	*In Fast Company*
(we) *submerged* (victorious)	*emerged*	*Crazy over Horses*
(back to your) *subnormal* (self)	*abnormal*	*The Bowery Boys Meet the Monsters*
(let's) *subposition**	*suppose*	*Fighting Fools*
(like being) *sub-tul**	*subtle*	*Jail Busters*
(she's absolutely) *suburban*	*superb*	*Mr. Hex*
(that is) *succinctly* (correct)	*distinctly*	*Jalopy*
supercilious	*superstitious*	*Mr. Hex*
(enough of this) *superflooish** (yakety yak)	*superfluous*	*Smugglers' Cove*
*superstitional**	*superstitious*	*Spook Busters*
support (with me)	*rapport*	*Mr. Hex*
suppressed (permission)	*expressed*	*News Hounds*
(gave me the) *suppression*	*impression*	*Trouble Makers*
(to put a tail on somebody in) *supterraneum** (language means to follow them)	*subterranean*	*Spy Chasers*
*sup-tle**	*subtle*	*Trouble Makers*
(we gather here tonight to observe a very) *suspicious* (occasion)	*auspicious*	*Jalopy*
sympathize (our watches)	*synchronize*	*Angels' Alley*
sympathize (our watches)	*synchronize*	*Bowery Battalion*
sympathize (our watches)	*synchronize*	*Feudin' Fools*
(my) *synthetic* (nervous systems) [Sach corrects him. Slip retorts, "I was using the past tense."]	*sympathetic*	*No Holds Barred*
(magic) *syrup*	*serum*	*Jalopy*
tabooed (right on his back)	*tattooed*	*Bowery Buckaroos*
(shut your) *tator-trap**	*mouth*	*Bowery Buckaroos*

(wired for mental) *telegraphy*	*telepathy*	*Private Eyes*
(artistic) *temperature*	*temperament*	*Mr. Hex*
(termites) *termanited**	*terminated*	*Spook Busters*
termite (my speech)	*terminating*	*News Hounds*
(heard the) *term-e-ology*	*terminology*	*Jalopy*
terra-firmament*	*terra firma*	*Jungle Gents*
(my theory is beginning to) *theorize*	*materialize*	*Here Come the Marines*
(may have to) *thread* (water)	*tread*	*Ghost Chasers*
(force the) *tissue*	*issue*	*Angels in Disguise*
titsie (flies)	*tsetse*	*Jungle Gents*
(no time for) *tomsickery**	*tomfoolery*	*Bowery Battalion*
(park your) *tonnage*	*body*	*Loose in London*
(make a) *touché*	*connection*	*Hard Boiled Mahoney*
(the leaning) *Tower of Pizza*	*Tower of Pisa*	*Blues Busters*
Town and Country [refers to car]	*jalopy*	*Blonde Dynamite*
Town and Country [refers to car]	*jalopy*	*Trouble Makers*
(into a) *tranceum**	*trance*	*Master Minds*
(railroad) *transformation*	*transportation*	*Bowery Bombshell*
translact*	*transact*	*Jinx Money*
(don't flip your) *transmission*	*wig*	*Ghost Chasers*
(King's) *transom*	*ransom*	*Jungle Gents*
(you get in a) *transom*	*trance*	*Mr. Hex*
transpose (the job to you)	*transfer*	*Spy Chasers*
(keep your) *trap* (shut)	*mouth*	*Blonde Dynamite*
(good) *treading*	*threading*	*Jinx Money*
tree (of them)	*three*	*Bowery Battalion*
tree (days)	*three*	*Jungle Gents*
(as easy as "a" – "b" –) "*tree*"	"*c*"	*Jinx Money*
(one, two,) *tree*	*three*	*Feudin' Fools*
treepassing* (on my private property)	*trespassing*	*Smugglers' Cove*
(do we got to go) *trew** (this again)	*through*	*Bowery Battalion*
(when you two are) *trew**	*through*	*Let's Go Navy!*
trigger wacky	*trigger happy*	*Bowery Buckaroos*
(maybe if I cut your) *troat**	*throat*	*Blues Busters*
(a) *tropic-graphical* (error)	*typographical*	*Clipped Wings*
trow* (in a couple of meatballs)	*throw*	*Ghost Chasers*

Glossary of Selected Malaprops and Other Twisted Wordplays • 159

(you can't) *trow** (us out)	throw	*Blues Busters*
*trow** (you)	throw	*Smugglers' Cove*
(you get) *trown** (in the can)	thrown	*Bowery Battalion*
(serve tea and) *trumpets*	crumpets	*Loose in London*
(upper) *trust*	crust	*High Society*
truth cereal	truth serum	*Clipped Wings*
(the feeling is) *unanimous*	mutual	*Angels' Alley*
(I was) *unbeknownst to* (the fact)	unaware of	*Crashing Las Vegas*
(stop speaking in the) *unconfirmative**	affirmative	*Crazy over Horses*
unconscious (mind)	subconscious	*Jinx Money*
(I don't like to sound) *unfortuitous**	unappreciative	*Spy Chasers*
un-identify (the body)	identify	*Trouble Makers*
(will not be) *uninhibited*	unrewarded	*Mr. Hex*
(new planet in the) *Universal*	Universe	*Trouble Makers*
unirrigated (liar)	unmitigated	*News Hounds*
*unperfect** (day)	imperfect	*Feudin' Fools*
*un-premedicated**	unpremeditated	*Jinx Money*
un-secret (it)	reveal	*Clipped Wings*
unstrained (spy)	untrained	*Spy Chasers*
(it's an) *urgency*	it's urgent	*News Hounds*
*variclose** (veins)	varicose	*Dig That Uranium*
varnishing (Americans)	vanishing	*Bowery Buckaroos*
vaulted (millionaires)	vaunted	*Live Wires*
*veemenous**	venomous	*Jungle Gents*
vegetarian	veterinarian	*Hold That Baby*
vegetarian	veterinarian	*Jungle Gents*
(the boys seem to be in) *venison*	unison	*Bowery Battalion*
*vervacity**	audacity	*News Hounds*
(Sometimes I doubt my own) *vervacity* (whatever that means).	veracity	*Hold That Baby*
*vervacity**	tenacity	*Mr. Hex*
vices versa	vice a versa	*Angels in Disguise*

vicious anemia [see also *delicious anemia*]	*pernicious anemia*	*Angels in Disguise*
(he'll) *vilify* (everything I said)	*verify*	*Jail Busters*
(Southern fried) *vitals*	*vittles*	*Feudin' Fools*
(that was) *vociferous* [re: singing]	*mellifluous*	*Mr. Hex*
vociferous (applause)	*loud*	*Blues Busters*
wedlocked* (to me)	*married*	*Hard Boiled Mahoney*
(suspicions were) *well-allocated*	*well-founded*	*Loose in London*
(happen to be very) *well-deformed*	*well-informed*	*Bowery Battalion*
well-mannerismed*	*well-mannered*	*Loose in London*
well-naturedly*	*well naturally*	*Jinx Money*
Wild Phil Hiccup	*Wild Bill Hickok*	*Crazy over Horses*
(no time for) *wittikisms**	*witticisms*	*Hold That Baby*
[spells out word] "*w – o – i – k?*"	*work*	*Live Wires*
(we got to) *wreckanoiter** (out the enemy)	*reconnoiter*	*Feudin' Fools*
wrestle (up some business)	*rustle*	*Trouble Makers*
(shut up you big) *yerk**	*jerk*	*Loose in London*

Selected Mispronunciations:

a-come-pen-ied = *accompanied* (*Private Eyes*)
airay = *array* (*Blonde Dynamite*)
a la carteé = *a la carte* (*Hard Boiled Mahoney*)
apper-ray-tus woiks = *apparatus works* (*Crazy over Horses*)
auspic-a-ces = *auspices* (*Fighting Fools*)
boid = *bird* (*Clipped Wings*)
cata-strophies = *catastrophes* (*Jalopy*)
cat-tis tro-fee = *catastrophe* (*High Society*)
ca-stroph = *catastrophe* (*Bowery Battalion*)
cata-strophe-e = *catastrophe* (*The Bowery Boys Meet the Monsters*)
constellations: *Capracorny* for *Capricorn*, *Pieces* for *Pisces*, *Aquarium* for *Aquarius* (*Trouble Makers*)

Glossary of Selected Malaprops and Other Twisted Wordplays • 161

cos-mop-o-lite (socialite) = *cosmopolitan* (*Paris Playboys*)
E-Litey Detective Agency = *Elite* (*Hard Boiled Mahoney*)
femme fa-tally = *femme fatale* (*Jalopy*)
fig-u-rine = *figurine* (*Smugglers' Cove*)
finds out = *find out* (*Loose in London*)
foim = *firm* (*Crazy over Horses*)
frequently free-quented = *frequently frequented* (*Hard Boiled Mahoney*)
fugitive (pronounced with g sound) (*Bowery Bombshell*)
goim = *germ* (*Hold That Line*)
G-rux = *Geroux* (*Paris Playboys*)
hair = *heir* (*Smugglers' Cove*)
hoit = *hurt* (*Hold That Line*)
idi-o-syn-cra-shes = *idiosyncrasies* (*Lucky Losers*)
infrences = *inferences* (*Mr. Hex*)
in-so-mania = *insomnia* (*Triple Trouble*)
in-so-maniac = *insomniac* (*Triple Trouble*)
Long champs – pronounces location wrong, then correctly, *Longchamps* (*Paris Playboys*)
loined = *learned* (*Paris Playboys*)
loirn = *learn* (*Bowery Battalion*)
pal-latay = *palette* (*Paris Playboys*)
purnt = *point* (*The Bowery Boys Meet the Monsters*)
ra-kay = *racket* (*Hard Boiled Mahoney*)
regukarly = *regularly* (*Jalopy*)
sick = *seek* (*Jinx Money*)
surl = *soil* (*Smugglers' Cove*)
soitently = *certainly* (*Bowery Buckaroos*)
soitan = *certain* (*News Hounds*)
stratergy = *strategy* (*Spy Chasers*)
thoity = *thirty* (*Ghost Chasers*)
woik = *work* (*Hold That Baby*)
woiks = *works* (*Bowery Battalion*)
woik, w – o – i – k = *work* (*High Society*)
woim = *worm* (*Bowery Battalion*)
woim = *worm* (*Crazy over Horses*)
woim = *worm* (*Smugglers' Cove*)

MATTERS OF MISSPELLING:
criticized for writing the word *dumb* as *dumm*: "I was using the plural tense" (*News Hounds*)
Spells out *final* as "P-H-Y-N-U-L" (*Bowery to Bagdad*)
"going home, h – o – m!" (*The Bowery Boys Meet the Monsters*)
"And you know *nutin*, N – u – t – i – n" = *nothing* (*Jungle Gents*)
"He was saying *nutin* - N – u – t – i – n" = *nothing* (*Paris Playboys*)
"*N-u-t- i- n*, absolutely *nothing*" = *nothing* (*Clipped Wings*)
"Just go, G – o – o" = *go* (*Dig That Uranium*)

10 Afterword

> "I miss an awful lot of things that people say. I miss an awful lot of things I do not see. But most of all, when I'm gone, I'm gonna miss me."
>
> – from Leo Gorcey's autobiography
> *An Original Dead End Kid Presents Dead End Yells, Wedding Bells, Cockle Shells, and Dizzy Spells.*
> (Vantage Press, 1967).

THE ACCOUNT PROVIDED by Gorcey's son, Leo Jr., reveals to fans that his father, the man who acted as the cool and endearing Muggs McGuiness or Slip Mahoney, had an unnerving and shocking dark side that often reared its ugly head. The dominating force that surfaced in Gorcey in his private life exhibited itself as an overpowering ego that might pull out the gun to control the situation, or at least instill and/or exert some sort of feeling of control over others.

Interestingly, the characters that Gorcey played in films (even considering his toughest bad boy role in the Dead End films), never seemed to be as "potentially dangerous" as Gorcey the man is described in many riveting real life moments. On the contrary, in the movies he was not a gun-toting nut. His character had redeeming qualities, never totally brutal or self-destructive.

However, real life seemed more dramatic and threatening as far as his interaction with others. For example, a showdown with the authorities over his wife trying to retrieve her belongings from their home is a case in point. As recounted by Leo Jr., Gorcey repeatedly refused permission for her to have access to get her belongings. On multiple occasions he showed what a stubborn man he could be, even with the legal authorities demanding he do so. He seemed to want to win this one, even if it meant that the potential for a violent showdown seemingly likely. No matter what might happen, Gorcey insisted that he was going to stand his ground.

He did not seem to consider the repercussions, or immediately back down from challenging the legal authorities, as you would think any reasonable man would do. One wonders that if he persisted just a little more, what would have happened? Admirably, each time the authorities showed fine restraint and decided not to cross the "do not cross the line" that he drew. However, what would have happened if they forced his hand? Would he have fired his guns? Would the authorities taken action that would have been tragic as so often happens in these situations nowadays? Would a shootout have been the result with someone dying, with Gorcey imprisoned for hurting or killing one of the officers? It seemed possible from this account that these confrontations were heading to that inevitable outcome.

Fortunately, nothing bad came of that incident. Nevertheless, heavy drinking unfortunately took its toll on a very remarkable man. Indeed, Gorcey's amazing life ended too soon. He has departed this earth now nearly forty years ago, leaving behind both good and bad memories. The life he led, as it must be for all, is forever locked in the past. Sadly, it cannot be altered. The pains he suffered and caused cannot be erased— only forgiven.

However, it is hoped that the frailties that he exhibited that wounded those most close to him could be something that can teach a lesson to each one of us. Indeed, we can and do at times descend to the depths of inhumanity; most often inflicting pain on those we love the most. We must all deal with our weaknesses and find a way to ameliorate and even try to overcome them. We are bound by the histories we create for others. Unfortunately, it is sad that the hurts we inflict on others, no matter how accidental or unintended, leave such indelible imprints.

A number of times Slip in the Bowery Boys films would forcefully exclaim, "Alright! Alright! Alright!" Yes, Slip knew that at times it is necessary to look to what really matters in the end. I believed that it is quite healing for us to dwell on whatever Leo Gorcey did in his life that made people smile and feel good inside as a part of the bigger human condition. That is what we must appreciate and perhaps even celebrate. His truly funny comedy of fractured language is a superb contribution to the world of films that must be remembered above all else. In addition, in his characters, particularly Muggs McGuiness and Slip Mahoney, we see his joy and zest for life, besides his sincere kindness to make things better for his friends. That spirit will always be the "Leo Gorcey" we dearly cherish and continue to enjoy!

Leo Gorcey's characters preserved on film gave my dad, myself, and so many other people over the years so much joy. It is sadly ironic that this same Leo Gorcey personally suffered so much misery and inner tears while making us laugh so much. I hate to think of those years spent intoxicated and escaping from the painful realities of his life. We the audience laughed all the while he cried a slow, but most certain premature death.

Brandy: "Unlike Gary (Hall), I wouldn't have traded my dad for anyone else. I would have had him live longer and would like to have seen him treat Leo Jr. and Jan like he did me, but I have no misgivings or regrets."

Who could have known that it was possible that the man who gave out so much pleasure with his comedic energies could have suffered so much pain? If only Leo Gorcey could somehow now know how much he has meant to so many people he never even knew so many years after he has departed, and that despite his human failings and fractured life, he made us all feel "Alright!"

Thank you, Leo Gorcey, for the fractured world you have given us! Undoubtedly, all of us who love your film characters will keep laughing all the days of our lives! Alright! Alright! Alright!

APPENDICES

BIBLIOGRAPHY

Gorcey, Leo B. *An Original Dead End Kid Presents Dead End Yells, Wedding Bells, Cockle Shells, and Dizzy Spells.* NY: Vantage Press, 1967.

Gorcey, Jr., Leo. *Me and the Dead End Kid.* Irvine, CA: Leo Gorcey Foundation, Spirit of Hope Publishing, 2003.

Lamparski, Richard. *Interview with Leo Gorcey. Whatever Became Of...* (WBAI-FM, New York City, dial 99.5), July, 1968.

Manago, Jim. *Behind Sach: The Huntz Hall Story.* Albany, GA: BearManor Media, 2015.

Williams, Coy "Don't Take Him Back to Brooklyn!" *Radio Life*, May 12, 1946.

Zeisemer, Brandy Jo: *Unpublished thesis* in partial fulfillment for a Master's degree in English, University of California, Chico, 1983.

Zinman, David. *Saturday Afternoon at the Bijou.* New Rochelle, NY: Arlington House, 1973.

BIBLIOGRAPHY

Selected Radio Show Transcripts

The following shows only offer the scenes with Gorcey. Please note that they are derived from listening to the shows. They are not taken from the radio scripts.

Pabst Blue Ribbon Town, January 29, 1944. Vera Vague (Barbara Jo Allen) guests.

Episode synopsis: Groucho needs a cook and housekeeper so he decides to get married. What the matrimonial agency sends over is Vera Vague (Allen), who's none of those things.

Gorcey's first appearance at 7:25 minutes.

Gorcey: Hey Marxy, hey Marxy are you home?

Marx: Well, well if it isn't *Blue Ribbon Town's* overaged problem child, Leo Gorcey. Come in Leo.

Gorcey: Hey I just heard the good news about you getting hitched.

Marx: Getting hitched? That's a fine way to talk about the sacred institution of matrimony.

Gorcey: Oh, excuse me. I meant I heard the news of you entering the blissful state of holy deadlock. (Audience laughs)

Marx: Well maybe hitched was the better way to put it. (Audience laughs) How did you find out about my so-called marriage?

Gorcey: Hey, it's all over town. The headlines in every paper says Groucho Marx to marry. Hey, Mr. RCA just signed announcement.

Marx: The theater marquee announcing my marriage, what did it say?

Gorcey: It didn't say nothing. I had to read it. (Audience laughs)

Marx: Oh, come, come. Come, come. Come, come Gorcey what did it say about my marriage?

Gorcey: Well it said; double feature next week: "A Lady Takes A Chance with the Wolfman." (Audience laughs) Anyway Marxy, I want you to know I think you're doing the right thing. Ah love. I love it! Wonderful to be in love, especially when you're in love with someone you like. (Audience laughs)

Marx: Leo that's a very astute remark. And I might add it comes from a very astupid person. (Audience laughs) Have you any other pearls of wisdom you like to dispose of?

Gorcey: Marxy, you're taking a very bitter *altitude* (*attitude*). If you're in love don't hide it, be gay. Love is a very beautiful thing, Marxy. Ah, when you're in love the birds are always singing, the bees is always buzzing, and the little butterflies is always making butter. (Audience laughs.)

Marx: You can save coupons that way. (Audience laughs) Gorcey, you don't understand, I thought I was marrying a good housekeeper, but instead I'm stuck with a woman who isn't interested in anything but romance.

Gorcey: Yeah? Gee, that's *compressing* (*depressing*). (Audience laughs) You gotta do something drastic to get rid of that dame.

Marx: Exactly.

Gorcey: Hey, I got it! She wants romance, be insulting to the dame; burn her up, be the kind of a guy that's no good at lovemaking. Make her think you're just no good as a husband. Make her think you're just a useless jerk. (Audience laughs)

Marx: No I—I just rather be myself.

Gorcey: That's what I mean, that's what I mean! (Audience laughs)

(Gorcey's second appearance later at 20 minutes is part of a fantasy about what it would be like if Marx and Allen were married, with Gorcey as their son.)

Allen: Children, dear, dinner's ready. Come in darlings, sit down for dinner. (They loudly scamper in.) Not all in the same chair, you dopes, spread out! (Audience laughs)

Gorcey: Hi ya, Mom! (To Marx). Hi ya, cranky puss.

Marx: Greetings my obnoxious offspring.

Allen: Now come. Come Leo dear, aren't you going to kiss your mother?

Gorcey: Naah! Kissing is for girls.

Allen: Well what do you think I look like, a halibut? Don't answer that.

Gorcey: Eh come on quit the gabbing, quit the gabbing! Let's eat.

Allen: Now children, before anyone touches the food, I'm sure your father has something he wants to say. Speak, Father.

Marx: Pass the meatball. (Audience laughs)

Allen: Groucho, don't you remember what day this is?

Marx: No, pass the meatball. (Audience laughs)

Allen: Dear, you must remember, this is my birthday.

Marx: Then Happy Birthday, and pass the meatball.

Allen: Now Junior, don't be so careless with your food; you're soiling the tablecloth.

Gorcey: What are you talking about, I'm eating very neat.

Allen: You call that neat, hanging your lower lip under the plate and banking your peas in off the meatball? (Audience laughs)

Gorcey: Well, I couldn't make it off the carrots, it was a two-cushion shot. (Audience laughs)

Daughter (Faye McKenzie): Hey, Daddy this is Mommy's birthday. Aren't you gonna get her something?

Gorcey: Yeah. Aren't ya gonna buy her no presents?

Marx: That's exactly what I'm going to buy her, no presents. (Audience laughs)

Pabst Blue Ribbon Town, February 5, 1944, with guest Gene Tierney. Part 1.

Announcer: In Wisconsin, in celebration of Pabst 100th Anniversary, Pabst Blue Ribbon Beer Presents *Blue Ribbon Town*, starring Groucho Marx with his glamorous guest, 20th Century Fox star, Gene Tierney. (Opening music with chorus)

Announcer: With lovely Gene Tierney joining us and our war bond and service camp tour, we have a trainload of fun and music aboard the Blue Ribbon Special tonight. Waiting to be paged are Faye McKenzie, Leo Gorcey, Bill Days, Robert Arm Brewster and his Blue Ribbon Blenders, yours truly, Derwood Kirby, and here seated in the pullman admiring the scenery is persnickety passenger, Groucho Marx.

Gorcey: Hey Marxy! Hey Marxy! Where are ya?

Marx: Well, well, if it isn't Pabst's bad boy, Leo Gorcey.

Gorcey: Heya Marxy! What ya hear from the engineer?

Marx: Just choo-choo, baby. Did you want to talk with me Leo?

Gorcey: Naaah! I don't want to converse with you. I must report to decline my conversation to our glorious, luscious, beauteous guest, Gene Tunney.

Marx: In this corner, Gene Tunney! Gorcey, this is Gene Tierney. She's no boxer.

Gorcey: That's what you think. The dame's a knockout.

Tierney: Oh, thank you Mr. Gorcey. And I also want to thank you for getting me into the dining car.

Gorcey: Don't mention it fair lady. Your wish is my demand.

Marx: Listen, my crude Casanova, just how did you manage to get into that crowded dining car?

Gorcey: That was easy. Nothing to it. Just told him the conductor was my old man.

Tierney: And I'm very grateful to you, Mr. Gorcey, for seeing that my luggage was handled so carefully.

Gorcey: Ah, that was nothing, nothing at all. I did that the same way. Just told 'em the conductor was my old man.

Marx: Hey, that's a good trick, Gorcey. Whatever made you think of that?

Gorcey: The conductor is my old man! (Laughter and applause)

(Six minutes later, Gorcey re-enters.)

Gorcey: Hi ya Marxy! Hi ya Geney! Well, here I am, don't worry about a thing. All ready to take you to dinner. I've just been downstairs in the dining room and I got everything all deranged [arranged].

Marx: Well, I couldn't think of a better man for the job.

Tierney: Thank you, Leo. I'll be down in just a few minutes.

Gorcey: Hey Marxy, you oughta see the swell rooms I got. I'm in the bridal suit.

Marx: You mean the bridal suite! Suite!

Gorcey: You're kind a cute yourself. (Audience laughs)

Marx: Say, wait a minute, Gorcey. With rooms so hard to get, how did you ever rate the bridal suite?

Gorcey: Eh, it was easy. I just told 'em the manager of the hotel was my old man.

Marx: Gorcey, I don't understand this, you got all that service on the train because you said your father was a conductor. Now you tell me your father's a manager of the hotel.

Gorcey: Can I help it if my old man can't hold a job. (Audience laughs)

(The storyline continues until eight minutes later, when Gorcey returns as "Black Louie" in a western skit.)

Gorcey: Hey you, get away from that Injun girl or I'll plug ya.

Marx: Hold on there. I'm G. Boone Marx, I'm a mighty tough hombre.

Gorcey: Yeah, well I'm flatly, a mighty tough hamburger myself.

Marx: Listen Black Leo (Laughter) what you do put mustard on, the hamburger? (Laughter) Listen Black Leo or Louie whatever you name is, I love here this gal too. Let's talk it over man to man. Here, have a smoke.

Gorcey: Thanks.

Marx: Match?

Gorcey: Naw! I ain't no sissy. I light my smokes with my gun.

Marx: Aren't you 'fraid you might shoot your nose off?

Gorcey: Naaa! Not me. (Gunshot heard) Oh well, things didn't smell too good around here anyways. (Laughter)

Butler: I say, would you like another glass of my beer?

Marx: Well, its great beer partner, but now there's trouble a brewing.

Butler: In that case I must be off. Well ta, ta, tip, tip cheerio and number ten Downing Street.

Marx: Not Downing Street, Downing Beer, isn't it?

Gorcey: Look here G. Look here G. Boone Marx, nobody body takes a girl away from Black Leo without getting masacrayed (massacred). Well the last gunfight I was in I got my man in and both their hands and foot with one bullet.

Marx: Well how did you do that?

Gorcey: He was putting his socks on at the time. (Laughter)

Tierney: Please do not fight over me. Injun girl does not want men to die because of her.

Gorcey: I don't care, I'm a shootin'.

Marx: Well I'm a shootin'.

Tierney: No! No! Stop! Stop!

Marx: Don't try to stop us Injun girl, we're a shootin'.

Gorcey: Well go 'head and shoot.

Marx: Ok, I'm a shootin' two bucks.

Gorcey: I've got you covered. (Laughter)

Marx: Yes, and I've got you covered.

Tierney: What about Injun girl?

Gorcey: You got a blanket. Go cover yourself. (Laughter and applause)

In *Pabst Blue Ribbon Town*, February 12, 1944, Gorcey appeared in a mechanical age skit regarding a typical American family from 2044 featuring Groucho as father, Gene Tierney as mother, and Gorcey as their son. An excerpt follows:

Gorcey: Well here I am, Matter and Patter."

When asked what on Earth is he doing, he responds:

Gorcey: On Earth, nothing, but I just hid a heck of a time with a dame on Jupiter.

Gorcey's struggle to deliver his line leads Marx to respond:

Marx: Heck of a time with that line too. Why you so late?

Gorcey: Well, the dame wanted me to meet her family. You know them people on Jupiter. They all have bi pairs of arms. By the time you get through you get shaking hands with them people. It ain't exactly early in giving directions to Jupiter. (He refers to the Big Dipper diaper.) (Laughter)

Pabst Blue Ribbon Town, **February 26, 1944.**

Jack Benny guests. Gorcey is a regular cast member along with McKenzie, Bill Day, Robert Armbruster and his Blue Ribbon Blenders, and announcer, Ken Niles. In this show, it seems as if everyone wants to leave Marx's show to be on Benny's program. However, Benny came to Marx's show for a rest.

Gorcey's first line: Hey Marxy! Hey Marxy! Is our distinguished guest here yet?

Marx: Well, well, everybody's entitled to one mistake and here's Mother Nature's: Leo Gorcey. (Applause)

Gorcey: Hey Marxy, I just heard you're talking about Phil Harris. You know he's an old schoolmate of mine. Gee, I ain't seen Phil since we were in the 5th grade together.

Marx: You ain't?

Gorcey: No. Just think, two whole years have slipped by. (Laughter) Say Marxy, did you enjoy yourself at Jack Benny's house last Sunday?

Marx: Yes, I did Gorcey, but I'm always glad to be back here in *Blue Ribbon Town* with my own happy little family.… .

Gorcey: And Marxy, I like you likewise.

Marx: And Gorcey, I like you lengthwise. (Laughter)

Marx tells Day, Gorcey, and McKenzie not to mention a single word or anything about radio to arriving guest star, Jack Benny; that he has radio-itis…

Gorcey (referring to Benny): Oh I get it; you mean he's allergic—

Marx: Gorcey, I bet you don't even know what allergic means?

Gorcey: Hey, certainly I do. Benny's allergic to radio like I'm allergic to jail.

Marx: Allergic to jail? I don't quite see the connection.

Gorcey: Well, every time I'm in jail, I break out. (Laughter and applause) See ya later Marxy!

(Near the end of the show, Gorcey returns to pester Jack Benny to be on his radio show.)

Gorcey: Hi there, Marxy, Hi ya, Mr. B. Say, I've been listening to your program lots of times and I think it's great.

Benny: I'm glad you enjoyed it Mr. G, but I don't think I care to discuss—

Gorcey: There's one thing wrong how-so-sever. (Laughter) That guy, Phil Harris, extracts from the refinement and the culture of the program.

Benny: You really think so?

Gorcey: There ain't a participle of a doubt. And believe me the lack of culture is a terrible curse that can be visited on no man.

Marx: You're absolutely right, Gorcey Pooh. So please stop visiting me.

Gorcey: Not only is Phil Harris ignorant, but he also has a terrible vocal bearing. He sang "There was nothin' about nothin' especially grammar." Not only can't he conjugate conjugations, but he can't even conjunct conjunctions.

Benny: Boy, what a soliloquy. (Laughter)

Gorcey: See, what you should do, Benny, is to get someone to take Harris' place. Someone who's got class refinement and education. In other words, me. (Laughter)

Benny: That's more than I had on the whole program (Laughter and applause).... "While after listening to you, Gorcey, Phil Harris sounds like Anthony Eden. (Laughter)

Gorcey: Well, I know my speech ain't so hot. But my writing is very audible. See about that Benny. I'll see ya later.

The Bob Burns Show, June 7, 1945:

Shirley Ross: Oh, look, here comes Leo Gorcey. Maybe he'd like to go the opera too.

Burns: Yeah. We'll insist that he goes, it'll do the boy good.

Gorcey: (Comes in singing loudly) Oh, take me back to Brooklyn. (Applause over singing)

Burns: Hello, Leo.

Gorcey (to Ross): How are you, my little post office?

Ross: Post office?

Gorcey: Yeah. You're the little frail that sends this male. [Word play on sound-alike words mail and male]

Burns: Leo, if you listen a minute then you might hear this as it's quite a lull… if you listen a minute I got something to say to you son.

Gorcey: OK Pop. Start beating your chops.

Burns: Well, Shirley and I thought you might be interested in going to the opera with us.

Gorcey: Nothing doing, I went to the Metropolitan Opera House once. It's just like Grant's tomb with sound effects. Every time I rattled my popcorn sack I got nothing but dirty looks.

Ross: But Leo, it has to be quiet at the opera so you can hear every note of the music.

Burns: Sure, I learned the hard way too, Leo. First time I went, I took along a sack of peanuts. But the people around me got so annoyed when I cracked them that finally I had to put my peanuts in my mouth and poke the shell off.

Gorcey: Well that ain't for me, Pops. No sir. I like shows where I can yell and whistle.

Ross: Leo, how did it happen that you went to the opera even once?

Gorcey: Well, they got me in there under false pretenses. They advertised a chorus of twenty, but if you ask me, every one of them was over fifty. (Audience laughs)

Ross: That was an operatic chorus. They pick them for their voices, not for their ages.

Gorcey: Well the only kind of chorus I like is the kind that comes out on the runway. (Laughter)

Burns: Well, wait a minute Leo, maybe you didn't see a good opera. What was the name of the one you saw?

Gorcey: Well, I forget. I uh, think it was uh, "Madame Butterscotch." (Laughter) Oh, no. That wasn't it. Maybe it was "The Barber of DeMille."

Burns: "That's Barber of Seville."

Gorcey: Well I knew it was a barber of some kind because I certainly got clipped. (Laughter)

Ross: Well Leo, some opera is very entertaining. Well of course, I don't suppose you're familiar with the "Merry Wives of Windsor?"

Gorcey: No, but I get pretty familiar with some gay babes in Brooklyn.

Burns: Never mind, Leo. It takes real talent to be an opera star.

Gorcey: Oh well, all together different in radio, hey Pop?

Ross: Well I don't know about that. In fact, Leo, Robin possesses a lot of a qualities that a good opera star must have. He has a resonant voice, a fine tone quality.

Burns: Yeah you know most operatic bass singers have a barrel chest like mine.

Gorcey: Barrel chest? Don't look now Pop, but your hoops have slipped.

Burns: Just what do you mean by that?

Gorcey: Well to put it blandly, your barrel has gone to pot. (Laughter)

Ross: Well that's a fine way to talk to Robin after all he's done for you.

Gorcey: Yeah I think your right, Shirley. I'm sorry Pop; I didn't mean it. At least not in a *declamatory* [defamatory] way. And just to show you how I appreciate what you've done for me, I'm going to give you credit for my latest farm development.

Burns: Well thank you Leo. What is this latest creation of yours?

Gorcey: Well Pops, I'm going to cross a beaver with a parrot so when he gnaws down a tree he can holler T-I-M-B-E-R! (Laughter)

Burns: Well now, why don't you go a little further with that idea and cross the beaver with an electric eel, then we he builds a dam, he can install his own power plant? (Laughter)

Gorcey: That's a very silly idea, but I'll give it some thought.

Ross: Well Leo, how about giving some more thought to going to the opera.

Burns: Yeah Leo, it'll add to your education.

Gorcey: I don't need to be educated; I studied musical *depreciation* [*appreciation*] in school. (Laughter)

Ross: And just what did you learn about music?

Gorcey: I learned about how to chew a spitball in 4/4 time.

Burns: That's a fine education in music. Is that all you learned?

Gorcey: I learned other things. Uh, for instance, would you care to hear about "Bill the Stool Pigeon?"

Burns: Is that an opera?

Gorcey: Certainly, you ever hear about "Bill the Stool Pigeon," a-lie-es "Will the Squealer?"

Burns: That's alias, Leo.

Gorcey: Well I guess I was using the past tense. (Laughter) This guy was also known as "Billy the Snitch."

Burns: Let's see "Billy the Snitch." Uh that couldn't be William Tell.

Gorcey: Uhhmmm! (Abrupt Laughter) Exactly! You hit the hammer right on the thumb.

Burns: Well hit me with a story, Leo.

Gorcey: Once upon a time, there was a guy named William Tell. He lived in Switzerland. He used to watch the cheese. In fact, he was the original Swiss watch. Then one day the king suspected his movements. (Laughter) The king then tried to get Willie to sing, but Willie being Swiss could only yodel. This made the king mad. So taking off his hat to cool his head he told Willie to bow to it, but Willie refused. Why don't you bow? said the king. My girdle is too tight answered Willie. (Laughter) Which if you want to know something, is a very snappy reply. (Laughter.) Oh, OK said the king. I will bet your life against your sons that you can't shoot an apple off the kid's cranium, which is a very selfish way to bet. So Willie answered, those are very high Swiss stakes. (Laughter) Howsoever, I will take a shot even though the kid is my favorite tax exemption. (Laughter) Look, says Willie Jr., let's think this thing over because it is not very stylish with kids to go around with arrows in their noggins. (Laughter) Quiet, said his old man, and just close your mouth so I can tell your head from the apple. Well with that, he lets go his shot at the apple. It was a pippin; that is, until the arrow hit it.

Burns: Yeah Leo, just like your story, it ended up a lot of applesauce.

(Leo laughs along with audience laughter and applause.) (Musical interlude)

Burns (To Shirley and Leo): Well kids, I called up the ticket agent for some opera tickets and a salesman is coming right over to see us.

Ross: Oh wonderful, Robin. You know we ought to read up on opera's so we'll understand them. There's a swell book out called *The Opera Lovers Guide*.

Gorcey: You just guide me to the opera. I'll do the loving, Shirley.

Burns: Never mind, Leo. Now let's make up our minds where you want to sit before the man gets here.

Ross: Oh, gee. Isn't it exciting! The opera I mean. Gosh if I ever get a chance to be in one I'd probably get so excited I'd forget to speak my lines.

Gorcey: Don't worry sister, your lines speak for themselves. (Laughter at that suggestive remark.)

Burns: Hey, here comes somebody now from the ticket agency.

Ticket Agent: Pardon me, but does somebody want tickets for the summer opera season. (Sounds like Porky Pig, as played by Mel Blanc.) (LAUGHTER)

Gorcey: Run for the hills the dam has busted! (That's because the man spits so much when he talks.)

Burns: Well, we're the ones who want the tickets. Are you from the ticket agency?

Ticket Agent: That's me! Theater tickets, train tickets, flight tickets, and laundry agency.

Burns: Laundry agency?

Ticket Agent: That's right, we do handwork roughdry and family finish. (Audience laughs)

Burns: It all sounds like wet wash to me.

Ticket Agent: Our motto is service with a smile.

Gorcey: Right now you can serve us with a towel.

Ticket Agent: Just a minute, I didn't come over here to be ridiculed. Do you want something or don't you?

Burns: Say, ain't you the fellow we saw at the beach a few weeks ago?

Ticket Agent: No. That's my brother. He's the spitting image of me. (Laughter)

Burns: Tell me, what kind of opera tickets have you got?

Ticket Agent: Well, there's "Carmen." "Tristin Isolde." "Patchagalli" (trying to say "Pagliacci"). "Rigoletto." And so forth. And so forth. And so forth.

Burns: You better get your valve fixed, brother, your losing a lot of compression. (Laughter)

Ticket Agent: Maybe you'd like some tickets for a play. Would you like to see Rain? (Laughter)

Burns: You keep talking, we'll all need reservations for a lifeboat.

Ticket Agent: Well you folks better make up your mind what you want. I can't waste this time here. I gotta date. I gotta give a lecture on diction.

Burns: You mean you're gonna give a lecture on diction?

Ticket Agent: That's right. I'm [a] very good speaker. The last time I gave a speech it was [a] very, very sad story. You should see how I swayed the audience. When I was finished there wasn't a dry eye in the house. (Laughter and applause)

Burns (To Shirley and Leo): Well, now come on here. What opera would you kids like to see?

Gorcey: Eh! How should I know? I don't know one from the other.

Burns: Well, Shirley and I can sing a few for you; then you can make up your mind.

Gorcey: I wouldn't know anymore than I did in the first place. They're all in foreign languages anyway.

Ross: Oh, well Leo it's the music that's important. We can use words you'll understand. Let's show him, Robin.

Burns: Sure.

(Ross and Burns sing their own words to "Carmen.")

Ross (singing): Leo my boy, just lend an ear, we'll sing some opera for you to hear.

Burns (singing): With opera lovers, we'll get in Dutch, for we're going to give it a rural touch.

Ross (singing): If you will just sit still awhile, we'll just sing to you, habanero style.

Burns/Ross (singing): If you will just sit still awhile, we'll just sing to you, habanero style.

Burns (singing): On my farm in Canoga Park I got more stock than Noah's Ark. I have lots of steers, a whole barn full, and take it from me, that's a lot of bull.

Burns/Ross (singing): He's got lots of steers, the whole barn full and take it from me, that's a lot of bull.

Burns (singing): I've got a cat and a shaggy dog, a little red hen and a big bullfrog.

Ross (singing): You can't see the cat. You can't see the dog, but on a clear day you can see the fog.

Burns/Ross (singing): You can't see the cat. You can't see the dog.

Ticket Agent: (singing.) But on a clear day, you can see the fog.

Burns (singing): Just stepped in Canoga Park. Go right to bed when it gets dark.

Ross (singing): They raise their crops without the rain. They also raise a little Cain.

Burns/Ross: They raise their crops without the rain. They also raise a little Cain. So Leo, you see just what we mean with this rustic operatic scene.

Gorcey (singing): That wasn't so bad, but sing some more. (Deep voice) It ain't quite what I'm looking for.

Burns (singing): Well Leo, my boy, if you really want more here's some music from "El Toreador." (Music plays.)

Burns (singing): I make a profit of seven bucks a day, selling alfalfa, and that isn't hay.

Ross and Burns (singing): He sells alfalfa trying to get rich. And he can make it, you'll get in a fix.

Gorcey (singing): Wait a minute Pop, that song don't suit. Your voice is squeakier than a ten cents flute. I want something that's a little hep. Ain't there no opera that's got some pep.

Burns (singing): We'll finish without our rural theme and give you something on the beam.

Ross (singing): With an anvil chorus rondelet about something, we all should do today.

All (singing): Buy war bonds and help to lick the Japs of Nippon. We got 'em by the throat but we must keep our grip on. Every little start of the rising sun. To hear Hirohito, right on the street-o, by buying a bond today. So don't delay! Do this today! (Applause)

Additional Examples of Slip's Fancy Talk and Word Power

The following are additional examples of Slip's fancy words, misused words, or funny expressions not included in the listing earlier. What he was meaning to say is often uncertain. As a word game played by readers, one can try to decipher what Slip intended.

From *In Fast Company*:
"philosophied my psychology"
"synchronized action"

From *Bowery Bombshell*:
"dastardly spectacle"
"blossoming delinquent"
"by the Board of Equalization"
"manners are getting municipal"

From *Spook Busters*:
"was granulating"
[rabbit in hat]: "what is called legerdemains"
"the guy carries his own undertakers"
"strictly a jet job"

From *Mr. Hex*:
"don't be so obligatory"

From *Hard Boiled Mahoney*:
"deductible mind"
"unobstrusive details"

From *News Hounds*:
"maybe in a more denunciatory manner"
"vernacular of the press that's hit the town and country"
"that is, if the lady is acquiescent"
"leave in a very perckipitit hurry" [big?]
"he's my innuendo"
"a wingding with flourishes"
"them gregarious guys over there"
"premeditated tankeroo"
"bring this case to its indetermitable end"
"what I might call the procrastination of destiny"

From *Bowery Buckaroos*:
"fortly there was a map"
"peace parley"
"misdelusion"
"obstreperous"
"smarty pills"
"The coast might say the temperatures is fidgeting."

From *Angels Alley*:
"crooked as a corkscrew"
"that is about as funny as a crutch"
"do some corkscrew-looking myself"
"that deluded stuff"
"one carnivorous gangster"
"kind of smack drastic"

From *Jinx Money*:
"don't precipitate"
"that is such a distortional values"
"getting mercenary"
"twain shall meet"
"euphonious looking"
"authenticated residence"
"to enumerate some denominations"
"murder's been incinerating on Louie's nerves"
"basement of operations"
"hot as a mail carrier's feet"

Additional Examples of Slip's Fancy Talk and Word Power

"my little willory wisp"

From *Smugglers' Cove*:
"solitude and peacetude"
"under my domicile roof"

From *Trouble Makers*:
"contragion" [contrary?]
"I am official ready to detest the fact, the scene of the crime."

From *Fighting Fools*:
"brotherly conjecture" [contribution?]
"centrifical introduction"
"Louie, you're being very deductible." [negative?]
"put a couple of catastrophes on that slip"

From *Hold That Baby*:
"incapacitated fibula tissue"
"grade A acidopholis milk"

From *Angels in Disguise*:
"an impossible cog in a wheel"
"I had to remonstrate with him."
"but tempest is figid" [tempers are fidgety]

From *Master Minds*:
"a prophet—a prestigitator"
"good, it's positively condescending"
"it's absolutely gulgarian"
"stentatious"
[regarding the clouds]: "stimuli and the cumili"
"strain on his mental cavities"

From *Lucky Losers*:
"At first I misinterpreted the innuendo."
"My friend is trying to say in his monosyllabic and padalionistic delivery is we'll have him here tomorrow night."
"It's just a naviation then with a definite purpose." [investigation].

From *Blues Busters*:
"I don't like to be a filibuster."
"if those silvery tones is actually emulating from your kisser"
"come my happy hamalgamites" [partners?]

From *Bowery Battalion*:
"Adios maraches muc."
"It'll do a reverse reconnoiter."

From *Ghost Chasers*:
"evade a confidence" [invade]
"And don't try no prest-disitarinism."
"And before I splash you in your ectoplasmic head."

From *Let's Go Navy!*:
"…while the two sailors were living over Louie's Sweet Shop. That's what I call the millennium."

From *Jalopy*:
[Referring to his name]: "well, it is allegorically phonious."
[Referring to jalopy]: "symphony in agitated metal"

From *Clipped Wings*:
"analogist" [analyst?]
"a capital confession"
"while I survey the linerntype" [linotype]
"skinny up there boy"

From *Private Eyes*:
"hatch a little scratch" [get some money]
"precisely succinct"
"admit the degradation of a thought"
"But that's infiguratively what he did."
"Do a little renaissance work."

From *Jungle Gents*:
"much to my surprise and petrification"
"inedible body of water"
"inflammably combusts it"

"very discourteous news for you"
"waiting to make my head samporized"
"sometimes is going ashrew"

From *Bowery to Bagdad*:
"like you animated Turkish towel"

From *High Society*:
"ample remuneration"
"the crest of the Bowery"
"real fine tooth curry comb"
"see if you can fix this wreck abahesprus?"

From *Jail Busters*:
"doorbell award for journalism"
"never mind the reparteé"
"the greatest deportment"
"defuses like an atomic atomizer"
"and there are more supplications like it up there?"
"have lunch while we're dissolving"
"since Morpheus is not willing to disengage you"
"dissolve the whole trouble"
"disintegrate the clutch"
"we'll be richer than King Creaso"
"drink of aqua velvet"

From *Crashing Las Vegas*:
"Sach and me gotta do a little drizzing."

Credits

Feature Films

"The greatest gangster thriller that ever exploded from the screen!"
Dead End (1937) D: William Wyler

Sylvia Sidney, Joel McCrea, Humphrey Bogart, Wendy Barrie, Claire Trevor, Allen Jenkins, Marjorie Main, Billy Halop, Huntz Hall, Bobby Jordan, Leo B. Gorcey, Gabriel Dell, Bernard Punsly, Charles Peck, Minor Watson, James Burke, Ward Bond, Elisabeth Risdon, Esther Dale, George Humbert, Marcella Corday, Charles Halton, Robert E. Homans, Bill Dagwell, Wade Boteler, Jerry Cooper, Kath Ann Lujan, Gertrude Valerie, Tom Ricketts, Charlotte Treadway, Al Bridge, Maude Lambert, Bud Geary, Frank Shields, Lucile Brown, Mickey Martin, Wesley Girard, Esther Howard, Gilbert Clayton, Earl Askam, Mona Monet, Donald M. Barry, Sidney Kibrick, Larry Harris, Norman Salling.

Film adaptation of Sidney Kingsley's play about the inhabitants of a New York City slum. Laborer McCrea is torn between rich Barrie and down-to-earth Sidney. A dangerous, legendary gangster (Bogart) returns to find that his beloved mother has renounced him and his former girlfriend is now a prostitute. A gang of neighborhood toughs (including Gorcey as Spit) populates the streets.

> Screenplay written by Lillian Hellman.
> Produced by Samuel Goldwyn and Merritt Hulburd.
> Filmed at Samuel Goldwyn Studios.
> Songs:
> "Boo Hoo" (composed by Carmen Lombardo, John Jacob Loeb, Edward Heyman)
> "The Prisoner's Song" (Guy Massey) (performed on kazoo by Bobby Jordan and sung by Gorcey and the boys)

"Girl of My Dreams" (Sunny Clapp)
Academy Award Nominations:
   (Supporting Actress) Claire Trevor
   (Cinematography) Gregg Toland
   (Art Direction) Richard Day
Music by Alfred Newman, (uncredited Edward B. Powell).
Released on August 27.
(93 minutes/Western Electric Mirrophonic Recording/video/
   laserdisc/DVD)
Samuel Goldwyn Productions/United Artists

"Will not interest children!"
Portia on Trial (1937) D: George Nicholls Jr.

Walter Abel, Frieda Inescort, Neil Hamilton, Heather Angel, Ruth Donnelly, Barbara Pepper, Clarence Kolb, Anthony Marsh, Paul Stanton, George Cooper, John Kelly, Hobart Bosworth, Ian MacLaren, Chick Chandler, Bob Murphy, Inez Palange, Leo Gorcey, Huntley Gordon, Marion Ballou, Hooper Atchley, Nat Carr, Lucie Kaye.

A female attorney's hidden secret becomes known after her marriage ends and her son becomes an adult. Gorcey plays Joe Gannon.

   Screenplay by Samuel Ornitz and Edward E. Paramore, from a story
      by Faith Baldwin.
   Produced by Albert E. LeVoy.
   Academy Award Nomination:
   (Music—Score) Alberto Colombo
   Released on November 8.
   (85 minutes/RCA Victor High Fidelity Sound)
   Republic

"Crashing New York—to smash a crime trust!"
Headin' East (1937) D: Ewing Scott

Buck Jones, Ruth Coleman, Shemp Howard, Donald Douglas, Elaine Arden, Earle Hodgins, John Elliott, Stanley Blystone, Harry Lash, Frank

Faylen, Dick Rich, Al Herman, Leo Gorcey, Kit Guard, Henry Hall, Forrest Taylor, Robert Taylor.

When racketeers cause problems for produce farmers, Cowboy Jones travels to the big city and confronts the crooks. Gorcey is the boy boxer in the gym.

>Screenplay by Ethel LaBlanche and Paul Franklin, from a story by Monroe Shaff.
>Produced by L.G. Leonard [Leonard Goldstein] and Monroe Shaff.
>Music by (uncredited Edward Kilenyi).
>Released on December 13.
>(67 minutes)
>Coronet/Columbia

"The romance of a shopgirl's millions!"
Mannequin (1938) D: Frank Borzage

Joan Crawford, Spencer Tracy, Alan Curtis, Ralph Morgan, Mary Phillips [Philips], Oscar O'Shea, Elizabeth [Elisabeth] Risdon, Leo Gorcey, Paul Fix, Phillip Terry, George Chandler, Bert Roach, Marie Blake [Blossom Rock], Matt McHugh, Helen Troy, Gwen Lee, Donald Kirke, Virginia Blair, Jim [James] Baker, Ruth Dwyer, Frank Jaquet, Jimmy Conlin, Granville Bates, Wade Boteler, James Flavin, Francis Ford, Chester Gan, Mary Gordon, Frank Puglia.

Crawford, a girl from the tenements, finds her way to the Broadway stage and into the arms of wealthy Tracy—but not before being sidetracked by a bad marriage. Gorcey plays Clifford Cassidy.

>Screenplay by Lawrence Hazard (and uncredited Frank Borzage), from a story by Katherine Brush.
>Produced by Joseph L. Mankiewicz (who was also an uncredited collaborating writer) (and uncredited Frank Borzage).
>Song:
>"Always and Always" (Edward Ward, Bob Wright, Chet Forrest) (Academy Award Nominee)
>Music by Edward Ward (uncredited Alex Hyde, Herbert Stothart).
>Released on January 21.

(95 minutes/Western Electric Sound/video/laserdisc/DVD)
Metro-*Goldwyn*-Mayer

"Beloved...she's a darling you want to hug to your heart! Brat...she's a devil whose neck you want to wring!"
The Beloved Brat (1938) D: Arthur Lubin

Bonita Granville, Dolores Costello, Donald Crisp, Natalie Moorhead, Lucille [Lucile] Gleason, Donald Briggs, Emmett Vogan, Loia Cheaney, Leo Gorcey, Ellen Lowe, Mary Doyle, Paul Everton, Bernice Pilot, [Matthew] Stymie Beard, Meredith White, Gloria Fischer [Fisher], Carmencita Johnson, Doris Brenn, Patsy Mitchell, Priscilla Lyon, Betty Compson, John Herron, Ottola Nesmith.

A teen girl's rich parents do not know how to handle her and it takes the intervention of an understanding teacher to make things right. Gorcey is Spike Matz.

>Screenplay by Lawrence Kimble, from the story *Too Much of Everything* by Jean Negulesco.
>Produced by Jack L. Warner, Hal Wallis, and Bryan Foy.
>Music by (uncredited Howard Jackson).
>Released on April 30.
>(62 minutes)
>Warner Brothers-First National

Crime School (1938) D: Lewis Seiler

Humphrey Bogart, Gale Page, Billy Halop, Bobby Jordan, Huntz Hall, Leo Gorcey, Bernard Punsley [Punsly], Gabriel Dell, George Offerman Jr., Weldon Heyburn, Cy Kendall, Charles Trowbridge, Spencer Charters, Donald Briggs, Frank Jaquet, Helen MacKellar, Al Bridge, Sybil Harris, Paul Porcasi, Frank Otto, Ed [Edward] Gargan, James B. Carson, John Ridgely, Harry Cording, Hally [Hal E.] Chester, Ethan Laidlaw, Vera Lewis, Clayton Moore.

Bogart becomes the warden of a reformatory and tries to clean out the corrupt administrators running the facility. He receives help from a group of boys recently sent there. Gorcey is Spike.

Screenplay by Crane Wilbur and Vincent Sherman, from a story by Wilbur.
Produced by Bryan Foy. A remake of the 1933 film *The Mayor of Hell*.
Songs
"Rain, Rain, Go Away!" (traditional, composer unknown)
"Put on Your Old Grey Bonnet" (Percy Wenrich, Stanley Murphy)
Music by Max Steiner (uncredited Leo F. Forbstein, Hugo Friedhofer, George Parrish)
Released on May 28.
(86 minutes/DVD)
Warner Brothers-First National

"The saga of America's dirty-faced kids…and the breaks that life won't give them!"
Angels with Dirty Faces (1938) D: Michael Curtiz

James Cagney, Pat O'Brien, Humphrey Bogart, Ann Sheridan, George Bancroft, Billy Halop, Bobby Jordan, Leo Gorcey, Gabriel Dell, Huntz Hall, Bernard Punsley [Punsly], Joe Downing, Edward Pawley, Adrian Morris, Frankie Burke, William Tracy, Marilyn Knowlden, William Worthington, Earl Dwire, Oscar O'Shea, Harris Berger, William Pawley, John Hamilton, Mary Gordon, Vera Lewis, Robert [E.] Homans, John Harron, George Offerman Jr., Harry Hayden, Dick Rich, Steven Darrell, Joseph A. Devlin, Frank Coghlan Jr., Dick Wessel, Dave Durand, Charles Trowbridge, Lane Chandler, Jack Perrin, Sonny Bupp, St. Brendan's Church Choir [The Robert Mitchell Boy Choir].

Tough gangster, Cagney, revisits his old neighborhood to find a group of slum boys idolizing him and his illegal exploits. Slowly seeing himself as a bad influence, Jimmy decides to do something about it. Gorcey plays Bim.

Screenplay by John Wexley and Warren Duff (with uncredited contributions from Ben Hecht and Charles MacArthur), from a story by Rowland Brown.
Produced by Samuel Bischoff. Portions filmed at Sing Sing Penitentiary, Ossining, New York.
Songs:
"Angels with Dirty Faces" (Maurice Spitalny, Fred Fisher).

"In My Merry Oldsmobile" (Gus Edwards, Vincent Bryan).
"The Sidewalks of New York" (instrumental) (Charles Lawrence).
"Shuffle Off to Buffalo" (instrumental) (Harry Warren).
"From Me to You" (instrumental) (Fabian Andre, Wayne King, Nat Conney).
Academy Award Nominations:
(Actor) James Cagney
(Director) Michael Curtiz
(Writing—Original Story) Rowland Brown
National Board of Review Award:
(Acting) James Cagney
New York Film Critics Circle Award:
(Best Actor) James Cagney
Music by Max Steiner, Hugo Friedhofer, Leo F. Forbstein.
Released on November 24.
(97 minutes/computer color version/video/laserdisc/DVD)
Warner Brothers-First National

"I am a fugitive...I am hunted by ruthless men! I am shunned by decent women! I am doomed to hide forever!"
They Made Me a Criminal (1939) D: Busby Berkeley

John Garfield, Claude Rains, Ann Sheridan, May Robson, Gloria Dickson, Billy Halop, Bobby Jordan, Leo Gorcey, Huntz Hall, Gabriel Dell, Bernard Punsley [Punsly], Robert Gleckler, John Ridgely, Barbara Pepper, William [B.] Davidson, Ward Bond, Louis Jean Heydt, Frank Riggi, Cliff Clarke [Clark], Dick Wessel, Raymond Brown, Sam Hayes, Robert Strange, Arthur Housman, Sam McDaniel, Clem Bevans, Doris Lloyd, Irving Bacon, John Harron, Ronald Sinclair.

Boxer Garfield fears he has killed a man in a brawl, so he flees westward and finds refuge at Robson's desert ranch. Gorcey is Spit, one of several delinquents undergoing rehabilitation at the spread.

Screenplay by Sig Herzig, from a novel by Bertram Millhauser and Bellah Marie Dix.
Produced by Hal B. Wallis. A remake of the 1933 film *The Life of Jimmy Dolan*. Portions filmed in Palm Desert, California.

Songs:
"M-O-T-H-E-R, a Word That Means the World to Me" (Theodore Morse, Howard Johnson)
"By a Waterfall" (Sammy Fain, Irving Kahal)
"Cowboy from Brooklyn" (instrumental) (Harry Warren)
"The Whip" (instrumental) (Abe Holzmann)
"Spirit of Independence" (instrumental) (Holzmann)
Music by Max Steiner, Leo F. Forbstein, (uncredited Hugo Friedhofer)
Released on January 28.
(92 minutes/RCA Sound/video/laserdisc/DVD)
Warner Brothers

"The right road...or the 'last mile'...which way are they headed?"
Hell's Kitchen (1939) D: Lewis Seiler, E.A. Dupont

Margaret Lindsay, Ronald Reagan, Stanley Fields, Billy Halop, Bobby Jordan, Leo Gorcey, Huntz Hall, Gabriel Dell, Bernard Punsley [Punsly], Frankie Burke, Grant Mitchell, Fred [Frederic] Tozere, Arthur Loft, Vera Lewis, Robert [E.] Homans, Charley Foy, Raymond Bailey, Clem Bevans, George Irving, Ila Rhodes, Lee Phelps, Jimmy O'Gatty, Don Turner, Joe A. Devlin, Jimmie Lucas, Jack Kenney, Sol Gorss, Cliff Saum, Charles Sullivan, Jack Gardner, Max Hoffman Jr., Dick Rich, Tom Wilson, Reid Kilpatrick, George O'Hanlon, Jack Mower, Ruth Robinson, George Offerman Jr.

Reagan befriends a gang of wayward teens when they are placed in a brutal youth shelter. Gorcey plays Gyp.

Screenplay by Crane Wilbur and Fred Niblo Jr., from a story by Wilbur.
Produced by Mark Hellinger and Bryan Foy. A remake of the 1933 film *The Mayor of Hell*.
Song:
"Auld Lang Syne" (traditional melody, lyrics by Robert Burns) (sung by Stanley Fields, Gorcey, and the boys)
Music by (uncredited Heinz Roemheld)

Released on July 8.
(81 minutes/DVD)
Warner Brothers

The Angels Wash Their Faces (1939) D: Ray Enright

Ann Sheridan, Billy Halop, Bernard Punsley [Punsly], Leo Gorcey, Huntz Hall, Gabriel Dell, Bobby Jordan, Ronald Reagan, Bonita Granville, Frankie Thomas, Henry O'Neill, Eduardo Ciannelli, Berton Churchill, Bernard Nedell, Dick Rich, Jack [Jackie] Searl, Margaret Hamilton, Marjorie Main, Minor Watson, Cyrus [Cy] Kendall, Grady Sutton, Aldrich Bowker, Robert Strange, Egon Brecher, Sybil Harris, Frank Coghlan Jr., Frankie Burke, John Hamilton, John Ridgely, William Hopper, Elliott Sullivan, Charles Trowbridge, John Harron, Howard Hickman, Lee Phelps, Jack Clifford, Tom Wilson, Edward Keane, Max Hoffman Jr., Wendell Niles.

A district attorney's son (Reagan) strives to smash an arson racket and gets help from the Dead End Kids (including Gorcey as Leo Finnegan).

> Screenplay by Michael Fessier, Niven Busch, and Robert Buckner, from a story by Jonathan Finn.
> Produced by Max Siegel. A follow-up to the 1938 film *Angels with Dirty Faces*.
> Songs:
> "A-Tisket, A-Tasket" (instrumental) (traditional, composer unknown)
> "In a Moment of Weakness" (instrumental) (Harry Warren)
> Music by Adolph Deutsch, Leo F. Forbstein, Ray Heindorf.
> Released on August 26.
> (84 minutes/RCA Victor Sound)
> Warner Brothers-First National

On Dress Parade (1939) D: William Clemens, (Noel Smith)

Billy Halop, Bobby Jordan, Huntz Hall, Gabriel Dell, Leo Gorcey, Bernard Punsley [Punsly], John Litel, Frankie Thomas, Cissie [Cecilia] Loftus, Selmer Jackson, Aldrich Bowker, Douglas Meins, William Gould, Don [Donald] Douglas, Eddie Acuff, Creighton Hale, John Hamilton, John

Harron, William Hopper, George Offerman Jr., George Reeves, John Ridgely, Dick Simmons.

At a military school, non-conformist Gorcey (as Slip Duncan) defies discipline with near-tragic results, ostracizing him from his fellow cadets.

    Screenplay by Tom Reed and Charles Belden.
    Produced by Bryan Foy. Portions filmed at Warner Ranch, Calabasas, California.
    Songs:
    "How Dry I Am" (instrumental) (traditional, composer unknown)
    "The Battle Cry of Freedom" (instrumental) (George Frederick Root)
    "My Buddy" (instrumental) (Walter Donaldson)
    "Home on the Range" (Daniel E. Kelley, Brewster M. Hickey)
    "You're in the Army Now" (traditional, composer unknown)
    Music by (uncredited Howard Jackson).
    Released on November 18.
    (62 minutes/DVD)
    Warner Brothers

"Oh please, Miss Detective...I want to be arrested by you!"
Private Detective **(1939) D: Noel Smith**

Jane Wyman, Dick Foran, Gloria Dickson, Maxie Rosenbloom, John Ridgely, Morgan Conway, John Eldredge, Joseph Crehan, William [B.] Davidson, Selmar [Selmer] Jackson, Vera Lewis, Julie Stevens, Jack Mower, Henry Blair, Willie Best, Leo Gorcey, Maris Wrixon.

A female shamus (Wyman) proves she is quite adept at detection when she is paired with a reluctant homicide investigator (Foran) on a case centered on a murdered millionaire. Gorcey plays a newsboy.

    Screenplay by Earle Snell and Raymond Schrock, from a story by Kay Krausse.
    Produced by Bryan Foy, uncredited.
    Music by (uncredited Rex Dunn).
    Released on December 9.
    (55 minutes)
    Warner Brothers-First National

"Three men and a girl...bound by invisible ties...branded by invisible stripes."
Invisible Stripes (1939) D: Lloyd Bacon

George Raft, Jane Bryan, William Holden, Humphrey Bogart, Flora Robson, Paul Kelly, Lee Patrick, Henry O'Neill, Frankie Thomas, Moroni Olsen, Margot Stevenson, Marc Lawrence, Joseph Downing, Leo Gorcey, William Haade, Tully Marshall, Victor Kilian, DeWolf [William] Hopper, Lane Chandler, Marion Martin, Raymond Bailey, John Ridgely, Bruce Bennett, Wade Boteler, Joseph Crehan, William B. Davidson, Frank Faylen.

Ex-con, Raft, wants to go straight, but discovers his kid brother (Holden) is part of Bogart's criminal gang. Gorcey is Jimmy.

> Screenplay by Warren Duff, from a story by Jonathan Finn and a book by Warden Lewis E. Lawes.
> Produced by Hal B. Wallis and Louis Edelman. Portions filmed at Sing Sing Penitentiary, Ossining, New York.
> Music by H. [Heinz] Roemheld, (uncredited Max Steiner).
> Released on December 30.
> (82 minutes/RCA Victor Sound/DVD)
> Warner Brothers-First National

"The story of men in the making by just plain American boys!"
Boys of the City (1940) D: Joseph H. Lewis

Bobby Jordan, Leo Gorcey, Hally [Hal E.] Chester, Frankie Burke, Vince Barnett, Inna Gest [Ina Guest], David [Dave] O'Brien, 'Sunshine' Sammy Morrison, Minerva Urecal, Dennis Moore, Donald Haines, David Gorcey, Eugene Francis, Forrest Taylor, Alden [Stephen/Guy] Chase, Jerry Mandy, George Humbert, Jack Cheatham, Jim Farley, Murdock MacQuarrie.

Muggs McGinnis (Leo Gorcey) and his pals are headed to a camp in the Adirondacks when they become entangled in a haunted house murder mystery. Entry in the *East Side Kids* series.

> Story and screenplay by William Lively.
> Produced by Sam Katzman.
> Music by (uncredited Lew Porter).

Released on July 15.
(65 minutes/Western Electric Mirrorphonic Recording/video/DVD)
Four-Bell/Monogram

"It's a riot in races!"
That Gang of Mine (1940) D: Joseph H. Lewis

Bobby Jordan, Leo Gorcey, Clarence Muse, Dave O'Brien, Joyce Bryant, 'Sunshine' Sammy Morrison, Milton Kibbee, David Gorcey, Donald Haines, Richard R. Terry, Wilbur Mack, Hazel Keener, Eugene Francis, Victor Adamson, Forrest Taylor, Nick Wall.

Leo Gorcey (as Mugs Maloney) sees his opportunity to become a jockey when a thoroughbred horse and its owner take refuge in a barn. Entry in the *East Side Kids* series.

Screenplay by William Lively, from a story by Alan Whitman.
Produced by Sam Katzman (and uncredited Pete Mayer).
Song:
"All God's Chillun Got Wings" (traditional, composer unknown)
Music by Lew Porter.
Released on September 23.
(62 minutes/Western Electric Mirrophonic Recording/video/DVD)
Four-Bell/Monogram

Hullabaloo (1940) D: Edwin L. Marin.

Frank Morgan, Virginia Grey, Dan Dailey Jr., Billie Burke, Nydia Westman, Ann Morriss, Donald Meek, Reginald Owen, Charles Holland, Leni Lynn, Virginia O'Brien, Curt Bois, Sara Haden, Larry Nunn, Barnett Parker, George Lessey, Cy Kendall, Connie Gilchrist, Leo Gorcey, Arthur O'Connell, Arthur Hoyt, Tim Ryan, Tom Seidel, Kay St. Germain, John Wald.

Morgan stars as a stage entertainer who wants to become a radio star. Gorcey is the bellhop at the apartment house.

Screenplay by Nat Perrin, from an idea by Bradford Ropes and Val
   Burton (Dorothy Yost contributed to the screenplay uncredited).
Choreography by Sammy Lee.
Produced by Louis K. Sidney.
Songs:
"We've Come a Long Way Together" (Sam H. Stept, Ted Koehler)
"A Handful of Stars" (Ted Shapiro, Jack Lawrence)
"Hullabaloo" (Earl K. Brent)
"Carry Me Back to Old Virginny" (James Allen Bland)
"You Were Meant for Me" (Nacio Herb Brown, Arthur Freed)
"My Mammy" (Walter Donaldson, Sam Lewis, Joe Young)
"When My Baby Smiles at Me" (Bill Munro, Ted Lewis, Andrew B.
   Sterling)
"Jeanie with the Light Brown Hair" (Stephen Foster)
"Vesti la Giubba" from *I Pagliacci* (Ruggerio Leoncavallo)
Music by (uncredited George Bassman and David Snell).
Released on October 25.
(78 minutes/Western Electric Sound/DVD)
Metro-*Goldwyn*-Mayer

Gallant Sons (1940) D: George B. Seitz

Jackie Cooper, Bonita Granville, Gene Reynolds, Gail Patrick, Ian Hunter, June Preisser, Leo Gorcey, William Tracy, Tommy Kelly, Edward Ashley, El Brendel, Minor Watson, Ferike Boros, Charlotte Wynters, Donald Douglas, George Lessey, Joe Yule, King Baggot, Marie Blake [Blossom Rock], Frank Hagney, Selmer Jackson, Frank Orth, William Tannen.

Comedy and mystery blend in this whodunit centering on a group of youths, including Gorcey as Doc Reardon, determined to solve a murder.

Screenplay by William R. Lipman and Marion Parsonnet.
Produced by Frederick Stephani.
Song:
"Carry Me Back to Old Virginny" (James Allen Bland)
Music by David Snell.
Released on November 15.
(71 minutes/Western Electric Sound/DVD)
Metro-*Goldwyn*-Mayer

Pride of the Bowery (1940) D: Joseph H. Lewis

Leo Gorcey, Bobby Jordan, Kenneth Howell, Mary Ainslee, Bobby Stone, Donald Haines, David Gorcey, 'Sunshine' Sammy Morrison, Kenneth Harlan, Nick Stuart, Lloyd Ingraham, Carleton [S.] Young, Eugene Francis.

Muggs Maloney (Leo Gorcey) is at odds with the other boys at a Civilian Conservation Corps camp when he concentrates on his boxing 'career.' Entry in the *East Side Kids* series.

> Screenplay by George Plympton, from William Lively's adaptation of a Steven Clensos story.
> Produced by Sam Katzman and Pete Mayer.
> Music by Johnny Lange, Lew Porter, (uncredited Milan Roder).
> Released on December 15.
> (61 minutes/Western Electric Mirrophonic Recording/video/DVD)
> Banner/Monogram

"There's a laugh and thrill each second...as slum kids turn 'aero-nuts' to battle saboteurs for Uncle Sam!"
Flying Wild (1941) D: William West

Leo Gorcey, Bobby Jordan, Joan Barclay, Dave O'Brien, George Pembroke, 'Sunshine' Sammy Morrison, David Gorcey, Donald Haines, Eugene Francis, Bobby Stone, Herbert Rawlinson, Dennis Moore, Forrest Taylor, Bob [Robert F.] Hill, Alden [Stephen/Guy] Chase, Mary Bovard, Bud Osborne.

Muggs (Leo Gorcey) suspects that espionage is afoot at an airplane plant, perpetrated by the physician-owner of a flying ambulance. When no one takes his suspicions seriously, Muggs and his friends set out to trap the spies. Entry in the *East Side Kids* series.

> Story and screenplay by Al Martin.
> Produced by Sam Katzman and Pete Mayer. Portions filmed at Alhambra Airport, California.
> Music by Johnny Lange, Lew Porter, (uncredited Milan Roder).
> Released on March 10.
> (62 minutes/video/DVD)
> Banner/Monogram

"The sky's the limit…for fun as five little angels raise the devil in the looniest, tuniest, laugh and love festival to come out of Hollywood in many a moon!"
Angels with Broken Wings (1941) D: Bernard Vorhaus

Binnie Barnes, Gilbert Roland, Mary Lee, Billy Gilbert, Jane Frazee, Edward Norris, Katharine Alexander, Leo Gorcey, Lois Ranson, Leni Lynn, Marilyn Hare, Sidney Blackmer, Tom Kennedy, Billy Bletcher, Tim Ryan, Rolfe Sedan, Clarence Wilson.

Alexander's children take it upon themselves to arrange a romance and marriage between her and Blackmer. Gorcey plays Punchy Dorsey. Screenplay by George Carleton Brown and Bradford Ropes, from a story by Brown. Produced by Albert J. Cohen

>Jule Styne and Eddie Cherkose songs:
>"Three Little Wishes"
>"In Buenos Aires"
>"Has to Be"
>"By Lo Baby"
>"Where Do We Dream from Here"
>Music by (uncredited Mort Glickman).
>Released on May 27.
>(72 minutes/RCA Sound)
>Republic

Out of the Fog **(1941) D: Anatole Litvak**

John Garfield, Ida Lupino, Thomas Mitchell, Eddie Albert, George Tobias, John Qualen, Aline MacMahon, Jerome Cowan, Odette Myrtil, Leo Gorcey, Robert E. Homans, Bernard Gorcey, Paul Harvey, Charles Drake, Charles Wilson, Jack Mower, Konstantin Sankar, Ben Welden, Murray Alper, Barbara Pepper, Frank Coghlan Jr., Richard Kipling, Eddie Graham, Jack Wise, Alexander Leftwich, Jimmy Conlin, Creighton Hale, Walter Tetley.

Gangster Garfield invades the lives of two fishermen and steals money the pair of men saved to buy a boat and falls in love with one of their daughters. Despite their fear, the victimized fishermen plot to eliminate their tormentor. Leo Gorcey portrays Eddie.

Screenplay by Robert Rossen, Jerry Wald, and Richard Macauley,
   from the play *The Gentle People* by Irwin Shaw.
Produced by Hal B. Wallis and Henry Blanke.
Music by (uncredited Heinz Roemheld and Max Steiner).
Released on June 14.
(93 minutes/RCA Sound/video/DVD)
Warner Brothers-First National

"Six kids on a spy chase in this boom-town-by-the-Pacific."
Down in San Diego (1941) D: Robert B. Sinclair

Bonita Granville, Ray McDonald, Dan Dailey, Leo Gorcey, Charles Smith, Dorothy Morris, Rudolph Anders, Joe Sawyer, Anthony Warde, Stanley Clements, Henry O'Neill, William Tannen, Frederick Worlock, Connie Gilchrist, Hobart Cavanaugh, Ludwig Stossel, Veda Ann Borg, James Millican, Jack Norton, Wade Boteler, Ken Christy, James Craven, Robert Kellard, Milton Kibbee, Walter Sande.
   Gorcey (as Snap Collins) and his buddies go into action when Dailey, former hood-turned-Marine, gets involved with a nest of spies.

Screenplay by Harry Clork and Franz Spencer [Schulz].
Produced by Frederick Stephani. Portions filmed on location.
Music by David Snell, (uncredited Daniele Amfitheatrof, Murray
   Cutter).
Released in August.
(69 minutes/Western Electric Sound)
Metro-*Goldwyn*-Mayer

Bowery Blitzkrieg (1941) D: Wallace Fox

Leo Gorcey, Bobby Jordan, Huntz Hall, Key[e] Luke, Warren Hull, Charlotte Henry, Bobby Stone, Donald Haines, Sunshine Sammy Morrison, David Gorcey, Martha Wentworth, Jack Mulhall, Eddie Foster, Dennis Moore, Tony Carson, Pat Costello, Dick Ryan, Minerva Urecal.
   Some crooks try to persuade Muggs (Leo Gorcey) to throw an upcoming prizefight. Entry in the *East Side Kids* series.

Screenplay by Sam Robins (and an uncredited Carl Foreman), from a story by Brendan Wood and Don Mullahy.
Produced by Sam Katzman.
Song:
"Jeanie with the Light Brown Hair" (Stephen Foster) (sung by Huntz Hall)
Music by Johnny Lange, Lew Porter.
Released on September 8.
(62 minutes/Glen Glenn Sound/video/DVD)
Banner/Monogram

Spooks Run Wild (1941) D: Phil Rosen

Bela Lugosi, Leo Gorcey, Bobby Jordan, Huntz Hall, Sunshine Sammy Morrison, David [Dave] O'Brien, Dorothy Short, David Gorcey, Donald Haines, Dennis Moore, P.J. Kelly, Angelo Rossitto, Guy Wilkerson, Rosemary Portia, Slim Andrews, Pat Costello, George Eldredge, Joe Kirk, James Sheridan.

The East Side Kids (with Leo Gorcey as Muggs) stumble onto a New England mansion that houses a mysterious Mr. Nardo (Lugosi), who may or may not be the Monster Killer.

Story and screenplay by Carl Foreman and Charles R. Marion; additional dialogue by Jack Henley.
Produced by Sam Katzman.
Music by Johnny Lange, Lew Porter, (uncredited Milan Roder).
Released on October 24.
(69 minutes/Glen Glenn Sound/video/DVD)
Banner/Monogram

"All we need is a theater…a singer…and an audience."
Born to Sing (1942) D: Edward Ludwig.

Virginia Weidler, Ray McDonald, Leo Gorcey, Douglas McPhail, Rags Ragland, Sheldon Leonard, Henry O'Neill, Larry Nunn, Margaret Dumont, Beverly Hudson, Richard [Dickie] Hall, Darla Hood, Joe Yule, Lester Matthews, Ben Carter, Lee Phelps, Connie Gilchrist, Cy Kendall, Maria Flynn, Barbara Bedford, Lane Chandler, James Flavin, Richard Haydel, Charles Lane, May McAvoy, Mel [Melville] Ruick, Robert Ryan, Ian Wolfe.

Gorcey reprises his role of Snap Collins from *Down in San Diego* to help put on a show that will hopefully give a boost to a struggling songwriter.

>Screenplay by Franz G. Spencer [Schulz] and Harry Clork, from a story by Spencer.
>Choreography by Sammy Lee.
>Produced by Frederick Stephani. Busby Berkeley directed the finale "Ballad for Americans" (composed by Earl Robinson and John Latouche).

Additional songs:
"You Are My Lucky Star" (Nacio Herb Brown, Arthur Freed)
"I've Got You Under My Skin" (Cole Porter)
"I'll Love Ya" (Lennie Hayton, Earl Brent)
"I Hate the Conga" (Brent) (performed by Leo Gorcey and Beverly Hudson)
"Here I Am, Eight Years Old" (Brent)
"Two A.M." (Robinson, Latouche)
"Alone" (Brown, Freed)
Music by (uncredited Lennie Hayton, David Snell).
Released on February 18.
(82 minutes/Western Electric Sound)
Metro-*Goldwyn*-Mayer

Mr. Wise Guy (1942) D: William Nigh

Leo Gorcey, Bobby Jordan, Huntz Hall, Billy Gilbert, Guinn [Big Boy] Williams, Douglas Fowley, Joan Barclay, Warren Hymer, Ann Doran, Jack Mulhall, Gabriel Dell, Sidney Miller, David Gorcey, Bobby Stone, Dick Ryan, Benny Rubin, Bill Lawrence, Sunshine Sammy Morrison, Joe Kirk, Stanley Blystone, Kit Guard, Frank O'Connor, Charles Sullivan.

The East Side Kids (including Leo Gorcey as Muggs) are accused of a truck robbery and sent to reform school. Learning that the same gang has framed an innocent Fowley for theft and murder, the boys break out to clear both themselves and the falsely condemned man.

>Screenplay by Sam Robins, Harvey Gates, and Jack Henley, from a story by Martin Mooney.

Produced by Sam Katzman and Jack Dietz.
Music by Johnny Lange, Lew Porter.
Released on /February 20.
(70 minutes/Western Electric Mirrophonic Recording/video/DVD)
Banner/Monogram

Sunday Punch (1942) **D: David Miller**

William Lundigan, Jean Rogers, Dan Dailey Jr., Guy Kibbee, J. Carrol Naish, Connie Gilchrist, Sam Levene, Leo Gorcey, Rags Ragland, Douglass Newland, Anthony Caruso, Tito Renaldo, Michael Browne, Dave Willock, Marcia Ralston, Floyd Shackleford, Lester Matthews, Alfred Hall, Charles Lane, Duke York, Sammy Shack, Edward Earle, Pat West, Robin Raymond, Steve Pendleton, Ava Gardner, Bernard Zanville [Dane Clark], George Offerman Jr., Cy Kendall, John Raitt, Robert Ryan.

A boarding house that caters to boxers has something new added when the pretty daughter of the owner moves in and immediately wins the attentions of two young pugilists. Gorcey is seen as Biff.

Screenplay by Fay and Michael Kanin and Allen Rivken, from a story by the Kanins.
Produced by Irving Starr.
Music by (uncredited Daniele Amfitheatrof, David Snell).
Released on May 8.
(76 minutes/Western Electric Sound)
Metro-*Goldwyn*-Mayer

"Those East Side shock troops deliver a 'kiss' to Hitler's and Hirohito's henchmen over here…and smash a giant spy ring."
Let's Get Tough (1942) **D: Wallace Fox**

Leo Gorcey, Bobby Jordan, Huntz Hall, Gabriel Dell, Tom Brown, Florence Rice, Robert Armstrong, David Gorcey, Sunshine Sammy Morrison, Bobby Stone, Sam Bernard, Philip Ahn, Jerry Bergen, Pat Costello, George Eldredge, Patsy Moran, Beal Wong, Jack Cheatham, Moy Ming.

The East Side Kids' mischief leads them to uncover a secret Japanese Black Dragon Society operating against America. Leo Gorcey is Muggs.

Screenplay by Harvey Gates, from his story *"I Am an American."*
Produced by Sam Katzman and Jack Dietz.
Music by (uncredited Johnny Lange, Lew Porter, Milan Roder).
Released on May 29.
(62 minutes/Glen Glenn Sound/video/DVD)
Banner/Monogram

Maisie Gets Her Man **(1942) D: Roy Del Ruth**

Ann Sothern, Red Skelton, Leo Gorcey, Allen Jenkins, Donald Meek, Lloyd Corrigan, Walter Catlett, Fritz Feld, Ben Weldon [Welden], 'Rags' Ragland, Frank Jenks, Pamela Blake, Frank Faylen, Willie Best, Florence Shirley, Monte Collins, Esther Dale, William Haade, Lou Lubin, Kay Medford, Robert Emmett O'Connor, William Tannen, Philip Van Zandt, Joe Yule.

Maisie partners with hick, Skelton, in a stage act when she joins a theatrical agency in Chicago. Gorcey plays Ceecil.

> Screenplay by Mary C. McCall Jr. and Betty [Elizabeth] Reinhardt, from a story by Reinhardt and Ethel Hill; based on a character created by Wilson Collison.
> Choreography by Daniel Dare.
> Produced by J. Walter Ruben.
> Song:
> "Cookin' with Gas" (Lennie Hayton, Roger Edens)
> Music by Lennie Hayton.
> Released in June.
> (85 minutes/Western Electric Sound/AFI Laughs Nominee/DVD)
> Metro-*Goldwyn*-Mayer

"Compared to the East Siders, a gorilla is a house pet! Wait'll you see them slug it out to a finish with Maxie Rosenbloom! And what a finish!
Smart Alecks (1942) D: Wallace Fox

Leo Gorcey, Bobby Jordan, Huntz Hall, Gabriel Dell, Maxie Rosenbloom, Gale Storm, Roger Pryor, [Sunshine] Sammy Morrison, Stanley Clements, David Gorcey, Bobby Stone, Herbert Rawlinson, Walter

Woolf King, Sam Bernard, Dick Ryan, Joe Kirk, Marie Windsor, Betty Sinclair, Tiny Jones.

A need for baseball uniforms leads Muggs (Leo Gorcey), Hall, and the gang into taking dishonest jobs to earn the money. When Jordan is severely beaten, the boys go after the crooks. Entry in the *East Side Kids* series.

>Screenplay by Harvey H. Gates.
>Produced by Sam Katzman and Jack Dietz.
>Song:
>"When You and I Were Young, Maggie" (J.A. Butterfield, George W. Johnson)
>Music by Edward J. Kay.
>Released on August 7.
>(60 minutes/Glen Glenn Sound/video/DVD)
>Banner/Monogram

"They're the 'Bridge Gang'…the screen's rowdiest rascals in a smashing story of crime and terror in the seething shadows of New York's famous landmark!"
'Neath Brooklyn Bridge (1942) D: Wallace Fox

Leo Gorcey, Bobby Jordan, Huntz Hall, Gabriel Dell, Noah Beery Jr., Marc Lawrence, Ann Gillis, Dave O'Brien, Sunshine Sammy Morrison, Stanley Clements, Bobby Stone, Jack Raymond, Betty Wells, Dewey Robinson, Patsy Moran, Jack Mulhall, Bud Osborne, J. Arthur Young, Betty Sinclair, 'Snub' Pollard, Franklyn Farnum.

A young woman's abusive stepfather winds up dead, with suspicion for the murder centered on Jordan. The East Side Kids (including Gorcey as Muggs) find a witness who can identify the real killer.

>Story and screenplay by Harvey Gates.
>Produced by Sam Katzman and Jack Dietz.
>Music by Edward [J.] Kay.
>Released on November 20.
>(61 minutes/Glen Glenn Sound/video/DVD)
>Banner/Monogram

"Those tenement terrors are in for the scrap of their lives!"
Kid Dynamite (1943) D: Wallace Fox

Leo Gorcey, Huntz Hall, Bobby Jordan, Gabriel Dell, Pamela Blake, Benny Bartlett, Sunshine Sammy [Morrison], Bobby Stone, Dave Durand, Vince Barnett, Daphne Pollard, Charles Judels, Dudley Dickerson, Henry Hall, Minerva Urecal, Wheeler Oakman, Margaret [Marguerita] Padula, Jack Mulhall, Kay Marvis, Ray Miller, Mike Riley's Orchestra, Marion Miller, 'Snub' Pollard, Lafe McKee.

A misunderstanding causes Gorcey (as Muggs McGinnis) and Jordan to become bitter rivals, a situation complicated by a boxing match, crooked gamblers, and Jordan's desire to marry Gorcey's sister. Entry in the *East Side Kids* series.

> Screenplay by Gerald J. Schnitzer, from the *Saturday Evening Post* magazine story "The Old Gang" by Paul Ernst. Additional dialogue provided by Morey Amsterdam.
> Produced by Sam Katzman and Jack Dietz.
> Song:
> "Comin' Thro' the Rye" (traditional Scottish melody; lyrics by Robert Burns)
> Music by Edward [J.] Kay.
> Released on February 5.
> (73 minutes/Glenn Glenn Sound/video/DVD)
> Banner/Monogram

"Anything goes, everything happens in the funniest hit the tenement terrors have ever made!"
Clancy Street Boys (1943) D: William Beaudine

Leo Gorcey, Huntz Hall, Bobby Jordan, Noah Beery Sr., Lita [Amelita] Ward, Benny Bartlett, Rick Vallin, [William] Billy Benedict, J. Farrell McDonald [MacDonald], Jan Rubini, Martha Wentworth, [Sunshine] Sammy Morrison, Dick Chandlee, Eddie Mills, George DeNormand, Jimmy Strand, Johnny Duncan, Bernard Gorcey, Gino Corrado, Symona Boniface. Muggs (Leo Gorcey) and his pals try to make a good impression on visiting 'Uncle' Pete (Beery), a rich Texan. Entry in the *East Side Kids* series.

Screenplay by Harvey Gates.
Produced by Sam Katzman and Jack Dietz. Filmed at Hal Roach Studios, Culver City, California.
Songs:
"Happy Birthday to You" (Mildred J. Hill, Patty Hill) (sung by Leo Gorcey and the gang)
"One O' Clock Jump" (instrumental) (Count Basie)
"Home on the Range" (Daniel E. Kelley, Brewster M. Higley)
Music by Edward [J.] Kay.
Released on April 23.
(66 minutes/Glen Glenn Sound/video/DVD)
Banner/Monogram

"You'll yell with glee when these happy-go-lucky hooligans invade the shivery domain of the man of a thousand horrors! It's chill-arious!"
Ghosts on the Loose (1943) D: William Beaudine

Leo Gorcey, Huntz Hall, Bobby Jordan, Bela Lugosi, Ava Gardner, Rick Vallin, [Sunshine] Sammy Morrison, [William] Billy Benedict, Stanley Clements, Bobby Stone, Minerva Urecal, Wheeler Oakman, Peter Seal, Frank Moran, Jack Mulhall, Bill Bates, Kay Marvis, Robert F. Hill, 'Snub' Pollard.

Helping out newlywed relatives of Hall, the East Side Kids (including Gorcey as Muggs) go to the wrong house—one filled with sinister Lugosi and his Nazi spies.

Screenplay by Kenneth Higgins.
Produced by Sam Katzman and Jack Dietz.
Songs:
"Drink to Me Only with Thine Eyes" (R. Melish, Ben Jonson) (played on the organ
by Bill Bates and sung by Gorcey and the Kids)
"Bridal Chorus (Here Comes the Bride)" (instrumental) (Richard Wagner)
"The Wedding March" (instrumental) (Felix Mendelssohn-Bartholdy)
Music by (uncredited Edward J. Kay).
Released on July 30.

(65 minutes/Glen Glenn Sound/video/laserdisc/DVD)
Banner/Monogram

"You'll always remember…and never forget…Destroyer."
Destroyer (1943) D: William A. Seiter, (uncredited Ray Enright)

Edward G. Robinson, Glenn Ford, Marguerite Chapman, Edgar Buchanan, Leo Gorcey, Regis Toomey, Ed [Edward] Brophy, Warren Ashe, Craig Woods, Curt Bois, Bobby Jordan, Pierre Watkin, Lloyd Bridges, Roger Clark, John Merton, Virginia Sale, Dale Van Sickel, Kenneth MacDonald, Larry Parks, Neil Reagan, Milburn Stone, Addison Richards, Dennis Moore, Charles McGraw, Edmund Cobb, Tristram Coffin, Lester Dorr, Bud Geary, Eddy Waller, Stanley Brown, Benson Fong, David Holt, Richard Loo.

World War I veteran Robinson's vision of the way things should work clashes with the way things are so when he re-enlists in the Navy during World War II. Gorcey plays Sarecky.

> Screenplay by Frank Wead, Lewis Meltzer, and Borden Chase, from a story by Wead.
> Produced by Louis F. Edelman.
> Music by Anthony Collins.
> Released on August 19.
> (99 minutes/Western Electric Mirrophonic Recording/video/DVD)
> Columbia

"From police blotter to social register in 10 easy lessons!"
Mr. Muggs Steps Out (1943) D: William Beaudine

Leo Gorcey, Huntz Hall, Gabriel Dell, [William] Billy Benedict, Joan Marsh, Bobby Stone, Bud [Buddy] Gorman, Dave [David] Durand, Jimmy Strand, Patsy Moran, Eddie Gribbon, Halliwell Hobbes, Stanley Brown, Betty Blythe, Emmett Vogan, Nick Stuart, Noah Beery [Sr.].

Serving a court sentence to find work, Gorcey (as Muggs) is hired as a chauffeur in a rich woman's offbeat household. When the other East

Side Kids are rung in as additional servants for a party, they are blamed for stealing a valuable necklace.

> Screenplay by William X. Crowley [William Beaudine] and Beryl Sachs.
> Produced by Sam Katzman and Jack Dietz.
> Music by Edward J. Kay.
> Released on October 29.
> (63 minutes/RCA Sound)
> Banner/Monogram

"It's their fight of fights! They've got the toughest guys in town on the run!"
Million Dollar Kid (1944) D: Wallace Fox

Leo Gorcey, Huntz Hall, Gabriel Dell, [William] Billy Benedict, Louise Currie, Noah Beery Sr., Iris Adrian, Herbert Hayes [Heyes], Robert Grieg [Greig], Johnnie [Johnny] Duncan, Stanley Brown, Patsy Moran, Mary Gordon, Al Stone, Dave [David] Durand, Jimmy Strand, Bud [Buddy] Gorman, Pat Costello, Bobby Stone, Bernard Gorcey.

The East Side Kids help a millionaire by trying to reform his son, who has turned to street crime. Leo Gorcey is Muggs McGinnis.

> Screenplay by Frank H. Young.
> Produced by Sam Katzman and Jack Dietz.
> Music by Edward [J.] Kay.
> Released on February 28.
> (65 minutes/RCA Sound/video/DVD)
> Banner/Monogram

"Follow 'em for fun...and thrills aplenty while the Kids put a hoodoo on the hoodlums!"
Follow the Leader (1944) D: William Beaudine

Leo Gorcey, Huntz Hall, Gabriel Dell, [William] Billy Benedict, Joan Marsh, Jack LaRue, Mary Gordon, J. Farrell MacDonald, Dave [David] Durand, Bobby Stone, Jimmy Strand, Bud [Buddy] Gorman, Gene Austin,

The Sherrill Sisters (Doris, Grace), [Sunshine] Sammy Morrison, Bernard Gorcey, Bryant Washburn, Marie Windsor.

Muggs and Glimpy (Leo Gorcey, Hall) return from war service to discover one of their former cohorts is in jail charged with robbery. When murder follows, the East Side Kids get together and find the deadly thugs who framed their pal.

>Screenplay by William X. Crowley [William Beaudine] and Beryl Sachs, from the story "East Side of the Bowery" by Ande Lamb.
>Produced by Sam Katzman and Jack Dietz.
>Songs:
>"Now and Then" (Gene Austin)
>"All I Want to Do Is Play the Drums" (Sammy Stern)
>Music by Edward [J.] Kay.
>Released on June 3.
>(64 minutes/Glen Glenn Sound)
>Banner/Monogram

Block Busters (1944) D: Wallace Fox

Leo Gorcey, Huntz Hall, Gabriel Dell, [William] Billy Benedict, Fred Pressel, Jimmy Strand, Bill Chaney, Roberta Smith, Noah Beery Sr., Harry Langdon, Minerva Urecal, Jack Gilman, Kay Marvis, Tom Herbert, Bernard Gorcey, Charlie Murray Jr., Robert F. Hill, Jimmy Noone and His Orchestra, The Ashburns.

The East Side Kids regret taking a French boy onto their baseball team when he turns out to be a showoff. Muggs (Leo Gorcey) crashes a masquerade party with Hall.

>Screenplay by Houston Branch.
>Produced by Sam Katzman and Jack Dietz.
>Music by Edward J. Kay.
>Released on July 22.
>(60 minutes/Glen Glenn Sound)
>Banner/Monogram

"Wuxtra! Wuxtra! It's a case of moider and you're the victim! You'll die laffing as the sidewalk sockers blast the tenement terror!"
Bowery Champs (1944) D: William Beaudine

Leo Gorcey, Huntz Hall, Gabriel Dell, Bill [William 'Billy'] Benedict, Bobby Jordan, Jimmy Strand, Bud [Buddy] Gorman, Evelyn Brent, Ian Keith, Thelma White, Frank Jacquet, Anne Sterling, Wheeler Oakman, Fred Kelsey, Bill [William] Ruhl, Kenneth MacDonald, Betty Sinclair, Francis Ford, Eddie Cherkose, Joe Bautista, Bernard Gorcey, Jack Mulhall.

Muggs (Leo Gorcey) has a chance to rise from copy boy to reporter when he and the East Side Kids get involved with a murder case.

> Screenplay by Earle Snell, with additional dialogue by Morey Amsterdam.
> Produced by Sam Katzman and Jack Dietz.
> Song:
> "Hotcha Chornia Brown" (Sam H. Stept, Bud Green)
> Music by Edward [J.] Kay.
> Released on November 25.
> (62 minutes)
> Banner/Monogram

"Thrills...adventure...as exciting as the city in which they're located!"
Docks of New York (1945) D: Wallace Fox

Leo Gorcey, Huntz Hall, [William] Billy Benedict, Georgia Pope, Carlyle Blackwell Jr., Betty Blythe, Cy Kendall, George Meeker, Joy Reese, Pierre Watkin, Patsy Moran, Bud [Buddy] Gorman, Mende Koenig, Maurice St. Clair, Leo Borden, Betty Sinclair, Charles King.

Glimpy (Hall) finds a valuable necklace beside a dead body, plunging the East Side Kids (including Gorcey as Muggs) into dangerous intrigue involving murderous foreigners.

> Screenplay by Harvey Gates.
> Produced by Sam Katzman and Jack Dietz.
> Music by Edward J. Kay.
> Released on February 24.
> (61 minutes/DVD)
> Banner/Monogram

Mr. Muggs Rides Again (1945) D: **Wallace Fox**

Leo Gorcey, Huntz Hall, [William] Billy Benedict, Johnny Duncan, Bud [Buddy] Gorman, Mende Koenig, Minerva Urecal, Nancy Brinckman, Bernerd [Bernard] Thomas, George Meeker, John H. Allen, Pierre Watkin, Milton Kibbee, Frank Jacquet, Bernard Gorcey, I. Stanford Jolley, Michael Owen, Betty Sinclair, Forrest Taylor.

Muggs (Leo Gorcey) is banned from horseracing due to false testimony from gangsters, but he and the East Side Kids catch a break when one of the crooks reforms and implicates his former cronies.

Screenplay by Harvey Gates.
Produced by Sam Katzman and Jack Dietz.
Music by (uncredited Edward J. Kay).
Released on July 15.
(63 minutes/Glen Glenn Sound)
Banner/Monogram

"She hid the body they all wanted in a wax museum!"
Midnight Manhunt/One Exciting Night (1945) D: **William C. Thomas**

William Gargan, Ann Savage, Leo Gorcey, George Zucco, Paul Hurst, Don Beddoe, Charles Halton, George E. Stone, Robert Barron, Edgar Dearing, Pat Gleason, Paul Harvey, Ben Welden.

Mystery abounds when a figure in a wax museum turns out to be the dead body of a racketeer. Gorcey is Clutch Tracy.

Screenplay by David Lang.
Produced by William H. Pine, William C. Thomas, and Maxwell Shane.
Music by Alexander Laszlo.
Released on July 27.
(69 minutes/Western Electric Mirrophonic Recording/DVD)
Pine-Thomas/Paramount

"You won't know whether to kiss 'em...or kill 'em!"
Come Out Fighting (1945) D: William Beaudine

Leo Gorcey, Huntz Hall, [William] Billy Benedict, Gabriel Dell, June Carlson, Amelita Ward, Addison Richards, George Meeker, Johnny Duncan, Bud [Buddy] Gorman, Fred Kelsey, Douglas Wood, Milton Kibbee, Pat Gleason, Robert [E.] Homans, Mende Koenig, Patsy Moran.

The East Side Kids undertake to 'toughen up' a boy whose police commissioner father thinks is not manly enough. However, the Kids are caught in a gambling raid while trying to steer their young charge away from criminals. Muggs (Leo Gorcey) almost starts a fight at the commissioner's office.

> Screenplay by Earle Snell.
> Produced by Sam Katzman and Jack Dietz.
> Music by Edward [J.] Kay.
> Released on September 29.
> (62 minutes/Western Electric Mirrophonic Recording)
> Banner/Monogram

"They'll short-circuit your funny bone!"
Live Wires (1946) D: Phil Karlson

Leo Gorcey, Huntz Hall, Mike Mazurki, Bobby Jordan, [William] Billy Benedict, William Frambes, Claudia Drake, Pamela Blake, John Eldredge, Patti Brill, Bernard Gorcey, Billy [Bill] Christy, Nancy Brinckman, Robert E. [Emmett] Keane, Earle Hodgins, Gladys Blake, William Ruhl, George Eldredge, John Indrisano, Pat Gleason, Frank Marlowe, Rodney Bell, Charles Sullivan, Henry Russell, Steve Taylor, Beverly Hawthorne, Jack Chefe, Malcolm McClean.

Leo Gorcey begins playing Slip Mahoney in this initial entry of the *Bowery Boys* series. While working for the district attorney, Slip learns that his former employer is a wanted racketeer with plans to skip the country.

> Screenplay by Tim Ryan and Joseph Mischel, from a story by Jeb [Dore] Schary.

Produced by Lindsley Parsons and Jan Grippo.
Song:
"The Right Sort of Man" (composer unknown)
Music by Edward J. Kay.
Released on January 12.
(64 minutes/Western Electric Mirrophonic Recording/DVD)
Monogram

"Fast, furious and funny...those riotous rascals are on the loose again!"
In Fast Company (1946) D: Del Lord

Leo Gorcey, Huntz Hall, Jane Randolph, Judy Clark, Bobby Jordan, [William] Billy Benedict, Douglas Fowley, David Gorcey, Marjorie Woodworth, Charles D. Brown, Paul Harvey, Luis Alberni, Mary Gordon, Bernard Gorcey, George Eldredge, William Ruhl, Dick Wessel, John Indrisano, Frank Marlowe, Judy Schenz, Charles Coleman, Stanley Price, Marcel De la Brosse, Walter Soderling, Lee Phelps, Jack Cheatham, Fred Aldrich, Mike Donovan, Wheeler Oakman, Paul Picerni, Harry Strang.

Slip (Leo Gorcey) and the Bowery Boys become cab drivers for an injured independent who is being targeted by the ruthless manager of a major taxi company.

Screenplay by Edmond Seward, Tim Ryan, Victor Hammond, and Ray Schrock; from a story by Martin Mooney.
Produced by Lindsley Parsons and Jan Grippo.
Music by Edward [J.] Kay.
Released on June 22.
(61 minutes/DVD)
Monogram

"Hey, girls, he's dynamite! When Leo gets his love wires crossed, look out!"
Bowery Bombshell (1946) D: Phil Karlson

Leo Gorcey, Huntz Hall, Bobby Jordan, [William] Billy Benedict, David Gorcey, Teala Loring, Sheldon Leonard, Dawn [Daun] Kennedy, James Burke, Vince Barnett, [William] 'Wee Willie' Davis, William Ruhl, Emmett Vogan, Bernard Gorcey, Milton Parsons, Lester Dorr, William

Newell, Eddie Dunn, Buddy Gorman, Nancy Brinckman, Charles Sullivan.

A photograph taken during a bank robbery may implicate an innocent Hall (as Sach), so Leo Gorcey (as Slip) attempts to destroy the picture's negative before the police see it.

Screenplay by Edmond Seward, from a story by Victor Hammond; additional dialogue provided by Tim Ryan.
Produced by Lindsley Parsons and Jan Grippo.
Song:
"I Love Him" (Lou and Ruth Herscher)
Music by Edward [J.] Kay.
Released on July 20.
(65 minutes/Western Electric Mirrophonic Recording/DVD)
Monogram

"The fun's getting fearocious! Mad doctors! Haunted houses! Gorillas!"
Spook Busters (1946) D: William Beaudine

Leo Gorcey, Huntz Hall, Douglass Dumbrille, Bobby Jordan, Gabriel Dell, [William] Billy Benedict, David Gorcey, Tanis Chandler, Maurice Cass, Vera Lewis, Charles Middleton, Chester Clute, Richard Alexander, Bernard Gorcey, Charles Millsfield, Arthur [Art] Miles, Tom Coleman.

Sach (Hall) falls into the hands of a mad scientist when Slip (Gorcey) and the Bowery Boys are sent to 'exterminate' some ghosts in a haunted mansion.

Screenplay by Edmond Seward and Tim Ryan.
Produced by Jan Grippo.
Music by Edward J. Kay.
Released on August 24.
(68 minutes/Western Electric Mirrophonic Recording/video/DVD)
Monogram

"The kid's got hex-appeal...he's hypnotic and she's exotic! There's bedlam in the Bowery as Leo and his rough-house rascals get all hex-cited about a beautiful gal and a heckling hypnotist!"
Mr. Hex (1946) D: William Beaudine

Leo Gorcey, Huntz Hall, Bobby Jordan, Gabriel Dell, [William] Billy Benedict, David Gorcey, Gale Robbins, Ben Weldon [Welden], Ian Keith, Sammy Cohen, Bernard Gorcey, William Ruhl, Danny Beck, Rita Lynn, Joe Gray, Eddie Gribbon, Meyer Grace, Gene Stutenroth [Roth], John Indrisano, Jimmy Aubrey, Dewey Robinson, Knox Manning.

Slip (Leo Gorcey) discovers a way to hypnotize Sach (Hall) into becoming a formidable prizefighter. Trouble comes when crooked managers use their own hocus-pocus to strengthen their boxer on the eve of a high-stakes bout.

Screenplay by Cyril [Cy] Endfield, from a story by Jan Grippo (who also produced).
Louis Herscher song:
"A Love Song to Remember"
Music by Edward J. Kay.
Released on December 7.
(63 minutes/Western Electric Mirrophonic Recording/video/DVD)
Monogram

"They're tip-top snoopers in the tip-toe racket!"
Hard Boiled Mahoney (1947) D: William Beaudine

Leo Gorcey, Huntz Hall, Bobby Jordan, Gabriel Dell, Betty Compson, [William] Billy Benedict, David Gorcey, Teala Loring, Dan Seymour, Byron Foulger, Patti Brill, Pierre Watkin, Danny Beck, Bernard Gorcey, Carmen De Antonio [D'Antonio], Noble Johnson, Bill [William] Ruhl, Ted Pavelec, Pat O'Malley, Jack Cheatham, Bob Faust, 'Snub' Pollard.

The Bowery Boys enter their own world of *film noir* as Slip and Sach (Leo Gorcey, Hall) are mistaken for detectives, and they go on a search for a woman; their caper leads to a dangerous blackmailer.

Screenplay by Cyril [Cy] Endfield, with additional dialogue provided by Edmond Seward and Tim Ryan.

Produced by Jan Grippo.
Music by Edward J. Kay.
Released on May 10.
(63 minutes/Western Electric Sound/video/DVD)
Monogram

News Hounds (1947) D: William Beaudine

Leo Gorcey, Huntz Hall, Bobby Jordan, Gabriel Dell, [William] Billy Benedict, David Gorcey, Christine McIntyre, Tim Ryan, Anthony Caruso, Bill Kennedy, Ralph Dunn, Nita Bieber, John Hamilton, Terry Goodman, Robert Emmett Keane, Bernard Gorcey, Buddy Gorman, Russ Whiteman, Emmett Vogan Jr., John H. Elliott, Leo Kaye, Emmett Vogan [Sr.], Meyer Grace, Gene Roth.

Would-be reporter Slip (Leo Gorcey) and his photographer Sach (Hall) delve into the story of racketeers fixing sports events.

Screenplay by Edmond Seward and Tim Ryan, from a story by Seward, Ryan, and George Cappy.
Produced by Jan Grippo.
Music by Edward J. Kay.
Released on September 13.
(68 minutes/Western Electric Recording/DVD)
Monogram

Bowery Buckaroos (1947) D: William Beaudine

Leo Gorcey, Huntz Hall, Bobby Jordan, Gabriel Dell, [William] Billy Benedict, David Gorcey, Julie Gibson, Russell Simpson, Minerva Urecal, Jack Norman [Norman Willis], Iron Eyes Cody, Bernard Gorcey, Rosa Turich, Chief Yowlachi[e], Sherman Sanders, Billy Wilkerson, Jack O'Shea, Cathy Carter, Bud Osborne, 'Snub' Pollard, Sueanne Ridgeway.

Slip (Leo Gorcey) passes as a deadly gunfighter when the Bowery Boys head west to clear Louie Dumbrowski (Bernard Gorcey) of a murder charge.

Screenplay by Tim Ryan, Edmond Seward, and Jerry Warner.
Produced by Jan Grippo.

Songs:
"Louie the Lout" (Eddie Cherkose)
"Two Gun Tillie" (Edward J. Kay; Cherkose)
"Oh Susanna" (Stephen Foster)
"Trail to Mexico (Bury Me Not on the Lone Prairie)" (instrumental) (traditional, composer unknown)
"Beautiful Dreamer" (Foster)
"Camptown Races" (Foster)
"Little Brown Jug" (Joseph E. Winner)
"Listen to the Mockingbird" (Alice Hawthorne [Septimus Winner])
"She'll Be Comin' 'Round the Mountain When She Comes"
    (traditional, composer unknown)
Music by Edward J. Kay.
Released on November 22.
(66 minutes/Western Electric Recording/video/DVD)
Monogram

"The Bowery Boys make it rough on racketeers!"
***Angels' Alley* (1948) D: William Beaudine**

Leo Gorcey, Huntz Hall, Gabriel Dell, [William] Billy Benedict, David Gorcey, Frankie Darro, Nestor Paiva, Rosemary LaPlanche, Geneva Gray, Bennie [Benny] Bartlett, John Eldredge, Nelson Leigh, Tommy [Thomas] Menzies, Mary Gordon, Richard [Dick] Paxton, Buddy Gorman, Robert Emmett Keane, John H. Elliott, William Ruhl, Dewey Robinson, Wade Crosby, Meyer Grace.

    Slip (Leo Gorcey) and his mother welcome Cousin Jimmy (Darro) into the household. Jimmy is a recently released convict whose misfortunes may lead him to commit more crimes if Slip cannot turn him around.

Screenplay by Edmond Seward, Tim Ryan, and Gerald Schnitzer.
Produced by Jan Grippo.
Music by Edward [J.] Kay.
Released on March 7.
(67 minutes/Western Electric Recording/DVD)
Monogram

"All the excitement and heartbreak of big-town guys and gals on the Great White Way!"
So This Is New York (1948) D: Richard O. Fleischer

Henry Morgan, Rudy Vallee, Bill Goodwin, Hugh Herbert, Leo Gorcey, Virginia Grey, Dona Drake, Jerome Cowan, Dave Willock, Frank Orth, Arnold Stang, William Bakewell, Dick Elliott, Jimmy Hunt, Al Kikume, Wilbur Mack, Will Wright.

Morgan takes his family to the Big Apple in search of a future spouse for his sister-in-law. One candidate is Gorcey (as Sid Mercer), a jockey.

> Screenplay by Carl Foreman and Herbert Baker, from the novel *The Big Town* by Ring Lardner.
> Produced by Stanley Kramer.
> Music by Dimitri Tiomkin.
> Released in June.
> (79 minutes/Western Electric Recording/DVD)
> Screen Plays Incorporated/Enterprise/United Artists

"They're crammed with cash! And flooded with fun!"
Jinx Money (1948) D: William Beaudine

Leo Gorcey, Huntz Hall, Gabriel Dell, Sheldon Leonard, Donald MacBride, Betty Caldwell, [William] Billy Benedict, David Gorcey, John Eldredge, Ben Welden, Lucien Littlefield, Bernard Gorcey, Benny Bartlett, Benny Baker, Ralph Dunn, Wanda McKay, Tom Kennedy, William Ruhl, Stanley Andrews, George Eldredge, William Vedder, Mike Donovan, Gertrude Astor.

The Bowery Boys (including Leo Gorcey as Slip) get involved with a cache of money won by a gambler who soon turns up murdered. The Boys hide the cash and two more killings occur.

> Screenplay by Edmond Seward, Tim Ryan, and Gerald Schnitzer.
>   Adapted from a story by Jerome T. Gollard.
> Produced by Jan Grippo.
> Music by Edward [J.] Kay.
> Released on June 27.
> (68 minutes/Western Electric Recording/DVD)

Smugglers' Cove (1948) D: William Beaudine.

Leo Gorcey, Huntz Hall, Gabriel Dell, Martin Kosleck, Paul Harvey, Amelita Ward, [William] Billy Benedict, David Gorcey, Jacqueline Dalya, Bennie [Benny] Bartlett, Eddie Gribbon, Andre Pola [Hans Schumm], Gene Stutenroth [Roth], Emmett Vogan, Buddy Gorman, John Bleifer, William Ruhl, George Meader, Leonid Snegoff.

Slip (Leo Gorcey) thinks he has inherited a house. When he goes to look it over, he and the Bowery Boys discover it is the headquarters of smugglers.

> Screenplay by Edmond Seward and Tim Ryan, from the *Bluebook* magazine story by Talbert Josselyn.
> Produced by Jan Grippo.
> Music by Edward [J.] Kay.
> Released on October 10.
> (66 minutes/Western Electric Recording/DVD)
> Monogram

"It's moider! You'll almost die laughing...when these keyhole watchers tangle with a killer!"
Trouble Makers (1949) D: Reginald LeBorg

Leo Gorcey, Huntz Hall, Gabriel Dell, Frankie Darro, Lionel Stander, John Ridgely, Helen Parrish, Fritz Feld, [William] Billy Benedict, David Gorcey, Benny Bartlett, Cliff Clark, Charles La Torre, Bernard Gorcey, William Ruhl, David Hoffman, Buddy Gorman, John Indrisano, Maynard Holmes, Pat Moran, Charles Coleman, Tom Coleman, Ken Lundy, Herman Cantor.

Slip (Leo Gorcey) and Sach (Hall) become bellhops in a motel after they witness a murder and do what they can to close in on the killer.

> Screenplay by Edmond Seward, Tim Ryan, and Gerald Schnitzer; from a story by Schnitzer.
> Produced by Jan Grippo.
> Music by Edward [J.] Kay.
> Released on January 2.
> (69 minutes/Western Electric Recording/DVD)
> Monogram

Fighting Fools **(1949) D: Reginald LeBorg.**

Leo Gorcey, Huntz Hall, Gabriel Dell, Frankie Darro, Lyle Talbot, [William] Billy Benedict, David Gorcey, Benny Bartlett, Bert Conway, Evelynn [Evelyn] Eaton, Bernard Gorcey, Teddy Infuhr, Ben Welden, Dorothy Vaughan, Sam Hayes, Bill Cartledge, Paul Maxey, Stanley Andrews, Frank Moran, Anthony Warde, Ralph Peters, Tom Kennedy, Eddie Gribbon, Martin Mason, Robert Wolcott, Meyer Grace, Frank Hagney, Bert Hanlon, Buddy Gorman, Rolland Dupree, Johnny Duncan, Mike Donovan, Jack Mower, John Indrisano.

Sach (Hall) is dispatched to find a kidnapped boy, held by gangsters as a control over a prizefighter who is managed by Slip (Leo Gorcey). The crooks demand that the boxer take a dive during an important bout.

> Screenplay by Edmond Seward, Gerald Schnitzer, and Bert Lawrence.
> Produced by Jan Grippo.
> Music by Edward [J.] Kay.
> Released on March 17.
> (69 minutes/Western Electric Recording/DVD)
> Monogram

"Leo is a 'little mother' now! The whole gang is diaper-daffy…when the infant heir to millions turns up in their washing machine!"
Hold That Baby! **(1949) D: Reginald LeBorg**

Leo Gorcey, Huntz Hall, Gabriel Dell, Frankie Darro, Anabel Shaw, John Kellogg, Edward Gargan, [William] Billy Benedict, Bennie [Benny] Bartlett, David Gorcey, Ida Moore, Florence Auer, Bernard Gorcey, Pierre Watkin, Torben Meyer, Fred Nurney, Frances Irvin, Emmett Vogan, Meyer Grace, Max Marx, Jody and Judy Dunn, William Ruhl, Lin Mayberry, William J. O'Brien, Danny Beck, Cay Forester, Herbert Patterson, John O'Connor, Harold Noflin, Roy Aversa, Buddy Gorman, Robert Cherry, Angi O. Poulos, Robert Strauss.

Slip and Sach (Leo Gorcey, Hall) find an abandoned baby and trace it back to a desperate mother who is trying to keep her unscrupulous aunts from pilfering the infant's fortune.

Screenplay by Charles R. Marion and Gerald Schnitzer.
Produced by Jan Grippo.
Music by Edward [J.] Kay.
Released on July 26.
(64 minutes/Western Electric Recording/DVD)
Monogram

"It's their funniest fightin-est film!"
Angels in Disguise (1949) D: Jean Yarbrough

Leo Gorcey, Huntz Hall, Gabriel Dell, Mickey Knox, Jean Dean, [William] Billy Benedict, David Gorcey, Bennie [Benny] Bartlett, Bernard Gorcey, Richard Benedict, Joseph [Joe] Turkel, Pepe Hern, Edward Ryan, Ray Walker, Rory Mallinson, Marie Blake [Blossom Rock], William Forrest, Don [C.] Harvey, Herbert Patterson, Roy Gordon, Jane Adams, Jack Mower, Lee Phelps, John Abbott, Tom Monroe, Jack Gargan, Peter Virgo, Doretta Johnson, Wade Crosby.

Slip and Sach (Leo Gorcey, Hall) go up against the Loop Gang, a bunch of criminals who have killed a policeman.

Screenplay by Charles R. Marion and Gerald Schnitzer, with
   additional dialogue by Bert Lawrence.
Produced by Jan Grippo.
Music by Edward J. Kay.
Released on September 25.
(63 minutes/Western Electric Recording/DVD)
Monogram

"The chills will electrify you when the Bowery Boys meet the monster."
Master Minds (1949) D: Jean Yarbrough.

Leo Gorcey, Huntz Hall, Gabriel Dell, Alan Napier, Jane Adams, [William] Billy Benedict, Bernard Gorcey, Glenn Strange, Bennie [Benny] Bartlett, David Gorcey, Skelton Knaggs, William Yetter [Sr.], Minerva Urecal, Chester Clute, Pat Goldin, Robert Coogan, Kit Guard, Whitey Roberts, Harry Tyler, Anna Chandler, Stanley Blystone, Tim O'Connor, Kent Odell.

A toothache seemingly gives Sach (Hall) the power to foretell the future. Slip (Leo Gorcey) quickly puts him in a carnival show, where he becomes a sensation. Unfortunately, Sach also becomes the target of a mad doctor hatching plans to transplant his brain into a werewolf-like monster named Atlas.

>Story and screenplay by Charles R. Marion, with additional dialogue by Bert Lawrence.
>Produced by Jan Grippo.
>Music by Edward J. Kay.
>Released on November 27.
>(64 minutes/Western Electric Recording/DVD)
>Monogram

"The escort bureau's goofiest gigolos! They're professional Romeos…to a gang of glamorous gun-girls!"
Blonde Dynamite (1950) D: William Beaudine

Leo Gorcey, Huntz Hall, Adele Jergens, Gabriel Dell, Harry Lewis, Murray Alper, Bernard Gorcey, Jody Gilbert, William ['Billy'] Benedict, Buddy Gorman, David Gorcey, John Harmon, Michael Ross, Lynn Davies [Davis], Beverlee [Beverly] Crane, Karin Randle, Stanley Andrews, Florence Auer, Constance Purdy, Dick Elliott, Tom Kennedy, Robert Emmett Keane.

The Bowery Boys have the run of the sweet shop when Louie Dumbrowski (Bernard Gorcey) goes on vacation. Slip (Leo Gorcey) and the gang turn it into an escort service and end up becoming patsies for bank-robbing gangsters—who distract the boys with a group of women.

>Screenplay by Charles [R.] Marion.
>Produced by Jan Grippo.
>Songs:
>"Overture" to *The Marriage of Figaro* (K. 492) (instrumental)
>   (Wolfgang
>Amadeus Mozart)
>"So You're the One" (Hy Zaret, Joan Whitney, Alex Kramer)
>Music by Edward J. Kay.
>Released on February 12.

(66 minutes/Western Electric Recording/DVD)
Monogram

"They're cheating the cheaters…but they don't know the dice…and the guns…are loaded!"
Lucky Losers (1950) D: William Beaudine

Leo Gorcey, Huntz Hall, Hillary Brooke, Gabriel Dell, Lyle Talbot, Bernard Gorcey, William ['Billy'] Benedict, Joseph [Joe] Turkel, Harry Tyler, Buddy Gorman, David Gorcey, Harry Cheshire, Frank Jenks, Douglas Evans, Wendy Waldron, Glen Vernon, Chester Clute, Selmer Jackson, Dick Elliott, Franklyn Farnum, Frank Hagney, Zon Murray, Mike Ragan.

The Bowery Boys (including Leo Gorcey as Slip) go from Wall Street brokers to gambling house croupiers as a brokerage owner's suspicious death leads them to syndicate members using a casino as a front.

>Screenplay by Charles R. Marion, with additional dialogue by Bert Lawrence.
>Produced by Jan Grippo.
>Music by Edward J. Kay.
>Released on May 14.
>(69 minutes/Western Electric Recording/DVD)
>Monogram

"If they had the wings of an angel over those prison walls they would fly! The big house becomes a fun house…when looney Leo and half-wit Huntz tangle with killer 'cons'…to prove they're as innocent as babes!"
Triple Trouble (1950) D: Jean Yarbrough

Leo Gorcey, Huntz Hall, Gabriel Dell, Richard Benedict, [G.] Pat Collins, Lyn Thomas, Bernard Gorcey, Paul Dubov, Joseph [Joe] Turkel, William ['Billy'] Benedict, Buddy Gorman, David Gorcey, George Chandler, Eddie Gribbon, Jonathan Hole, Joseph Crehan, Effie Laird, Edward Gargan, Eddie Foster, Frank Marlowe, Tom Kennedy, Lyle Talbot, Stanley Blystone, Paul Bryar, William Haade, William Ruhl.

When Slip and Sach (Leo Gorcey, Hall) try to stop a warehouse robbery, they are accused of taking part in it. The boys accept a jail term so they can follow a link between a con doing time and his shortwave messages to the gang guilty of the crime.

> Screenplay by Charles R. Marion, with additional dialogue by Bert Lawrence.
> Produced by Jan Grippo.
> Music by Edward J. Kay.
> Released on August 13.
> (66 minutes/Western Electric Recording/DVD)
> Monogram

"The most riotous night club kings you'll ever see!"
Blues Busters (1950) D: William Beaudine

Leo Gorcey, Huntz Hall, Adele Jergens, Gabriel Dell, Craig Stevens, Phyllis Coates, Bernard Gorcey, William ['Billy'] Benedict, Buddy Gorman, David Gorcey, Paul Bryar, Matty King, William [Sailor] Vincent, Franklyn Farnum, Bess Flowers, Frank Hagney, Hank Mann, Sam McDaniel.

Slip (Leo Gorcey) becomes a tuxedo-wearing master of ceremonies when Louie's sweet shop is converted into a nightspot featuring singing sensation Sach (Hall)—who acquires a suave singing voice after a tonsillectomy. The Bowery Boys think they have a moneymaking proposition until a rival nightclub owner schemes to put Sach under personal contract. Hall's singing voice is dubbed by John Laurenz.

> Story and screenplay by Charles R. Marion, with additional dialogue by Bert Lawrence.
> Produced by Jan Grippo.
> Songs:
> "Wasn't It You?" (Ben Raleigh, Bernie Wayne)
> "Bluebirds Keep Singing in the Rain" (Johnny Lange, Elliott Daniel)
> "Let's Have a Heart to Heart Talk" (Billy Austin, Edward Brandt, Paul Landers)
> "You Walk By" (Raleigh, Wayne)
> "Better Be Looking Out for Love" (Ralph Wolf, Johnny Lange)
> "Joshua Fit de Battle of Jericho" (traditional, composer unknown)
> "Dixie's Land" (Daniel Decatur Emmett)
> "Swanee River" (instrumental) (Stephen Collins Foster)

Music by Edward J. Kay.
Released on October 29.
(67 minutes/Western Electric Recording/DVD)
Monogram

"They're the daffiest draftees in history!"
Bowery Battalion (1951) D: William Beaudine

Leo Gorcey, Huntz Hall, Donald MacBride, Virginia Hewitt, Russell Hicks, Bernard Gorcey, William ['Billy'] Benedict, Buddy Gorman, David Gorcey, John Bleifer, Al Eben, Frank Jenks, Selmer Jackson, Michael Ross, Emil Sitka, Harry Lauter, George Offerman Jr., William Ruhl.

Slip (Leo Gorcey) and the Bowery Boys are army privates who are assigned to protect Louie Dumbrowski (Bernard Gorcey) during a mission to net foreign spies.

Screenplay by Charles R. Marion, with additional dialogue by Bert Lawrence.
Produced by Jan Grippo.
Music by Edward J. Kay.
Released on January 24.
(69 minutes/Western Electric Recording/DVD)
Monogram

"They've got ants in their trance at a séance!"
Ghost Chasers (1951) D: William Beaudine

Leo Gorcey, Huntz Hall, Lloyd Corrigan, Lela Bliss, Philip Van Zandt, Bernard Gorcey, [William] Billy Benedict, Robert Coogan, Buddy Gorman, David Gorcey, Jan Kayne, Argentina Brunetti, Marshall Bradford, Michael Ross, Donald Lawton, Hal Gerard, Doris Kemper, Belle Mitchell, Paul Bryar, Pat Gleason, Bob Peoples, Bess Flowers, Maudie Prickett.

Slip (Leo Gorcey) and the Bowery Boys attempt to expose phony spiritualists, resulting in a ghost (Corrigan) helping Sach (Hall) when trouble looms.

Screenplay by Charles R. Marion, with additional dialogue by Bert Lawrence.
Produced by Jan Grippo.
Music by Edward J. Kay.
Released on April 29.
(69 minutes/video/DVD)
Monogram

"The fleet's all fouled up…because of their sea-going shenanigans and hilarious hi-jinks!"
Let's Go Navy! (1951) D: William Beaudine.

Leo Gorcey, Huntz Hall, Allen Jenkins, Tom Neal, Charlita, Richard Benedict, Paul Harvey, Jonathan Hale, William ['Billy'] Benedict, Bernard Gorcey, Buddy Gorman, David Gorcey, Emory Parnell, Douglas Evans, Frank Jenks, Dave Willock, Ray Walker, Tom Kennedy, Murray Alper, Dorothy Ford, Harry Lauter, Peter Mamakos, Paul Bryar, Richard Monahan, Billy Lechner, George Offerman Jr., Mike Lally, Russ Conway, Harry Strang, Sailor Vincent, Lee Graham, Pat Gleason, George Eldredge, William Hudson, Bob Peoples, John Close, Emil Sitka, Ray Dawe, Jimmy Cross, Bill Chandler, Don Gordon, Neyle Morrow, Joey Ray.

When two sailors steal a charity fund, Slip (Leo Gorcey) and the Bowery Boys join the Navy to find the thieves.

Screenplay by Max Adams, with additional dialogue by Bert Lawrence.
Produced by Jan Grippo.
Music by Edward J. Kay.
Released on July 29.
(68 minutes/Western Electric Recording/DVD)
Monogram

"It's hee-hawlarious! Nutty nags take to their heels when the boys start horsin' around!"
Crazy Over Horses (1951) D: William Beaudine

Leo Gorcey, Huntz Hall, Ted de Corsia, Allen Jenkins, Gloria Saunders, Tim Ryan, William ['Billy'] Benedict, Bernard Gorcey, David Condon

[Gorcey], Bennie [Benny] Bartlett, Mike [Michael] Ross, Russell Hicks, Peggy Wynne, Sam Balter, Leo 'Ukie' Sherin, Bob Peoples, Ray Page, Darr Smith, Smoki Whitfield, Perc Launders, Wilbur Mack, Gertrude Astor, Bill Cartledge, Whitey Hughes, Delmar Thomas, Bernard Pludow, Ben Frommer.

The Bowery Boys end up owning a stake in a racehorse which Slip (Leo Gorcey) thinks is a thoroughbred, but crooked gamblers want the animal for their own scheme.

>Screenplay by Tim Ryan.
>Produced by Jerry Thomas.
>Portions filmed at Hollywood Racetrack, Inglewood, California.
>Song:
>"William Tell Overture" (instrumental) (Gioachino Rossini)
>Music by Edward J. Kay.
>Released on November 18.
>(65 minutes/Western Electric Recording/DVD)
>Monogram

"They're a razzle-dazzle riot as collegiate cut-ups!"
Hold That Line (1952) D: William Beaudine

Leo Gorcey, Huntz Hall, John Bromfield, Veda Ann Borg, Mona Knox, Gloria Winters, Taylor Holmes, Bernard Gorcey, Gil Stratton Jr., David Condon [Gorcey], David [Benny] Bartlett, Francis Pierlot, Pierre Watkin, Bob [Robert] Nichols, Paul Bryar, Percival Vivian, Tom Kennedy, Bert Davidson, Marjorie Eaton, Jean Dean, Steve Wayne, Ted Jordan, George Sanders, Marvelle Andre, Franklyn Farnum.

Sach (Hall) develops a vitamin in a college chemistry class that gives him an athletic edge on the football field. Unfortunately, before the big game he is kidnapped. Slip (Leo Gorcey) puts on a helmet and takes the field to help the team.

>Screenplay by Tim Ryan and Charles R. Marion, with additional dialogue by Bert Lawrence.
>Produced by Jerry Thomas. Portions filmed at Los Angeles City College, California.
>Music by Edward J. Kay.

Released on March 23.
(64 minutes/DVD)
Monogram

"They're loaded for laughs...with bombs and blondes!"
Here Come the Marines (1952) D: William Beaudine

Leo Gorcey, Huntz Hall, Hanley Stafford, Myrna Dell, Murray Alper, Arthur Space, Tim Ryan, Bernard Gorcey, Gil Stratton Jr., David Condon [Gorcey], Bennie [Benny] Bartlett, Paul Maxey, William Newell, Lisa Wilson, Riley Hill, James Flavin, Robert Coogan, Leo 'Ukie' Sherin, Bob Peoples, Sammy Finn, Buck Russell, Stanley Blystone, Wayne Mallory, Perc Launders, Alan Jeffrey, Bob Cudlip, Sailor Vincent, Jack Wilson, Dick Paxton, Court Shepard, William Bailey, Paul Bradley.

The Bowery Boys follow Slip (Leo Gorcey) into the military, but it is not long before they find a murdered soldier and a playing card clue that leads them to a suspect gambling house.

Screenplay by Tim Ryan, Charles R. Marion, and Jack Crutcher.
Produced by Jerry Thomas.
Music by Edward J. Kay.
Released on June 29.
(66 minutes/DVD)
Monogram

Feuding Fools (1952) D: William Beaudine.

Leo Gorcey, Huntz Hall, Dorothy Ford, Lyle Talbot, Benny Baker, Anne Kimbell, Oliver Blake, Bernard Gorcey, David Condon [Gorcey], Bennie [Benny] Bartlett, Fuzzy Knight, Robert Easton, O.Z. Whitehead, Paul Wexler, Russell Simpson, Leo 'Ukie' Sherin, Arthur Space, Bob [Robert] Bray, Bob [Robert] Keyes, Stanley Blystone, Elizabeth Russell.

Sach (Hall) inherits a farm in Kentucky, which is smack-dab in the middle of a shooting feud between the Smiths and Jones clans. Slip (Leo Gorcey) raises the ire of the Smiths when he talks about his expertise in money matters.

Screenplay by Bert Lawrence and Tim Ryan.
Produced by Jerry Thomas.
Music by Edward J. Kay.
Released on September 21.
(63 minutes/Western Electric Sound/DVD)
Monogram

No Holds Barred **(1952) D: William Beaudine**

Leo Gorcey, Huntz Hall, Marjorie Reynolds, Bernard Gorcey, Leonard Penn, Henry Kulky, Hombre Montana, David Condon [Gorcey], Bennie [Benny] Bartlett, Sandra Gould, Tim Ryan, Lisa Wilson, Murray Alper, Barbara Grey, Leo 'Ukie' Sherin, Ray Walker, Nick Stewart, Mike Ruby, John Indrisano, 'Brother' Frank Jares, Ted Christy, John Smith, Pat Fraley, Bob Cudlip, Mort Mills, William Page, John Eldredge, Meyer Grace, Johnny Cross, Beverly Michaels.

The Bowery Boys grapple with the wrestling world when Sach (Hall) discovers he has the ability to take down any opponent. Slip (Leo Gorcey) finds himself taking a beating each time Sach demonstrates a new wrestling technique he has acquired.

Screenplay by Tim Ryan, Jack Crutcher, and Bert Lawrence.
Produced by Jerry Thomas.
Music by Edward J. Kay.
Released on November 23.
(65 minutes/DVD)
Monogram

"You'll blow your gasket howling at these dizzy whizzes of the racing world!"
Jalopy **(1953) D: William Beaudine**

Leo Gorcey, Huntz Hall, Bernard Gorcey, Bob Lowry [Robert Lowery], Leon Belasco, Richard Benedict, Jane Easton, Murray Alper, David Condon [Gorcey], Bennie [Benny] Bartlett, Tom Hanlon, Mona Knox, Conrad Brooks, Bob Rose, George Dockstader, George Barrows, Fred Lamont, Teddy Mangean, Bud Wolfe, Carey Loftin, Louis Tomei, Dude Criswell, Dick Crockett, Pete Kellett, Carl Saxe.

The Bowery Boys get into the auto racing game. After Slip loses the first race, Sach (Hall) develops a fuel formula, which speeds up a car's performance. Slip (Leo Gorcey) has to drive a car backwards in order to win a race.

> Screenplay by Tim Ryan, Jack Crutcher, and Edmond Seward Jr., from a story by Ryan and Crutcher; additional dialogue provided by Bert Lawrence.
> Produced by Ben Schwalb.
> Portions filmed at Culver City Speedway, California.
> Song:
> "(Hail, Hail) The Gang's All Here" (instrumental) (Theodore F. Morse, Theodora
> Morse, Dolly Morse)
> Music by (uncredited Marlin Skiles).
> Released on February 15.
> (62 minutes/Western Electric Recording/DVD)
> Allied Artists

"They're panics in Piccadilly! Making merrie with the shapeliest plum in the royal pudding!"
Loose in London (1953) D: Edward Bernds

Leo Gorcey, Huntz Hall, Bernard Gorcey, Angela Greene, Walter Kingsford, Norma Varden, John Dodsworth, William Cottrell, David Gorcey, Benny Bartlett, Rex Evans, James Logan, Alex Fraser, Charles Keane, Clyde Cook, Joan Shawlee, James Fairfax, Wilbur Mack, Teddy Mangean, Gertrude Astor, Matthew Boulton, Charles Wagenheim, Bess Flowers.

The Bowery Boys go across the pond to Merry Olde England when Sach (Hall) learns he is the heir to a dying earl. After they arrive, the boys discover the earl is a victim of his relatives' scheme to do away with him. Slip (Leo Gorcey) accidentally tears a girl's skirt at an art auction.

> Screenplay by Elwood Ullman and Edward Bernds.
> Produced by Ben Schwalb.
> Music by (uncredited Marlin Skiles).
> Released on May 24.

(63 minutes/DVD)
Allied Artists

"A jet-propelled joyride of laughs, WAFs, and daffy thrills!"
Clipped Wings **(1953) D: Edward Bernds**

Leo Gorcey, Huntz Hall, Bernard Gorcey, Renie Riano, Todd Karns, June Vincent, Fay Roope, Mary Treen, Anne Kimbell, David Condon [Gorcey], Bennie [Benny] Bartlett, Elaine Riley, Lou Nova, Philip Van Zandt, Lyle Talbot, Ray Walker, Frank Richards, Michael Ross, Jean Dean, Henry Kulky, Arthur Space, Conrad Brooks, Tristram Coffin, Tommy Cook, William Tannen.

Slip and Sach (Leo Gorcey, Hall) mistakenly join the Air Force, but manage to round up enemy agents while helping a friend.

> Screenplay by Charles R. Marion and Elwood Ullman, from a story by Marion.
> Produced by Ben Schwalb.
> Music by (uncredited Marlin Skiles).
> Released on August 14.
> (65 minutes/video/DVD)
> Allied Artists

"You'll yock and yowl…as those half-wit hawkshaws go on the prowl for a missing blonde minx in a mink!"
Private Eyes **(1953) D: Edward Bernds**

Leo Gorcey, Huntz Hall, Bernard Gorcey, Robert Osterloh, Joyce Holden, William ['Bill'] Phillips, Rudy Lee, William Forrest, Chick Chandler, David Condon [Gorcey], Bennie [Benny] Bartlett, Lou Lubin, Tim Ryan, Peter Mamakos, Edith Leslie, Myron Healey, Emil Sitka, Gil Perkins.

A belt in the nose turns Sach (Hall) into a mind reader, a skill he uses to aid him and Slip (Leo Gorcey) in setting up a detective agency. They quickly get a client who is blonde, beautiful, and neck-deep in underworld intrigue.

> Screenplay by Elwood Ullman and Edward Bernds.
> Produced by Ben Schwalb.
> Music by (uncredited Marlin Skiles).

Released on December 6.
(64 minutes/DVD)
Allied Artists

"A zany laff spree in gay Paree!"
Paris Playboys (1954) D: William Beaudine

Leo Gorcey, Huntz Hall, Bernard Gorcey, Veola Vonn, Steven Geray, John E. Wengraf, Marianna [Mari] Lynn, David Condon [Gorcey], Bennie [Benny] Bartlett, Gordon B. Clark, Alphonse Martell, Fritz Feld, Jack Chefe, Bess Flowers, Robin Hughes, Charles La Torre, Roy Gordon, Cosmo Sardo.

Hall plays a dual role as Sach is mistaken for a lookalike French scientist who disappeared while working on rocket formula. The Bowery Boys discover that spies are eager to get their hands on the valuable papers. Slip (Leo Gorcey) consumes a Gallic cocktail that makes his bowtie spin.

Screenplay by Elwood Ullman and Edward Bernds.
Produced by Ben Schwalb.
Music by (uncredited Marlin Skiles and Arthur Morton).
Released on March 7.
(62 minutes/DVD)
Allied Artists

"The scariest, screwiest laugh riot since Frankenstein gave up the ghost!"
The Bowery Boys Meet the Monsters (1954) D: Edward Bernds

Leo Gorcey, Huntz Hall, Bernard Gorcey, Lloyd Corrigan, Ellen Corby, John Dehner, Laura Mason, Paul Wexler, David Condon [Gorcey], Bennie [Benny] Bartlett, Norman Bishop, Steve Calvert, Rudy Lee, Paul Bryar.

Slip and Sach (Leo Gorcey, Hall) become fodder for experiments conducted by a family of mad scientists whose household includes a gorilla, a robot, a cleaver-wielding butler, and a lady vampire.

Screenplay by Elwood Ullman and Edward Bernds.
Produced by Ben Schwalb.
Music by (uncredited Marlin Skiles).

Released on June 6.
(65 minutes/DVD)
Allied Artists

"You'll go wild with laffs! As the boys go native and cut-up monkeyshines on a wacky safari!"
Jungle Gents (1954) D: Edward Bernds

Leo Gorcey, Huntz Hall, Bernard Gorcey, Laurette Luez, Patrick O'Moore, Rudolph Anders, Harry Cording, David Condon [Gorcey], Bennie [Benny] Bartlett, Eric Snowden, Woody Strode, Joel Fluellen, Murray Alper, Emory Parnell, Jett Norman [Clint Walker], Emil Sitka, Roy Glenn, John Harmon, Pat Flaherty.

The Bowery Boys take an expedition to Africa, where Sach (Hall) demonstrates he can use his sense of smell (heightened by some sinus medication) to detect valuable diamonds. Slip (Leo Gorcey) and the gang also expose a 'spirit' fakir who is scaring the superstitious natives.

Screenplay by Elwood Ullman and Edward Bernds.
Produced by Ben Schwalb.
Music by (uncredited Marlin Skiles).
Released on September 5.
(64 minutes/Western Electric Recording/DVD)
Allied Artists

"The Bowery Boys run riot as harem hot-shots with Babylonian babes in the land of enchantment and dancing girls!"
Bowery to Bagdad (1955) D: Edward Bernds

Leo Gorcey, Huntz Hall, Bernard Gorcey, Joan Shawlee, Eric Blore, Jean Willes, Robert Bice, Richard [Dick] Wessel, Michael Ross, Rayford Barnes, Rick Vallin, Paul Marion, David Condon [Gorcey], Bennie [Benny] Bartlett, Charles Lung, Leon Burbank.

Slip and Sach (Leo Gorcey, Hall) receive a bevy of wishes when Sach buys an ancient lamp and releases a genie. The boys' mystical windfall comes in handy as crooks set out to steal the magic curio.

Story and screenplay by Elwood Ullman and Edward Bernds.
Produced by Ben Schwalb.
Music by (uncredited Marlin Skiles).
Released on January 2.
(64 minutes/Western Electric Recording/DVD)
Allied Artists

"What a ball! What a brawl! Those half-baked lowbrows crash the upper crust!"
High Society (1955) D: William Beaudine

Leo Gorcey, Huntz Hall, Bernard Gorcey, Amanda Blake, David Condon [Gorcey], Addison Richards, Paul Harvey, Dayton Lummis, Ronald Keith, Gavin Gordon, Dave Barry, Bennie [Benny] Bartlett, Kem Dibbs, James Conaty.

Slip and Sach (Leo Gorcey, Hall) side with a young heir who is threatened with the loss of his wealthy inheritance due to the machinations of his scheming relatives.

> Screenplay by Bert Lawrence and Jerome S. Gottler, from a story by Elwood Ullman and Edward Bernds.
> Produced by Ben Schwalb.
> Academy Award Nomination*:
> (Writing—Motion Picture Story) Edward Bernds, Elwood Ullman.
> *Withdrawn from the final Academy Award ballot due to assumed confusion with the 1956 film *High Society*, which starred Bing Crosby, Grace Kelly, and Frank Sinatra.
> Music by (uncredited Marlin Skiles and Arthur Morton).
> Released on April 17.
> (61 minutes/DVD)
> Allied Artists

"The Iron Curtain is cracked with laughter!"
Spy Chasers (1955) D: Edward Bernds

Leo Gorcey, Huntz Hall, Bernard Gorcey, Leon Askin, Sig Ruman, Veola Vonn, Lisa Davis, David Condon [Gorcey], Bennie [Benny] Bartlett,

Richard Benedict, Frank Richards, Linda Bennett, Paul Burke, Mel Welles, John Bleifer.

The Bowery Boys aid an exiled king and his daughter from being usurped by traitors. Slip (Leo Gorcey) forms his gang into a 'royal army' and puts them through a military drill.

> Story and screenplay by Bert Lawrence and Jerome S. Gottler.
> Produced by Ben Schwalb.
> Music by Marlin Skiles.
> Released on July 31.
> (66 minutes/DVD)
> Allied Artists

"It's real crazy, stir-crazy fun!"
Jail Busters (1955) D: William Beaudine

Leo Gorcey, Huntz Hall, Bernard Gorcey, Barton MacLane, Anthony Caruso, Percy Helton, David Condon [Gorcey], Bennie [Benny] Bartlett, Lyle Talbot, Michael Ross, John Harmon, Murray Alper, Fritz Feld, Henry Kulky, Emil Sitka, Harry Tyler, Ray Walker.

Slip and Sach (Leo Gorcey, Hall) help their reporter friend Chuck (David Gorcey) expose prison corruption by having themselves jailed on a phony robbery charge.

> Screenplay by Edward Bernds and Elwood Ullman.
> Produced by Ben Schwalb.
> Music by Marlin Skiles.
> Released on September 18.
> (61 minutes/Western Electric Recording/DVD)
> Allied Artists

"They're on the trail of those crazy hot rocks!"
Dig That Uranium (1955) D: Edward Bernds

Leo Gorcey, Huntz Hall, Bernard Gorcey, Mary Beth Hughes, Raymond Hatton, Harry Lauter, Myron Healey, Richard Powers [Tom Keene], Paul Fierro, David Condon [Gorcey], Bennie [Benny] Bartlett, Francis

McDonald, Frank Jenks, Don C. Harvey, Carl 'Alfalfa' Switzer.

Some nasty varmints set their sights on the uranium mine that the Bowery Boys have purchased. Slip (Leo Gorcey) becomes a tough western hombre in Sach's dream sequence.

>Screenplay by Elwood Ullman and Bert Lawrence.
>Produced by Ben Schwalb.
>Music by Marlin Skiles.
>Released on December 25.
>(61 minutes/Western Electric Recording/DVD)
>Allied Artists

"The jokers were never wilder! They're breaking the laff bank!"
Crashing Las Vegas (1956) D: Jean Yarbrough

Leo Gorcey, Huntz Hall, Mary Castle, Don Haggerty, David Condon [Gorcey], Terry Frost, Jimmy Murphy, Mort Mills, Jack Rice, Nicky Blair, Doris Kemper, Bob Hopkins, John Bleifer, Emil Sitka, Dick Foote, Don Marlowe, Jack Grinnage, Minerva Urecal, Frank J. Scannell, Joey Ray, Jack Chefe, Frank Hagney, Speer Martin, Jim Brandt, Cosmo Sardo, Alfred Tonkel.

Sach (Hall) suffers an electric shock and becomes a whiz at predicting numbers, so the Bowery Boys are off to Las Vegas to win big. A batch of crooks are also along, and they gain influence over Sach when they convince him he killed a man. Slip (Leo Gorcey) and the gang work to prove to their pal that his 'crime' is a hoax.

>Story and screenplay by Jack Townley.
>Produced by Ben Schwalb.
>Portions filmed on location.
>Music by Marlin Skiles.
>Released on April 22.
>(62 minutes/Western Electric Recording/DVD)
>Allied Artists

"Everybody who's ever been funny is in it!"
It's a Mad, Mad, Mad, Mad World (1963) D: Stanley Kramer

Spencer Tracy, Milton Berle, Sid Caesar, Buddy Hackett, Ethel Merman, Mickey Rooney, Dick Shawn, Phil Silvers, Terry-Thomas, Jonathan Winters, Edie Adams, Dorothy Provine, Eddie 'Rochester' Anderson, Jim Backus, Ben Blue, Joe E. Brown, Alan Carney, Chick Chandler, Barrie Chase, Lloyd Corrigan, William Demarest, Andy Devine, Selma Diamond (voice), Peter Falk, Norman Fell, Paul Ford, Stan Freberg, Louise Glenn (voice), Leo Gorcey, Sterling Holloway, Marvin Kaplan, Edward Everett Horton, Buster Keaton, Don Knotts, Charles Lane, Mike Mazurki, Charles McGraw, Cliff Norton, ZaSu Pitts, Carl Reiner, Madlyn Rhue, Roy Roberts, Arnold Stang, Nick Stewart, The Three Stooges, Sammee Tong, Jesse White, Jimmy Durante, Morey Amsterdam, Jack Benny, Paul Birch, Noble 'Kid' Chissell, Stanley Clements, King Donovan, Minta Durfee, Roy Engel, James Flavin, Stacy Harris, Don C. Harvey, Allen Jenkins, Robert Karnes, Tom Kennedy, Harry Lauter, Jerry Lewis, Tyler McVey (voice), Barbara Pepper, Elliott Reid (voice), Eddie Ryder, Paul Sorensen, Doodles Weaver, Lennie Weinrib (voice).

Slapstick comedy about a group of strangers who learn about $350,000 in hidden loot from a dying gangster and set off on a madcap cross-country race to find it. Gorcey is seen as the first cab driver, who drops Caesar and Adams off at a department store.

Story and screenplay by William and Tania Rose.
Produced by Stanley Kramer.
Portions filmed at numerous locations in California and in Miami Shores, Florida.
Songs:
"It's a Mad, Mad, Mad, Mad World" (Ernest Gold, Mack David) (Academy
Award Nominee) (Winner of a Golden Laurel Award)
"You Satisfy My Soul" (Gold, David)
"Thirty-One Flavors" (Gold, David)
Academy Award:
(Effects—Sound Effects) Walter Elliott
Additional Academy Award Nominations:
(Cinematography—Color) Ernest S. Laszlo
(Sound) Gordon Sawyer

(Film Editing) Frederic Knudtson, Robert C. Jones, Gene Fowler Jr.
(Music—Score) Ernest Gold
Golden Globe Nominations:
(Motion Picture—Musical/Comedy) Stanley Kramer
(Motion Picture Actor—Musical/Comedy) Jonathan Winters
American Cinema Editors Award Nomination ('Eddie'):
(Edited Feature Film) Frederic Knudtson, Robert C. Jones, Gene Fowler Jr.
Edgar Allan Poe Award Nomination:
(Motion Picture) William and Tania Rose
Additional Golden Laurel Award:
(Top Roadshow) Stanley Kramer
New York Film Critics Circle Award Nomination:
(Best Film) Stanley Kramer (3rd place, tied with *The Birds* and *To Kill a Mockingbird*)
Released on November 7.
(154 minutes [TV print], 175 minutes [video]/Westrex Recording/Technicolor/Ultra Panavision 70/Super-Cinerama/Rated [G]/AFI America's Greatest Movies Nominee/AFI Laughs 40/video/laserdisc/DVD)
Casey Productions/United Artists

Second Fiddle to a Steel Guitar (1966) D: Victor Duncan

Pamela Hayes, Leo Gorcey, Huntz Hall, Arnold Stang, Homer and Jethro, Kitty Wells, Webb Pierce, Faron Young, Minnie Pearl, Lefty Frizzell, Sonny James, Bill Monroe, George Hamilton IV, Del Reeves, Carl Butler, Pearl Butler, Merle Kilgore, Little Jimmy Dickens, Johnnie Wright, Dottie West, Billy Walker, Connie Smith, Old Joe Clark, Delores Smiley, Marilyn Gallo, Pete Drake, Bill Phillips, Buddy Spicher, Murv Shiner, Curly Fox, Clyde Smith, Lamar Morris, Dave Lewis, Bob Perry.

Musical comedy about a benefit performance, which has to switch from opera to country music. Gorcey plays Leo, a stagehand (along with his old Bowery Boy pal Hall).

Screenplay by Seymour D. Rothman.
No producer credited.
Music by Audrey Williams.

Released on December 29.
(107 minutes/Eastmancolor)
Marathon

"Of all the American heroes who served their country in its hour of need—only one had a great rock sound..."
The Phynx (1970) D: Lee H. Katzin

A. Michael Miller, Ray Chippeway, Dennis Larden, Lonnie [Lonny] Stevens, Lou Antonio, Mike Kellin, Michael Ansara, George Tobias, Joan Blondell, Martha Raye, Larry Hankin, Ted Eccles, Ultra Violet, Pat McCormick, Joseph Gazal, Robert Williams, Barbara Noonan, Rich Little, Sue Bernard, Ann Morell, Shirley Miles, Patty Andrews, Busby Berkeley, Xavier Cugat, Fritz Feld, John Hart, Ruby Keeler, Joe Louis, Marilyn Maxwell, Maureen O'Sullivan, Harold Sakata, Ed Sullivan, Rona Barrett, James Brown, Cass Daley, Leo Gorcey, Louis Hayward, Patsy Kelly, Guy Lombardo, Butterfly McQueen, Richard Pryor, Colonel Harland Sanders, Rudy Vallee, Johnny Weissmuller, Edgar Bergen, Dick Clark, Andy Devine, Huntz Hall, George Jessel, Dorothy Lamour, Trini Lopez, Pat O'Brien, Jay Silverheels, Clint Walker, Sally Struthers, I. Stanford Jolley, Jack Bannon.

A plethora of popular American celebrities (including Gorcey playing himself) have been kidnapped by communists, but don't worry—a rock group (Miller, Chippeway, Larden, Stevens) is sent behind the Iron Curtain to save them.

> Screenplay by Stan Cornyn, from a story by Bob Booker and George Foster (who also produced).
> Mike Stoller and Jerry Leiber songs:
> "What Is Your Sign?"
> "I've Got Them Feelin' Too Good Today Blues"
> "Hello"
> "You Know the Feeling"
> "Trip with Me"
> "They Say That You're Mad"
> "It Nearly Blew My Mind"
> "The Boys in the Band"
> Music by Mike Stoller, Sonny Burke.

Released on May 6.
(92 minutes/color/Rated [M-PG])
Cinema Organization/Warner Brothers

Short Subject

Swingtime in the Movies (1938) **D: Crane Wilbur**

Fritz Feld, Katherine [Kathryn] Kane, John Carroll, Charley Foy, Jerry Colonna, Helen Lynd, Irene Franklin, Humphrey Bogart, George Brent, Pat O'Brien, John Garfield, Leo Gorcey, Huntz Hall, Billy Halop, Stuart Holmes, Bobby Jordan, Eddie Kane, Priscilla Lane, Rosemary Lane, Frank Mayo, Fay McKenzie, Kansas Moehring, Jack Perrin, Marie Wilson.

Movie director Feld is trying to find an actress who can do a flawless Southern accent for his latest western. Besieged by a bevy of hopeful starlets, he spots a waitress who comes from the South. Gorcey is a "Crime School Kid" being made to conform by Bogart. Entry in the *Broadway Brevities* series.

Written by Crane Wilbur.
Choreography by William O'Donnell.
Songs:
"You Oughtta Be in Pictures" (instrumental) (Dana Suesse)
"Swingin' Through the Kitchen Door" (M.K. Jerome, Jack Scholl)
"Queen of the Border Cantina" (Jerome, Scholl)
"The Toast of the Texas Frontier" (Jerome, Scholl)
"Look Out for Love" (Jerome, Scholl)
Academy Award Nomination:
(Short Subject—Two Reel) Warner Brothers.
(20 minutes/Vitaphone Sound/Technicolor)
Vitaphone/Warner Brothers

Stage Appearances

Dead End (1935-37) D: Sidney Kingsley

Elspeth Eric, Joseph Downing, Margaret Mullen, Sheila Trent, Martin Gabel, Marjorie Main, Billy Halop, Huntz Hall, Bobby Jordan, Leo Gorcey, Gabriel Dell, Bernard Punsly, Charles Bellin, Carroll Ashburn, Robert J. Mulligan, George Cotton, Sidonie Espero, Philip Bourneuf, Marc Daniels, Francis DeSales, Dan Duryea, David Gorcey, Sidney Lumet, Elizabeth [Betty] Wragge, Bernard Zanville [Dane Clark].

A gang of kids grows up on the streets of a slum as a notorious gangster returns to take up with his former girlfriend.

> Written by Sidney Kingsley.
> Produced by Norman Bel Geddes.
> Run: October 28, 1935 to June 12, 1937 (687 performances)
> Belasco Theater, New York City

(Untitled revue) circa February 1940.

Leo Gorcey, Bernard Punsley [Punsly], Gabriel Dell, Huntz Hall.

A live show billed as "Here they are on stage: the toughest little hoodlums that ever made you howl out loud."

(Note: Apparently, this show traveled to various cities, this entry came from a Milwaukee newspaper).

Radio Appearances

Elza Schallert Interviews (Blue) May 26, 1938

Elza reviews the film *Alexander's Ragtime Band* and interviews the Dead End Kids (Billy Halop, Leo Gorcey, Huntz Hall, Bobby Jordan, Gabriel Dell, Bernard Punsly).

The Kate Smith Hour (CBS) October 20, 1938

> Host: Ted Collins. Stars: Kate Smith, Bud Abbott and Lou Costello, Parker Fennelly and Arthur Allen.

Vocalists: The Kate Smith Singers.
Announcer: Andre Baruch.
The Jack Miller Orchestra.
The Dead End Kids perform in an original drama written by Norman Corwin.
Leo Gorcey, Huntz Hall, Gabriel Dell, Bernard Punsly.

***Texaco Star Theater* (CBS) November 9, 1938**
Host: Adolphe Menjou.
Stars: Una Merkel, Charles Ruggles, Ned Sparks. Vocalists: Jane Froman, Kenny Baker, the Texaco Star Chorus.
Announcer: Jimmy Wallington.
The David Broekman Orchestra.
Max Reinhardt presents the Dead End Kids (Billy Halop, Leo Gorcey, Bobby Jordan) in a dramatic segment "Out of Thin Soil," written for radio by Harry Kronman from a story by Jess Oppenheimer.
Directed by William A. Bacher.
Paula Winslowe. Thelma Hubbard.

***Pabst Blue Ribbon Town* (CBS) (Series) November 27, 1943 to June 17, 1944**
Comedy and variety focused on the zany doings of a town's offbeat citizen.

Cast
Star: Groucho Marx
Regular: Leo Gorcey
Vocalists: Fay McKenzie, Bill Days, The Blue Ribbon Blenders
Announcer: Dick Joy
Ken Niles Orchestra: Robert Armbruster
Produced by Dick Mack.

November 27, 1943.
Star: Groucho Marx.
Vocalist: Fay McKenzie.
The Robert Armbruster Orchestra.
Leo Gorcey joins the regular cast. Groucho discusses the servant problem with guest Edward Everett Horton.

December 4, 1943
Stars: Groucho Marx, Leo Gorcey.
Vocalist: Fay McKenzie.
The Robert Armbruster Orchestra.
Guest: Adolphe Menjou, the dapper supporting player of film and no mean comedian, jousts in quips with Groucho. Announcing a series of awards for post-war employment plans.

December 11, 1943
Stars: Groucho Marx, Leo Gorcey.
Vocalist: Fay McKenzie.
The Robert Armbruster Orchestra.
Frances Gifford, once a jungle girl of the movies, meets the man who was once Captain Spaulding, the African explorer.

December 18, 1943
Star: Leo Gorcey.
Vocalist: Fay McKenzie.
The Robert Armbruster Orchestra.
Broadcast from Camp Santa Anita, California. Chico Marx subs for his absent brother Groucho. The guest is man-chasing Vera Vague (Barbara Jo Allen). Also, a talk by Beardsley Ruml, treasurer of R.H. Macy and Company and chairman of the Federal Reserve Bank of New York; he discusses the Post-War Employment Awards.

December 25, 1943
Stars: Groucho Marx, Leo Gorcey.
Vocalists: Fay McKenzie, Bill Days.
The Robert Armbruster Orchestra.
Donald Dickson, former male vocalist on the series, returns as a guest when Groucho holds a Christmas open house at 33 Blue Ribbon Lane.

January 1, 1944
Stars: Groucho Marx, Leo Gorcey.
Vocalist: Fay McKenzie.
The Robert Armbruster Orchestra.
Edward Everett Horton of the film *The Gang's All Here*, pays a

return visit. Hilarious doings are in store as the mad pair of Groucho and Edward go to work on problems of the day. Also, a talk by Beardsley Ruml.

January 8, 1944
Stars: Groucho Marx, Leo Gorcey.
Vocalist: Fay McKenzie.
The Robert Armbruster Orchestra.
Guest: actor Charles Laughton, who starred in the film comedy *The Man from Down Under*.
Note: Charles Laughton stepped in for the previously announced guest, Basil Rathbone.

January 15, 1944
Stars: Groucho Marx, Leo Gorcey.
Vocalists: Fay McKenzie, Bill Days.
The Robert Armbruster Orchestra.
Guest Lionel Barrymore runs for mayor of Blue Ribbon Town. With Fay leading the way, Groucho and Lionel trek to the Hollywood Canteen where they agree to help Fay with her chores of serving visiting servicemen.

January 22, 1944
Stars: Groucho Marx, Leo Gorcey.
Vocalists: Fay McKenzie, Bill Days.
The Robert Armbruster Orchestra.
Guest Betty Hutton, blonde bombshell, indulges in comic antics as a singing comedienne.

January 29, 1944
Stars: Groucho Marx, Leo Gorcey.
Vocalists: Fay McKenzie, Bill Days.
Announcer: Ken Niles.
The Robert Armbruster Orchestra.
Groucho advertises for a cook and gets love-starved guest Vera Vague (Barbara Jo Allen). Mr. Marx envisions what life would be like married to Vera and how things would work out in his altered household.
Directed by Dick Mack.

February 5, 1944
Stars: Groucho Marx, Leo Gorcey.
Vocalists: Fay McKenzie, Bill Days.
Announcer: Durward Kirby.
The Robert Armbruster Orchestra.
Broadcast from Milwaukee Auditorium in Wisconsin. The film actress Gene Tierney makes the first of a pair of guest appearances as she accompanies Groucho and his gang to sponsor Pabst Beer's headquarters. They help the brewing company celebrate 100 years in business. The cast goes back a century in time, where Groucho becomes a rough, tough hombre—G. Boone Marx. He sings "Don't Forget There's a War Going On."

February 12, 1944
Stars: Groucho Marx, Leo Gorcey.
Vocalists: Fay McKenzie, Bill Days.
Announcer: Durward Kirby.
The Robert Armbruster Orchestra.
Broadcast from the Shrine Mosque in Peoria, Illinois. Groucho and guest Gene Tierney have a full supply of madness in store as the show visits Midwestern Pabst beer plants. The cast takes a guess at what things will be like 100 years in the future. Directed by Dick Mack.

February 19, 1944
Stars: Groucho Marx, Leo Gorcey.
Vocalists: Fay McKenzie, Bill Days.
The Robert Armbruster Orchestra.
Guest Orson Welles and Groucho engage in a heated discussion of high rent and lease terms. Leo complicates matters when he enters into the negotiations. Bill sings "Spring Will Be a Little Late This Year." Fay offers "Besame Mucho."

February 26, 1944
Stars: Groucho Marx, Leo Gorcey.
Vocalists: Fay McKenzie, Bill Days.
Announcer: Ken Niles.
The Robert Armbruster Orchestra.

Groucho plays host to Jack Benny. Benny visits Mr. Marx in the hope of getting away from radio shoptalk, but he does not quite succeed. In fact, he steals the show (literally) when the gang wants to quit Groucho and go to work for Jack.

March 4, 1944
Stars: Groucho Marx, Leo Gorcey.
Vocalists: Fay McKenzie, Bill Days.
The Robert Armbruster Orchestra.
Guest Edward Everett Horton, the befuddled bumbler of the movies, is an income tax advisor who assists Groucho, but as expected is tangled up in the return forms.

March 11, 1944
Stars: Groucho Marx, Leo Gorcey.
Vocalists: Fay McKenzie, Bill Days.
The Robert Armbruster Orchestra.
Groucho's dual personality surfaces when guest Miriam Hopkins brings her Southern accent to Blue Ribbon Town; they do a "Dr. Jekyll and Mr. Hyde" sketch.
Note: Miriam Hopkins played Ivy Pearson in the 1932 film version of *Dr. Jekyll and Mr. Hyde*.

March 18, 1944
Stars: Groucho Marx, Leo Gorcey.
Vocalists: Fay McKenzie, Bill Days.
The Robert Armbruster Orchestra.
Cinema blonde Carole Landis drops by. Groucho turns mystical and sings a new song, "Groucho, the Swami." He and Carole visit the San Pedro Marine Base in California.

March 25, 1944
Stars: Groucho Marx, Leo Gorcey.
Vocalists: Fay McKenzie, Bill Days.
The Robert Armbruster Orchestra.
Guest George Jessel, comedian, toastmaster, and film producer, helps Groucho start his second year in radio.

April 1, 1944
Stars: Groucho Marx, Leo Gorcey.
Vocalists: Fay McKenzie, Bill Days.
The Robert Armbruster Orchestra.
Broadcast from Santa Monica Air Force Base in California. Weather being what it is, Groucho goes afloat as a showboat captain and stages some April 1 tomfoolery.
Songs: "Holiday for Strings," "Good Night, Wherever You Are," "My Shining Hour."

April 8, 1944
Stars: Groucho Marx, Leo Gorcey.
Vocalists: Fay McKenzie, Bill Days.
The Robert Armbruster Orchestra.
Beauteous Lynn Bari of film is Groucho's guest when the show goes to the Marine Air Base at Miramar, California.

April 15, 1944
Stars: Groucho Marx, Leo Gorcey.
Vocalists: Fay McKenzie, Bill Days.
The Robert Armbruster Orchestra.
Groucho looks out from behind his 'ceegar' and sees guest Laird Cregar when the screen bogeyman visits the man with the stogie. Leo does his best to scare the daylights out of the film menace.

April 22, 1944
Stars: Groucho Marx, Leo Gorcey.
Vocalists: Fay McKenzie, Bill Days.
The Robert Armbruster Orchestra.
Guest: Actress Martha Scott who went west in the film *In Old Oklahoma*.

April 29, 1944
Stars: Groucho Marx, Leo Gorcey.
Vocalists: Fay McKenzie, Bill Days.
The Robert Armbruster Orchestra.
Groucho and guest Nancy Walker mind a baby and are charged with kidnapping.

May 6, 1944
Stars: Groucho Marx, Leo Gorcey.
Vocalists: Fay McKenzie, Bill Days.
The Robert Armbruster Orchestra.
Groucho's company, finding itself temporarily out of pants, puts on bed sheets and goes Arabian. The mad Marx introduces "Sultan Groucho Marx." Other songs include "Good Night, Soldier" and "Amor, Amor, Amor."
Verna Felton.

May 13, 1944
Stars: Groucho Marx, Leo Gorcey.
Vocalists: Fay McKenzie, Bill Days.
The Robert Armbruster Orchestra.
Groucho and Fay don costumes to play the parts of a Mexican bandit and his senorita.
Songs: "I Wish That I Could Hide Inside This Letter" and "I'm in the Mood for Love."

May 20, 1944
Stars: Groucho Marx, Leo Gorcey.
Vocalists: Fay McKenzie, Bill Days.
The Robert Armbruster Orchestra.
Groucho is tangled up in a court affair when a neighbor sues him for custody of a melon patch.

May 27, 1944
Stars: Groucho Marx, Leo Gorcey.
Vocalists: Fay McKenzie, Bill Days.
The Robert Armbruster Orchestra.
Groucho gives a comedy-infested lawn party at 33 Blue Ribbon Lane in honor of Leo and his girlfriend Jennifer Schultz.

June 3, 1944
Stars: Groucho Marx, Leo Gorcey.
Vocalists: Fay McKenzie, Bill Days.
The Robert Armbruster Orchestra.
Film fright-master, Boris Karloff, is the one to tremble when Groucho catches the fiend murdering his egg-laying hen

red-handedly (a Rhode Island Red). Before turning the cold-blooded actor over to the authorities, Groucho and Leo wring a confession from him. Fay sings "I'll Get By." Bill renders "It Had to Be You." The orchestra and chorus give us "Bye, Bye, Bessie."

June 10, 1944
Stars: Groucho Marx, Leo Gorcey.
Vocalists: Fay McKenzie, Bill Days.
The Robert Armbruster Orchestra.
Groucho gets Leo's girlfriend and a draft headache when he unwittingly brags to the chairman of the local induction board that he is only twenty-five years old.

June 17, 1944
Stars: Groucho Marx, Leo Gorcey.
Vocalists: Fay McKenzie, Bill Days.
The Robert Armbruster Orchestra.
Harpo Marx, the silent but horn-blowing brother, comes to 33 Blue Ribbon Lane and performs "Stardust" on his harp. Groucho presents singer-actor Kenny Baker, who replaces Groucho as star of this series beginning next week.

The Bob Burns Show **(NBC) (Series) March 1, 1945 to June 27, 1946**
Comedy-variety with rustic comedian Burns in skits and musical interludes, often playing solos on his homemade instrument he calls a 'bazooka'.

Cast
Star: Bob Burns
Regular: Leo Gorcey
Vocalists: Shirley Ross, The Suitcase Six
Announcer: Doug Gorlay
Orchestra: Gordon Jenkins.

The Bob Burns Program **March 1, 1945**
Star: Bob Burns.
Vocalist: Shirley Ross.

Leo Gorcey, one of the original Dead End Kids of the movies, makes his first appearance.
Song: "Let's Fall in Love"

The Bob Burns Program March 8, 1945
Stars: Bob Burns.
Vocalist: Shirley Ross.
Leo Gorcey returns for a second week.

The Bob Burns Program March 15, 1945
Stars: Bob Burns, Leo Gorcey.
Vocalist: Shirley Ross.
Leo officially becomes one of the regulars at Bob's San Fernando Valley ranch. Shirley sings "I Knew It Would Be This Way."

The Bob Burns Program March 22, 1945
Stars: Bob Burns, Leo Gorcey.
Vocalist: Shirley Ross.
No further information available.

The Bob Burns Program March 29, 1945
Stars: Bob Burns, Leo Gorcey.
Vocalist: Shirley Ross.
No further information available.

The Bob Burns Program April 5, 1945
Stars: Bob Burns, Leo Gorcey.
Vocalist: Shirley Ross.
Leo is shown the wonders of the circus when Bob takes him for a visit to the big top.

The Bob Burns Program April 12, 1945
Pre-empted by coverage of President Franklin D. Roosevelt's death.

The Bob Burns Program April 19, 1945
Bob opens a hayseed theater guild in his barn.

***The Bob Burns Program* April 26, 1945**
Pre-empted by an address at the United Nations conference in San Francisco, California.

***The Bob Burns Program* May 3, 1945.**
Stars: Bob Burns, Leo Gorcey.
Vocalist: Shirley Ross.
Bob's guest is radio comedienne Arlene Harris, the 'human chatterbox' of *The Al Pearce Show*.

***The Bob Burns Program* May 10, 1945**
Stars: Bob Burns, Leo Gorcey.
Vocalist: Shirley Ross.
No further information available.

***The Bob Burns Program* May 17, 1945**
Stars: Bob Burns, Leo Gorcey.
Vocalist: Shirley Ross.
Bob takes Shirley and Leo to the state fair.

***The Bob Burns Program* May 24, 1945**
Stars: Bob Burns, Leo Gorcey.
Vocalists: Shirley Ross, The Suitcase Six.
Bob has something to say about wartime shortages and costs, "There's too much beefing about gas and gassing about beef." The shortage of pork, as Bob sees it is "caused by too few hogs on one side of the counter and too many hogs on the other." Bob's guest is Norma Nilson, seven-year-old actress. Shirley sings "Who" during a surprise birthday party for Leo.

***The Bob Burns Program* May 31, 1945**
Stars: Bob Burns, Leo Gorcey.
Vocalist: Shirley Ross.
No further information available.

***The Bob Burns Program* June 7, 1945**
Stars: Bob Burns, Leo Gorcey.
Vocalist: Shirley Ross.

Bob gives his thoughts on romance. Bob and Shirley want to take Leo to the opera.

The Bob Burns Program June 14, 1945
Stars: Bob Burns, Leo Gorcey.
Vocalist: Shirley Ross.
Bob and Shirley once again deal with their 'problem child', Leo.

The Bob Burns Program June 21, 1945
Stars: Bob Burns, Leo Gorcey.
Vocalists: Shirley Ross, The Suitcase Six.
The Paul Baron Orchestra.
Bob and the gang discuss upcoming vacation plans. Shirley sings "Out of Nowhere." The Suitcase Six introduce a new tune penned by Gordon Jenkins, "Every Time."

The Bob Burns Program June 28, 1945
Stars: Bob Burns, Leo Gorcey.
Vocalist: Shirley Ross.
Bob and the cast say goodbye for the summer with a review of the season's broadcasts. *Last show of the season.*

The Bob Burns Program October 4, 1945
Stars: Bob Burns, Leo Gorcey.
Vocalist: Shirley Ross.
The Gordon Jenkins Orchestra.
First show of the season. Bob tells of his vacation exploits.

The Bob Burns Program October 11, 1945
Stars: Bob Burns, Leo Gorcey.
Vocalist: Shirley Ross.
The Gordon Jenkins Orchestra.
No further information available.

The Bob Burns Program October 18, 1945
Stars: Bob Burns, Leo Gorcey.
Vocalist: Shirley Ross.
The Gordon Jenkins Orchestra.

Bob demonstrates to Leo and Shirley how an old 'end man' puts on a real minstrel show.

The Bob Burns Program October 25, 1945
Stars: Bob Burns, Leo Gorcey.
Vocalist: Shirley Ross.
The Gordon Jenkins Orchestra.
Bob, the fellow with the Ozark drawl, once again recalls the minstrels.

The Bob Burns Program November 1, 1945
Stars: Bob Burns, Leo Gorcey.
Vocalist: Shirley Ross.
The Gordon Jenkins Orchestra.
What happened on the Burns ranch during the ghostly night of Halloween when Bob and Leo put on masks to make some spooky house calls?

The Bob Burns Program November 8, 1945
Stars: Bob Burns, Leo Gorcey.
Vocalist: Shirley Ross.
The Gordon Jenkins Orchestra.
No further information available.

The Bob Burns Program November 15, 1945
Stars: Bob Burns, Leo Gorcey.
Vocalist: Shirley Ross.
The Gordon Jenkins Orchestra.
Bob gives listeners the lowdown on the post-war car models.
Songs: "It's Been a Long, Long Time" and "Blue Skies."

The Bob Burns Program November 22, 1945
Stars: Bob Burns, Leo Gorcey.
Vocalist: Shirley Ross.
The Gordon Jenkins Orchestra.
Leo cooks Thanksgiving dinner.
Songs: "Homesick, That's All" and "San Antonio Rose."

***The Bob Burns Program* November 29, 1945**
Stars: Bob Burns, Leo Gorcey.
Vocalists: Shirley Ross, The Suitcase Six.
The Gordon Jenkins Orchestra.
Bob starts his Christmas shopping early, but discovers that even June would not have been early enough this year. Bob and Shirley serve as shopping guides for Leo in a tour through the department store maze. Shirley's solo (probably in answer to the question, "When is the best time to do your Christmas shopping?") is the song "It Seems to Be Spring." Leo receives a letter from his girlfriend that contains matrimonial hints. Also in tonight's cast is Charles Kemper.

***The Bob Burns Program* December 6, 1945**
Stars: Bob Burns, Leo Gorcey.
Vocalist: Shirley Ross.
The Gordon Jenkins Orchestra.
Leo sees his first rodeo.
Songs: "Slowly" and "Coquette."

***The Bob Burns Program* December 13, 1945**
Stars: Bob Burns, Leo Gorcey.
Vocalist: Shirley Ross.
The Gordon Jenkins Orchestra.
Bob takes Leo to have him professionally photographed.
Songs: "Out of Nowhere" and "Cherry."

***The Bob Burns Program* December 20, 1945**
Stars: Bob Burns, Leo Gorcey.
Vocalist: Shirley Ross.
The Gordon Jenkins Orchestra.
Bob gives an old-fashioned Christmas party in Canoga Park that provides mirth and melody. The highlight of the fun comes when Bob attempts to light his Christmas tree just as Santa Claus drops by.

***The Bob Burns Program* December 27, 1945**
Stars: Bob Burns, Leo Gorcey.
Vocalist: Shirley Ross.

The Gordon Jenkins Orchestra.
Leo plans to start a newspaper with the printing press he received for Christmas. Shirley sings "Symphony."

***The Bob Burns Program* January 3, 1946**
Stars: Bob Burns, Leo Gorcey.
Vocalist: Shirley Ross.
The Gordon Jenkins Orchestra.
Bob looks in on the stock market.

***The Bob Burns Program* January 10, 1946**
Stars: Bob Burns, Leo Gorcey.
Vocalist: Shirley Ross.
The Gordon Jenkins Orchestra.
Leo hopes to up his culture quotient by making himself familiar with the classics.

***The Bob Burns Program* January 17, 1946**
Stars: Bob Burns, Leo Gorcey.
Vocalist: Shirley Ross.
The Gordon Jenkins Orchestra.
Leo continues his study of the classics. Shirley sings "You've Got Me Crying Again."

***The Bob Burns Program* January 24, 1946**
Stars: Bob Burns, Leo Gorcey.
Vocalist: Shirley Ross.
The Gordon Jenkins Orchestra.
Bob faces an accusation of having a higher ham content than the Berkshire hogs he raises when Shirley and Leo heckle him. Shirley sings "You've Got Me Crying Again."

***The Bob Burns Program* January 31, 1946**
Stars: Bob Burns, Leo Gorcey.
Vocalist: Shirley Ross.
The Gordon Jenkins Orchestra.
Leo shops for baby things when he learns he is to become an uncle. Song: "I'm Waiting for the Train to Come In."

***The Bob Burns Program* February 7, 1946**
Stars: Bob Burns, Leo Gorcey.
Vocalist: Shirley Ross.
The Gordon Jenkins Orchestra.
Bob observes the Boy Scouts' birthday by showing Leo and Shirley how much he remembers from his early scout training.

***The Bob Burns Program* February 14, 1946**
Stars: Bob Burns, Leo Gorcey.
Vocalist: Shirley Ross.
The Gordon Jenkins Orchestra.
Leo includes a pound of butter substitute in his valentine to his girlfriend.

***The Bob Burns Program* February 21, 1946**
Stars: Bob Burns, Leo Gorcey.
Vocalist: Shirley Ross.
The Gordon Jenkins Orchestra.
Broadcast from New York City. Bob and Shirley tell of their plane trip from Hollywood to the Big Apple. Leo gets together with some of the old Brooklyn friends.

***The Bob Burns Program* February 28, 1946**
Stars: Bob Burns, Leo Gorcey.
Vocalist: Shirley Ross.
Leo describes his visit to relatives in Brooklyn as the show airs its final broadcast from New York City. Bob offers an earful about the shopping he has done for Aunt Boo and Uncle Slug. Bob, Leo, and Shirley make plans to return to Hollywood for next week's show.

***The Bob Burns Program* March 7, 1946**
Stars: Bob Burns, Leo Gorcey.
Vocalist: Shirley Ross.
The Gordon Jenkins Orchestra.
Back in Hollywood after a visit to New York and Bermuda, Bob hears a report from his foreman on conditions at his ranch and begins consideration of his campaign for re-election as mayor of Canoga Park.

The Bob Burns Program **March 14, 1946**
Stars: Bob Burns, Leo Gorcey.
Vocalist: Shirley Ross.
The Gordon Jenkins Orchestra.
Bob calls for help with his income taxes.

The Bob Burns Program **March 21, 1946**
Stars: Bob Burns, Leo Gorcey.
Vocalist: Shirley Ross.
The Gordon Jenkins Orchestra.
Leo and Shirley help Bob with his spring housecleaning.

The Bob Burns Program **March 28, 1946**
Stars: Bob Burns, Leo Gorcey.
Vocalist: Shirley Ross.
The Gordon Jenkins Orchestra.
The clothing shortage causes some dire results when Bob buys a loom so that he can weave his own attire.

The Bob Burns Program **April 4, 1946**
Stars: Bob Burns, Leo Gorcey.
Vocalist: Shirley Ross.
The Gordon Jenkins Orchestra.
Bob thinks he has succeeded in inventing the proverbial better mousetrap and is overwhelmed by the flood of people who beat a path to his door.

The Bob Burns Program **April 11, 1946**
Stars: Bob Burns, Leo Gorcey.
Vocalist: Shirley Ross.
The Gordon Jenkins Orchestra.
Bob has trouble with his hired man at the ranch. Shirley sings "Personality."

The Bob Burns Program **April 18, 1946**
Stars: Bob Burns, Leo Gorcey.
Vocalist: Shirley Ross. The Gordon Jenkins Orchestra.
No further information available.

***The Bob Burns Program* April 25, 1946**
Stars: Bob Burns, Leo Gorcey.
Vocalist: Shirley Ross.
The Gordon Jenkins Orchestra.
Bob advises Leo how to act when he is appointed judge during Boys' Week.

***The Bob Burns Program* May 2, 1946**
Stars: Bob Burns, Leo Gorcey.
Vocalist: Shirley Ross.
The Gordon Jenkins Orchestra.
Bob turns on the klieg lights on Leo's private and public past. Leo, who has appeared in fifty-two flickers since he started in show business with the Dead End Kids, receives a lecture on movie serials as Bob fondly reminisces on Pearl White and *The Perils of Pauline*.

***The Bob Burns Program* May 9, 1946**
Stars: Bob Burns, Leo Gorcey.
Vocalist: Shirley Ross.
The Gordon Jenkins Orchestra.
Bob redecorates his Canoga Park ranch house with help from Leo and Shirley.

***The Bob Burns Program* May 16, 1946**
Stars: Bob Burns, Leo Gorcey.
Vocalist: Shirley Ross.
The Gordon Jenkins Orchestra.
Bob collects old clothes for the post-war needy in Europe. Song: "I Fall in Love Every Day."

***The Bob Burns Program* May 23, 1946**
Stars: Bob Burns, Leo Gorcey.
Vocalists: Shirley Ross, The Suitcase Six.
The Gordon Jenkins Orchestra.
Bob is certain America needs more music when the Philadelphia Symphony inspires him. He takes to the piano to play "Love Is Like a Pretzel." It's the same old story with a new twist. Also in the cast is Eric Rolf, Jim Backus, and Clarence Nash.

The Bob Burns Program May 30, 1946
Stars: Bob Burns, Leo Gorcey.
Vocalist: Shirley Ross.
The Gordon Jenkins Orchestra.
Bob has a monologue about auto racing. Leo's duck celebrates his birthday with a party.

The Bob Burns Program June 6, 1946
Stars: Bob Burns, Leo Gorcey.
Vocalists: Shirley Ross, The Suitcase Six.
The Gordon Jenkins Orchestra.
A baby pops up at Bob's ranch. Reason for this arrival is that Leo, trying to raise money for Bob's Father's Day present, turns to baby-sitting as a source of revenue. Leo, with the help (?) of his duck Morton, creates a panic—or a reasonably accurate facsimile.

The Bob Burns Program June 13, 1946
Stars: Bob Burns, Leo Gorcey.
Vocalist: Shirley Ross.
The Gordon Jenkins Orchestra.
Bob discusses his vacation plans with Shirley and Leo.

The Bob Burns Program June 20, 1946
Stars: Bob Burns, Leo Gorcey.
Vocalist: Shirley Ross.
The Gordon Jenkins Orchestra.
Bob has a few words about the Joe Lewis-Billy Conn prizefight. Bob and Shirley plan to attend Leo's graduation.
Song: "Linger in My Arms a Little While Longer."

The Bob Burns Program June 27, 1946
Stars: Bob Burns, Leo Gorcey.
Vocalist: Shirley Ross.
The Gordon Jenkins Orchestra.
Bob and his cast finish the season with a resume of best songs and stories of the year. *Leo Gorcey leaves the series with this broadcast.*

The Bob Burns Show **(audition program for revival show) November 24, 1947**
Star: Bob Burns.
Vocalist: Shirley Ross.
The George Wyle Orchestra.
Leo Gorcey, that pugnacious Brooklynite, comes to visit Bob at his Canoga Park ranch in California. Bob performs a bazooka solo. Recorded by Star Transcriptions, Incorporated.
Jess Kirkpatrick.

Whatever Became Of… **(WBAI-FM, New York City, dial 99.5) July 1968**
Host: Richard Lamparski.
Richard interviews Leo Gorcey, with funny reminisces of films from his Dead End Kids and Bowery Boys days.

TELEVISION APPEARANCES

The Dick Powell Show **(NBC) "No Strings Attached" April 24, 1962**
Host/Star: Dick Powell.
When Judy Maxwell (Angie Dickinson) becomes involved in an accident case, the full weight of her father's distinguished law firm is brought to bear. However, glib attorney Mike Scott (Powell) is more than a match for them. Written by Ben Starr and Bob [Robert] O'Brien. Directed by Hy Averback.
Penny Nickels: Mamie Van Doren. Bunny Easter: Barbara Nichols.
Danny Cannon: Robert Strauss. Floyd Maxwell: John Litel. Billy Vale: Leo B. Gorcey.
Waiter: Herbie Faye. Andy Dugan: Buddy Lewis. Miss Talbot: Amzie Strickland.
George: Paul Smith. Janitor: Percy Helton. Judge Bender: Don Beddoe.
Bunny's Attorney: George Petrie. Hood 1: Martin Walker. Hood 2: Sid Curtis.

Mr. Smith Goes to Washington (ABC) "...But What Are You Doing for Your Country?" **October 13, 1962**
>Stars: Fess Parker, Sandra Warner, Red Foley, Stan Irwin, Rita Lynn.
>Senator Smith (Parker) meets a trio of hoboes and decides to rehabilitate them. He knows that the best way to talk to them is man-to-man…so he dresses like a hobo. Written by Hal Stanley.
>J.C. Stover: Jerome Cowan. Windy: Leo Gorcey. Spud: Richard Reeves. Jo-Jo: William Fawcett.

That Regis Philbin Show (Syndicated) **February 15, 1965**
>Host: Regis Philbin.
>Talk, music, and comedy with guests Leo Gorcey, Choo Choo Collins, Dennis James, and the Ramsey Lewis Trio.

The Tonight Show Starring Johnny Carson (NBC) **September 27, 1967**
>Host: Johnny Carson.
>Announcer: Ed McMahon.
>The Doc Severinsen Orchestra.
>Late-night talk and variety with guests: former Dead End Kid and Bowery Boy Leo Gorcey, singer-actress Liza Minnelli, and comic actor Louis Nye.

The Tonight Show Starring Johnny Carson (NBC) **January 9, 1968**
>Host: Johnny Carson.
>Announcer: Ed McMahon.
>The Doc Severinsen Orchestra.
>Guests: Leo Gorcey, Liza Minnelli, and NASA scientist Dr. Robert Jastrow.

SOURCES FOR CREDITS

Archives of the Airwaves (7 volumes) by Roger C. Paulson, BearManor Media, 2005-06.

Behind Sach: The Huntz Hall Story by Jim Manago, BearManor Media, 2015.

The Big Broadcast, 1920-1950, A New, Revised, and Greatly Expanded Edition of Radio's Golden Age, The Complete Reference Work by Frank Buxton and Bill Owen, Flare/Avon, 1972.

The Columbia Story by Clive Hirschhorn, Crown, 1989.

The Complete Directory to Prime Time Network and Cable TV Shows, 1946-Present, 9th Edition, by Tim Brooks and Earle Marsh, Ballantine, 2007.

Feature Films, 1940-1949, A United States Filmography by Alan G. Fetrow, McFarland, 1994.

Feature Films, 1950-1959, A United States Filmography by Alan G. Fetrow, McFarland, 1999.

Feature Films, 1960-69, A Filmography of English-Language and Major Foreign-Language United States Releases by Harris M. Lentz III, McFarland, 2001.

The Films of the Bowery Boys by David Hayes and Brent Walker, The Citadel Press, 1984.

The 5th Revised Ultimate History of Network Radio Programming and Guide to All Circulating Shows by Jay Hickerson, Presto Print II/Minuteman Press, 2015.

The Great American Broadcast, A Celebration of Radio's Golden Age by Leonard Maltin, Dutton/Penguin, 1997.

Handbook of Old-Time Radio, A Comprehensive Guide to Golden Age Radio Listening and Collecting by Jon D. Swartz and Robert C. Reinehr, The Scarecrow Press, 1993.

The Hollywood Reliables by James Robert Parish with Gregory W. Mank, Arlington House, 1980.

Hollywood Song, The Complete Film & Musical Companion, 3 volumes, by Ken Bloom, Facts On File, 1995.

Internet Movie Database, website at www.imdb.com.

JJ's Radio Logs, Internet website at www.jjonz.com.

Leonard Maltin's Classic Movie Guide, Second Edition, edited by Leonard Maltin, Plume, 2010.

The MGM Story, The Complete History of Fifty-Seven Roaring Years by John Douglas Eames, Crown, 1982.

The Monogram Checklist, The Films of Monogram Pictures Corporation, 1931-1952 by Ted Okuda, McFarland, 1987.

Old Time Radio Researchers Group, Internet website at www.otrr.org.

On the Air: The Encyclopedia of Old-Time Radio by John Dunning, Oxford University Press, 1998.

OTRRpedia, Internet website at www.otrrpedia.net.

RadioGOLDINdex, Internet website at www.radiogoldindex.com.

Radio Programs, 1924-1984, A Catalog of Over 1800 Shows by Vincent Terrace, McFarland, 1999.

Radio's Golden Years, The Encyclopedia of Radio Programs, 1930-1960 by Vincent Terrace, A.S. Barnes & Company, 1981.

Radio Speakers, Narrators, News Junkies, Sports Jockeys, Tattletales, Tipsters, Toastmasters, and Coffee Klatch Couples Who Verbalized the Jargon of the Aural Ether from the 1920s to the 1980s—A Biographical Dictionary by Jim Cox, McFarland, 2007.

The Republic Pictures Checklist, Features, Serials, Cartoons, Short Subjects and Training Films of Republic Pictures Corporation, 1935-1959 by Len D. Martin, McFarland, 1998.

Same Time...Same Station, An A-Z Guide to Radio from Jack Benny to Howard Stern by Ron Lackmann, Facts On File, 1996.

70 Years of the Oscar, The Official History of the Academy Awards by Robert Osborne, Abbeville Press, 1999.

Sold on Radio, Advertisers in the Golden Age of Broadcasting by Jim Cox, McFarland, 2008.

Sound Films, 1927-1939, A United States Filmography by Alan G. Fetrow, McFarland, 1992.

Tune in Yesterday, The Ultimate Encyclopedia of Old-Time Radio, 1925-1976 by John Dunning, Prentice-Hall, 1976.

TV Guide magazine, various issues 1962-68, Triangle Publications.

Vitaphone Films, A Catalogue of the Features and Shorts by Roy Liebman, McFarland, 2003.

The Warner Bros. Story by Clive Hirschhorn, Crown, 1979.

www.ingramcontent.com/pod-product-compliance
Lightning Source LLC
Chambersburg PA
CBHW060112170426
43198CB00010B/868